Crossing the Event Horizon:

Human Metamorphosis

and The Singularity Archetype

Edited by Austin Iredale

Eye Spirals by Tanner Dery

Interior Design by Mathael Robintree

To my mother and father,

and evolving mutants everywhere.

Boulder, Colorado

Copyright © 2012 by Jonathan Zap

Contents

Acknowledgments

First and foremost my parents, who raised me in a culturally vibrant, intellectually rigorous environment where investigation of any subject was encouraged, and unwarranted assumptions were always challenged. Dr. William Williamson, Chairman of the Ursinus College Philosophy Department and author of several books on religion and philosophy, one of a number of superb faculty members, as well as the college president, Dr. Richard Richter, who, though part of a conservative academic culture, provided crucial encouragement and support of my extremely divergent research. Novelist E.L. Doctorow, my writing mentor at NYU. My superb and ever vigilant editor, Austin Iredale, who, in this and other works, immersed himself in the mechanics of every sentence and citation and provided invaluable feedback on style, organization and the presentation of ideas. Webmaster extraordinaire and computer graphics expert, Tanner Dery, whose work ethic and talent provided invaluable, generous help to the dissemination of my work in cyberspace and who designed the eye spirals for the book. My endlessly patient and exceptionally capable agent Lisa Hagan, President of the Paraview Literary Agency, who knows everything about publishing. Rob Brezsny, who brought the glowing encouragement one expects of the philosopher of pronoia, as well as the practical suggestions and contacts of an accomplished and successful writer. John Major Jenkins, who, ever since we met through our late colleague, Terence McKenna, has been my companion researcher of mysteries. His archeo-astronomical investigations and ability to navigate disputatious fields distorted by collective projections has been a shining example. Daniel C. Jones, whose intuitive counsel and global insight has been a priceless resource in the completion of this, and many other life ventures. Code writing genius and cosmic thinker, Mathael Robintree, who created the infrastructure behind the Zap Oracle, inspired me with his insights and did a brilliant job with the layout of the book. Philosopher and Renaissance man, Michael Grosso, whose work, though I first encountered it when editing the final draft, and our recent correspondence, has brought exciting and humbling corroboration of my results. And, of course, Carl Jung, who, like a wizard bearing a torch, seemed to step out of his collected works when I first encountered him as a twenty-year-old, and who has served as a spiritual grandfather ever since. And all the thinkers, visionaries and researchers quoted throughout the book, those who shared dreams that revealed the thousands faces of the Singularity Archetype, readers who supplied insights, leads and moral support, and all those whom I have never encountered, but whose myriad contributions are helping the species move toward the event horizon.

I. Introduction: Through a Glass Darkly

MOST of us sense that the human species is hurtling toward some sort of event horizon. Images of apocalypse, extinction and metamorphosis haunt the collective imagination, but most efforts to look through the dark glass of the future and see what's up ahead have been dismal failures.

Looking through a glass darkly usually means that you see a distorted reflection of yourself — your projections and unconscious expectations, the distorted artifacts of your psyche misconstrued as images of the future. Later we'll examine the psychology of prophecy and why it has earned its reputation as the most fallible of human enterprises. All of us have seen people of various persuasions — religious, New Age, techno-futurist, etc. — step into the carnival funhouse-mirror world of future gazing. When they emerge it always seems to be with breathless enthusiasm to tell us all about the definitive vision they have had. But unless we are also newly emerged from the carnival funhouse we can't help but to think: What, another one? We've seen it all before, one after another steps out of the funhouse sure that they've seen things right, and yet they all see something a bit different, and whenever they attach a date to it they are always proven wrong.

Did anyone notice a "King of Terror" coming from the sky in 1999 as Nostradamus predicted? And where is Edgar Cayce's "Ring of Fire" predicted for the same end of the millennium that brought us nothing more dramatic than the revelation that Y2K was a big, fat wet cardboard dud? And for that matter why do we still hear about the whole phantasmagoria of the Book of Revelation when it was scheduled to happen in the First Century AD? Prophecies come toward us like a fleet of titanium alloy submarines confidently ready to expose the abyssal depths of the ocean with the most advanced and unerring sonar. But prophecy's service and reliability record is more like that of a fleet of iron and wood submarines with coal-fired engines and screen windows. The broken hulls of disconfirmed prophecies litter the ocean floor like iron turds, while up above people step aboard the latest and greatest of iron and wood submarines as confidently as ever.

And what are we to make of Carnival 2012, a frenzy of absurdities that has about as much to do with the Maya as French fries have to do with the French. It has become little more than the latest opportunity for present-day prophesiers to take their turn at history's most unreliable enterprise. For fifteen years I've watched the archaeoastronomical insights of my friend and colleague, John Major Jenkins, become drowned out by the nonsensical cacophony of Carnival 2012.[1] I've written extensively about the 2012 phenomenon elsewhere, but for now just a few items to set against the parade of misinformation. The Mayan calendar does not end in 2012. Like all calendars, it is perpetual. A great cycle of time ends in 2012 according to the Maya, but the calendar continues. Second, no one has ever found a Mayan prophecy about 2012. The actual, ancient Maya did not predict any particular happening in 2012 except the end of one cycle and the beginning of the next. The whole 2012 end-of-the-world song-and-dance comes from people, usually of Christian ancestry, projecting their unconscious, ancestral apocalypticism onto the unsuspecting artifact of another culture. "Mayan" has become a kind of brand name, a cool icon that people can put in front of whatever stares back at them from the carnival funhouse mirror. Mayan culture has less to do with them than Cuban Marxism has to do with the guy in your local coffee shop wearing a Che Guevara T-shirt. Sure it's become a tasteless, if accepted, pop culture tendency to appropriate meaningful items and make them into a bit of image or word bling, but at least it is done blatantly. For example, no one buys a Zen Republic Energy Drink® thinking that they are imbibing Zen Buddhism or supporting a republic.

But what if there were an image of the future, a primordial image, low resolution but so brilliant that it glitters from the misty depths of countless dreams, and shimmers from behind the distorting mirrors of religious traditions, the fever dreams of saucer cults, the futuristic imaginings of science fiction, fantasy and other artifacts of contemporary mythology? What if an essential image of the future were overlaid, like an iridescent hologram, onto everything we perceive? If we tear off a little piece of the hologram, we see a very blurry version of the original image. This little piece of the hologram has the Rorschach-like blur of an image about to come into focus. The iridescent blur of the almost-image invites the psyche to confabulate various visions. Is it a beast with seven heads? A Ring of Fire? A King of Terror? Something cool and kind of Mayan? Every projection onto the blurry hologram is a bit different, but all of them are right about one thing: There is something there, some sort of image, blurry though it might seem. The image squirms and scintillates before us, struggling to come into focus. If we are too attached to our little piece of the hologram, what comes into focus is our projection onto the hologram. Perhaps we got our projection from a religion, a tradition, a self-proclaimed prophet, or perhaps it came right out of our own imagination.

---

[1] For details on John's significant discoveries regarding the Mayan calendar, see "Carnival 2012: A Psychological Study of the 2012 Phenomenon and the 22 Classic Pitfalls and Blind Spots of Esoteric Research" at ZapOracle.com.

But there is another way to look at the hologram. Instead of gazing into little pieces of it, we can look at the pieces as a vast mosaic. All of the pieces are refractions of a single primordial image. If we don't fixate on any one of them, but allow them to flow back together we may see an image coalesce and emerge from the larger hologram. The image that emerges from the unfractured hologram is more than the superimposition of individual projections; it is a primordial image of a structure that exists within the potential of our species right now. This image is the seed of the future we are hurtling toward. I call this primordial image of the future the Singularity Archetype.[2]

The Singularity Archetype is a resonance, flowing backward through time, of an approaching Singularity[3] at the end of human history. Since the Singularity Archetype is a ubiquitous hologram, you don't have to see it through my eyes, through a tradition or the quirky gaze of any particular individual or group. The Singularity Archetype is like a mote of light you can see reflected in the eyes of multitudes. It is a mote of light reflecting in your eyes and mine right now. Some label this dancing mote of light 2012, others call it Rapture, or a variety of other names and labels.

If we allow the primordial image to reflect off of every sort of eye, then the reflection of each eye becomes like a pixel in a vast hologram.[4] The reassembled image subsumes the idiosyncrasies of particular reflections and coalesces them into the Singularity Archetype. The Singularity Archetype reflects back to us an essential image of the event horizon we are hurtling toward. Essential images do not provide dates or specifics, so it is not like reading a book, but more like seeing roughly formed elements within a future that is also largely unformed. As we

---

[2] For now I am emphasizing the evolutionary side of the archetype. Later, I will develop what it means for the life of the individual.

3 Some with a scientific background may object to this use of "singularity." For them singularity has a specific mathematical meaning: "In mathematics, and in particular singularity theory, an Ak, where $k \geq 0$ is an integer, describes a level of degeneracy of a function. The notation was introduced by V.I. Arnold." But other definitions include: the quality of being one of a kind; strangeness of being remarkable or unusual.
Technological singularity refers to a hypothesis that technological progress will become extremely fast, and so make the future unpredictable and qualitatively different from today. For example, here is a blurb from the webpage for the movie version of Ray Kurzweil's book *The Singularity is Near*, The Singularity is Near: The Movie Home: "The Onset of the 21st Century will be an era in which the very nature of what it means to be human will be both enriched and challenged as our species breaks the shackles of its genetic legacy and achieves inconceivable heights of intelligence, material progress, and longevity. While the social and philosophical ramifications of these changes will be profound, and the threats they pose considerable, celebrated futurist Ray Kurzweil presents a view of the coming age that is both a dramatic culmination of centuries of technological ingenuity and a genuinely inspiring vision of our ultimate destiny."
Similarly, "event horizon," which coined specifically in relation to blackhole physics is commonly used metaphorically as in a recent article on education: "Is this what is happening to education today? Did the current mandates create an event horizon? Is every dollar that is earmarked for education disappearing into the "is it on the test?" event horizon?"

[4] Yes, I know that pixel and hologram are incompatible. This in not optical physics, but rather a loose, extended metaphor.

come to see and understand the Singularity Archetype as a roughly formed template of our likely future and not a specific culture-bound prophecy, we find our free will enhanced. We need to be aware of the formed elements of our future — death, taxes, evolutionary transformation — but we also need to recognize the unformed aspects which give us the room to make choices. Recognizing that the future has both formed and unformed elements, we step out of the deterministic world of prophecy and its linear countdown calendars. We also stop getting dazzled and bedazzled by what was chiseled in stone or written in sacred books long ago and far away about a primordial image we can find reflected in our own eyes right now.

I don't claim that my vision and understanding of the Singularity Archetype is the definitive one, or that my mind is entirely free of distorting projections. My request is that you do what you would no doubt do anyway: scan every aspect of what I present about the Singularity Archetype with your penetrating inner truth sense. I believe your inner truth will reveal a holographic image already inside of you. You may discover aspects of the Singularity Archetype I have distorted or failed to locate. If so, your understanding can contribute to bringing the image into sharper focus, an added clarity for which I will be forever grateful.

The Intensifying Metabolism of Evolution

The metabolism of the species, and therefore the metabolism of events on this planet, has heated up to a feverish intensity. According to some estimates, there are more human beings alive right now than all the human beings that have ever died. The evolutionary process of our species seems to be heading rapidly toward critical mass. Consider how much change has occurred in just the last fifty or one hundred years. The most conservative of predictions is that we are hurtling toward dramatic changes on every level. But how can we contemplate the future development of our own species in a planetary situation that boils over with an infinite array of variables? And how can we possibly transcend the inherent subjectivity of being fully vested members of the species we're trying to contemplate?

To use the imperfect hologram analogy again, if the whole species is a hologram, the most logical subdivision is the single individual. Each of us is one of seven billion pixels comprising the species hologram. But unlike the pixels of a 2D image, each pixel, like each part of a fractal, recapitulates the whole. Switching metaphors to Russian nesting dolls — the largest doll is the species, the second smallest doll would be a single individual and if we open that doll up we find the smallest doll, a single strand of double helix DNA.

So if an entire species seems like an unwieldy object of contemplation, and DNA seems a bit too minute and hard to unravel in a single book, let's speculate about the future of a single individual. One rich source of information about our individual would be biometrics — we could have his DNA analyzed, and ask him to submit to MRIs and every sort of scan and medical test. Maybe we could even get him to accept wearing all sorts of sensors, astronaut style, so we could see how his blood pressure, heart rate, galvanic skin response and so forth fluctuate moment-by-moment. We might find out something very relevant about our individual's future, especially if we found something drastically wrong — a terminal disease or a misfiring brain perhaps. However, for reasons we'll discuss later, I am not of the persuasion that believes a human being is reducible to wetware. If I were limited to a single source of information about an individual, I would not consider biometrics to be the most primary. A source of information I would consider primary would be our individual's dreams.

For three or so hours a day our individual's psyche generates its own universe, a parallel dimension where the deepest aspects of his being are given form. What turns up in these dreams could range from that which is at the very surface of his waking personality to the vast undiscovered continents of his unconscious.

If dreams are the most primary source of information for an individual, what source of information would have the analogous function for a species? Swiss psychiatrist Carl Jung provided the answer that myths are to the collective what dreams are to the individual. A myth, therefore, is a collective dream, a glimpse into the primordial depths of our species.

The Archetypes of the Collective Unconscious

Jung and his colleagues have provided us with definitive evidence of a collective unconscious. From this collective layer of the unconscious emerge the great, primordial images Jung referred to as the "archetypes." Archetypes are "innate universal psychic dispositions that form the substrate from which the basic themes of human life emerge."[5] Across cultures and periods we find endless variations of these archetypes, such as the Self, Persona, Shadow, Hero, Great Mother, Trickster, Devil, etc. The archetypes may manifest in anyone but often show up most vividly in the fertile psyches of artists, poets, mystics, writers, shamans and prophets. Through such individuals the archetypes become myths and diffuse throughout a culture.

---

[5] Papadopoulos, Renos, ed. "The Archetypes". *The Handbook of Jungian Psychology*. New York: Routledge, 2006.

Edward Edinger, a Jungian analyst who wrote eloquently about the nature of archetypes, points out that although we can study archetypes as patterns, they are also living, dynamic agencies. Similarly, we could take a smear of human blood, dry it out on a glass slide, stain it, and illuminate it on the stage of a powerful binocular microscope where we could observe the structure of the erythrocytes and leukocytes. But while we're looking at all the intriguing structures frozen in time on the glass slide, we need to also have a stereoscopic vision in which we see not only the slide but the inner reality of our bodies where blood exists as trillions of living cells pulsing through our veins and arteries. Archetypes are not merely things that we observe, they are living agencies as active, pulsing and alive within our psyches as the blood that is, pulsing and alive, coursing within our bodies. Edinger reminds us that the archetype,

> "is a living organism, a psychic organism that inhabits the collective psyche. And the fact that an archetype is both a pattern and an agency means that any encounter with an archetype will have these two aspects.
>
> "As a pattern, we can encounter an archetypal reality and speak about it as an object — an object of our knowledge and understanding. But as a dynamic living agency it appears to us as subject, as an entity like ourselves with intentionality and some semblance of consciousness."

Jung, in *Answer to Job*, describes the archetype as follows:

> "They are spontaneous phenomena which are not subject to our will, and we are therefore justified in ascribing to them a certain autonomy. They are regarded not only as objects but as subjects with laws of their own. [...] If that is considered, we are compelled to treat them as subjects; in other words, we have to admit that they possess spontaneity and purposiveness, or a kind of consciousness and free will."

Jung rejected the idea that the human psyche was born as a blank slate, a smooth, unpredisposed topography waiting to be carved by the forces of outer conditioning. Instead he envisioned the emerging psyche as a landscape riddled with dry riverbeds shaped by the dynamism of the collective psyche operating across the millennia. When new vitality appeared it would most likely flow into these established channels. This is why people from the most diverse cultures would all envision Heroes, Tricksters, Great Mothers and so forth. Archetypes are the essential, primordial images stored in the hologram of the collective psyche. Each individual refracts these primordial images a bit differently, but the essence is still quite apparent.

Jung points out: "The hypothesis of a collective unconscious belongs to the class of ideas that people at first find strange but soon come to possess and use as familiar conceptions."

Jung was an empiricist and he used empirical evidence to demonstrate the existence of the collective unconscious:

"The hypothesis of the collective unconscious is [...] no more daring than to assume there are instincts. One admits readily that human activity is influenced to a high degree by instincts, quite apart from the rational motivations of the conscious mind. So if the assertion is made that our imagination, perception, and thinking are likewise influenced by inborn and universally present formal elements, it seems to me that a normally functioning intelligence can discover in this idea just as much or just as little mysticism as in the theory of instincts. Although this reproach of mysticism has frequently been leveled at my concept, I must emphasize yet again that the concept of the collective unconscious is neither a speculative nor a philosophical but an empirical matter. The question is simply this: are there or are there not unconscious, universal forms of this kind? If they exist, then there is a region of the psyche one can call the collective unconscious."[6]

Seeds of the Future

"[For the alchemists] they were seeds of light broadcast in the chaos [...] the seed plot of a world to come." — Jung, on the archetypes[7]

The dreams of an individual in crisis will tend to be dynamic, highly charged, and revealing of the archetypes ascendant in their inner process. Similarly, the mythology of a culture in crisis will be intense and revealing of forces shaping collective destiny beneath the world of surfaces and appearances. Furthermore, the realms of dream and mythology will typically parallel or overlap. For example, while Jung worked as an analyst during the era of the Weimar Republic, he found that Wotan[8], the god of war and mayhem in German mythology, was occurring frequently in the dreams of his educated, highly civilized German patients. Jung was very disturbed by this phenomenon, which he called "Wotanism." Based on the emergence of this archetype, Jung was able to correctly predict the future shape of irrational forces brewing in the German psyche.

---

[6] Jung, C. *Collected Works of C. G. Jung, Vol. 9*. 2nd ed. Princeton University Press, 1968.
    For an introduction to the collective unconscious and the archetypes, see *Man and his Symbols*.
[7] Jung, C. *Collected Works of C. G. Jung, Vol. 8*. 2nd ed. Princeton University Press, 1968. 388.
[8] Some claim him as Nordic; he is also known as Odin.

Down the Rabbit Hole

Before we descend into the rabbit hole to encounter the Singularity Archetype, I would like to suggest an invaluable piece of equipment to bring along. Besides all the critical faculties that you bring to bear on this or any other document you read, an encounter with an archetype also requires, as we discussed earlier, a deeply intuitive truth sense. As you approach an archetype you will feel a resonance within, a sense of uncanny familiarity and recognition. *The Hero with a Thousand Faces* is the memorable title of Joseph Campbell's classic book on the hero archetype. Campbell was being numerically modest because every archetype has billions or trillions of faces. These myriad faces are the individual permutations or manifestations of the archetype, like facets allowing you to look into the prismatic depths of a jewel that can dazzle and overwhelm.

During our journey we will have time to look through only a tiny fraction of the available faces/facets of the Singularity Archetype. Hopefully these few vantages will allow the reader to triangulate the essence of an ever-shifting vision. At most, a fundamentalist looks through a single facet of an archetype and concretizes a single face he has been conditioned to see there. The Jungian approach, however, is to realize that each facet involves its own prismatic distortions of the archetype, like a series of cubist paintings of a single subject. Unlike the fundamentalist, the Jungian doesn't attach to the idiosyncratic reflections of particular versions, but attempts to see the essence that unites the myriad manifestations of the archetype.

Our first facet will give us an abstracted outline. Before we glimpse some manifestations of the Singularity Archetype, let's start with a definition and a generic template of how it manifests.

The Singularity Archetype Defined

The Singularity Archetype is a primordial image of human evolutionary metamorphosis which emerges from the collective unconscious. The Singularity Archetype builds on archetypes of death and rebirth and adds information about the evolutionary potential of both species and individual.

How the Archetype Manifests (a Composite Picture)

A rupture-of-plane event occurs, usually threatening the survival of the individual and/or species. The event is a shock that disrupts the equilibrium of body/physical world and also individual/collective psyche. It is an ontological shock that will be viewed as the worst thing possible by individual/ collective ego.

There is another rupture of plane that may actually be the same rupture as above but seen from a cosmic rather than a personal view. The shock is revealed to be a transcendent evolutionary event. The revelation of the transcendent aspect will often involve spiral motifs and unusual lights. Consciousness and communication metamorphose and with them core aspects — ego, individuality, connection to linear time, corporeality, gender identification, social order, etc. — fundamentally transform. There is a vision or actualization of release from some or all limits of corporeal incarnation and the emergence of "glorified bodies," which have enhanced powers and various degrees of etherialization. More visual and telepathic modes of consciousness and communication emerge, and this is part of a transformation of individuality into "Homo gestalt" — a new species where individual psyches are networked telepathically.

The Singularity Archetype may occur as a dream, vision or fantasy about eschaton — an end point of the species. The Singularity Archetype may also be experienced and even actualized to various degrees by an individual through transcendent and/or anomalous experiences such as near-death experiences (NDEs), UFO/abduction/close encounter experiences, kundalini and psychotropic episodes.

As with encounters with all archetypes, individuals and groups will attach idiosyncratic material to it, such as particular end dates and scenarios. But the Singularity Archetype cannot be located in linear time and is not reducible to a premonition of particular outcomes or predetermined futures. It could, however, be viewed as a "strange attractor,"[9] a not fully formed pattern associated with the future that is affecting individual and species in past and present. Another way of defining the Singularity Archetype (in its collective form) is as a resonance, flowing backward through time, of an approaching Singularity at the end of human history.

The Singularity Archetype is a critical point where transformation, in ways impossible to fully anticipate, will greatly shift human consciousness and therefore the nature of "reality." From an ordinary, grounded human perspective, this Singularity may be perceived as apocalyptic extinction. From a more cosmic perspective, the Singularity is revealed as a transcendent evolutionary threshold.

The Singularity Archetype, however, is not merely located in the future, but has also existed in the past and is very much alive in the

---

[9] This is a term that Terence McKenna borrowed from Chaos Mathematics, and I am using it in the same way he did, but I do not know if that corresponds to its mathematical meaning.

present as well. It reflects the potential that exists in the species in real time and has relevance to individuals whose lifespan does not extend to the event horizon of the species. As we will see later in the section on the Singularity Archetype and Near-Death Experience, the Singularity Archetype relates to both the evolutionary event horizon of the species and, for the individual, the event horizon of death.

As with all archetypes, visions of this approaching Singularity occur in a variety of permutations. When an archetype emerges from the collective unconscious, it is colored by the cultural conditioning, personal unconscious and unique individuality of the psyche perceiving it. Attached to the Singularity Archetype is a constellation of elements, a developing mythology of a new step in human evolution. These elements reflect changes occurring as we approach the Singularity. The Singularity Archetype is found in the prophecies of great religions and tribal cultures, and many who feel it approaching see it through the particular lens of their religious or cultural tradition. An evangelical Christian, for example, may speak of Armageddon and the Rapture.

While most perceive the Singularity Archetype through religious prophecy, it is also possible to view it from a nondenominational vantage (the Jungian method). We can do this by looking at a variety of manifestations of the Singularity Archetype from different periods, places, individuals and sources. We can look at dreams, individual and collective (myths), but also at consciously created visionary artifacts such as novels, movies, etc. In a later section we'll take a brief look at the Singularity Archetype through religious prophecies. It will be a brief look, because for me at least, looking at the Singularity Archetype through religious prophecy is another version of looking through a glass darkly. At best it is like looking through thick, semi-transparent stained-glass windows. The jigsaw pattern of lead solder forms a fixed template defining and segmenting your vision. Oxides of cobalt, copper and gold added long ago to molten glass predetermine the colors you will see. But to be fair, stained-glass windows are meant to be looked at with awe from a distance. They are certainly not made for looking through. I find it more useful to view the Singularity through the eyes of modern individuals. To start, let's consider a couple of dreams recorded by one of Jung's most brilliant colleagues, Marie Louise Von Franz, in Jung's classic introductory work: *Man and his Symbols*.

Two Dreams

Von Franz describes two dreams reported to her by someone she describes as "a simple woman who was brought up in Protestant surroundings..." In both dreams a supernatural event of great significance is viewed. But in one dream the dreamer views the event from above, in the other dream she views the same event standing on the earth.

The dreamer's painting of her earthbound dream.[10]

The dreamer's painting of her dream from the heavens.[10]

> "In the earthbound dream, the dreamer stands with a guide, looking down at Jerusalem. The wing of Satan descends and darkens the city. The occurrence in the Middle East of this uncanny wing of the devil immediately brings to mind Antichrist and Armageddon."

The dreamer witnesses the same cosmic event from the heavens. From this vantage she sees the white, wafting cloak of God. The white spiral appears as a symbol of evolution. Von Franz narrates: "the spectator is high up, somewhere in heaven, and sees in front of her a terrific split between the rocks. The movement in the cloak of God is an attempt to reach Christ, the figure on the right, but it does not quite succeed. In the second painting, the same thing is seen from below — from a human angle. Looking at it from a higher angle, what is moving and spreading is a part of God; above that rises the spiral as a symbol of possible further development. But seen from the basis of our human reality, this same thing in the air is the dark, uncanny wing of the devil.

> "In the dreamer's life these two pictures became real in a way that does not concern us here, but it is obvious that they may also contain a collective meaning that reaches beyond the personal. They may prophesy the descent of a divine darkness upon the Christian hemisphere, a darkness that points, however, toward the possibility of further evolution. Since the axis of the spiral

---

[10] From *Man and His Symbols*, a superb introduction to the work of C.G. Jung

does not move upward but into the background of the picture, the further evolution will lead neither to greater spiritual height nor down into the realm of matter, but to another dimension..."

Over many years of working with people on their dreams, I have observed many such visions of the Singularity Archetype. For example, a few years ago a young man reported to me the following dream:

"The sky is turning very dark. Underground tremors occur and escalate to where the earth seems to be shaking itself to pieces. There is fire and lightening, and it seems to be the end of the world. Then everything calms down. Sunlight breaks through the dark clouds and illuminates a large white eagle, which comes spiraling down from above. In its talons it holds a golden egg with a glowing aura. Carefully, it deposits this egg in a nest at the top of a great tree."

In this single, brief dream account we see many of the elements we saw in the two dreams recorded by Von Franz. There is the descent of darkness that seems to threaten the end of the world, but this transforms into a cosmic rebirth event associated with a spiral.

Childhood's End

We will now switch facets and view a third manifestation of the Singularity Archetype through a very different psyche and medium. The very different psyche belongs to Arthur C. Clarke, who was originally an astrophysicist and later became famous as a science-fiction writer. Clarke is a man of science and famously anti-religious. For example, *The New York Times* quoted him as saying: "Religion is a byproduct of fear. For much of human history, it may have been a necessary evil, but why was it more evil than necessary? Isn't killing people in the name of God a pretty good definition of insanity?"[11] In other words, Clarke's worldview is in dramatic contrast to the probable worldview of the Christian woman whose dreams we just looked at. Also, science fiction, a form that is consciously created with much effort during waking hours, would seem to be a very different source than dreams, which erupt spontaneously from the unconscious.

Clarke is best known for the novel and Stanley Kubrick film, *2001: A Space Odyssey. 2001* is one of the most brilliant visions of the Singularity Archetype but, we are going to consider an earlier example of Clarke's work, the classic science-fiction novel, *Childhood's End.* Science fiction is obviously a very different medium than dreams. But like dreams, science fiction is also a fertile and open imaginal realm

---

[11] http://www.celebatheists.com/wiki/Arthur_C._Clarke

where the collective unconscious can communicate with modern persons, and a new mythology, however unrecognized, can express itself. Since *Childhood's End* is as profound a manifestation of the Singularity Archetype as I've ever encountered, we'll give it a correspondingly more thorough look.

Childhood's End begins with extraterrestrial spacecraft appearing over the world's capitals. Beings from within these craft break through all communications and announce that they are "the Overlords" and have come to establish peace on earth. They claim to be superior beings who wish to establish peace and prosperity on earth through the formation of a world government, maintained by their supreme authority. They ask to be thought of as civil servants rather than dictators. In fact, they do advance man's material contentment, with the major religions standing as their only organized opposition. The Overlords succeed in establishing peace on earth and, excepting military aggression, do not curtail any human freedoms. To all appearances the Overlords are benevolent, but they remain a great unknown: "Speculations concerning the Overlords were pure guesswork. No one knew their motives; and no one knew toward what future they were shepherding mankind."

Much of the continuing distrust of the Overlords stems from the fact that they will not appear in public or even offer a description of their physical form. Eventually they promise to reveal themselves after two generations — fifty years.

These fifty years pass peacefully for the human species. Thanks to the Overlords, mankind has entered a golden age of affluence and everyone eagerly awaits the day when the Overlords will descend to earth and reveal themselves. When the long-anticipated day arrives the great spacecraft descend. With some ceremony, the Overlords emerge, and to the uneasy surprise of the human species their appearance is revealed:

> "The leathery wings, the little horns, the barbed tail — all were there. The most terrible of all legends had come to life out of the unknown past. Yet now it stood smiling, in ebon majesty, with the sunlight gleaming upon its tremendous body…" (65).

This decidedly mythological element is fascinatingly incongruous with the setting of technological materialism stereotypical of the science-fiction genre. What is the meaning of a specter from the Christian and pagan past reemerging in the world of the future? Clarke reveals that the Overlords' alarming physiognomy is simply the result of their evolutionary adaptation to the environmental conditions of their planet. The Overlords are actually perfectly benevolent and are far more rational and intelligent than humans. The novel explains their physical appearance as "a racial memory of a future event," accounting for their cross-cultural appearance in legend and myth. In other words, their physical form and association with evil is an archetype, but also a premonition. The association with evil, furthermore, is not a reflection of the Overlord's nature, as they are in fact benevolent, but rather a result of the event horizon of total transformation that the Overlord's arrival signifies. The instinctive and premonitory fear of the Overlord's physical form derives from the conservatism of an established genome recognizing that metamorphosis means the obsolescence and extinction of the species in its old form.

The Overlords are servants of the "Overmind," a cosmic intelligence permeating the universe that is Clarke's naturalistic God concept. The Overmind employs the Overlords as midwives. When the Overmind senses that an intelligent species is about to cross the evolutionary event horizon and make the jump into higher consciousness, it sends the Overlords to their planet to supervise the process. This evolutionary process is volatile and unstable, and if not properly supervised could result in disastrous consequences whose effects would reach far beyond the particular world on which the process occurs.

The Overlords, though infinitely superior to humans in every perceivable attribute, are themselves barren and unable to manifest the evolutionary birth process that it is their perpetual task to oversee. As one of the Overlords, Rasheverak, explains:

> "Probably, like most men, you have always regarded us as your masters. That is not true. We have never been more than guardians, doing a duty imposed upon us from — above. That duty is hard to define: perhaps you can best think of us as midwives attending a difficult birth. We are helping to bring something new and wonderful into being. [...] Yes, we are the midwives. But we ourselves are barren" (178).

Karellan, the chief Overlord, in a final speech to mankind, adds:

> "Our intellects are far more powerful than yours, but there is something in your minds that has always eluded us. [...] Our races have much in common — that is why we were chosen for this task. But in other respects, we represent the ends of two different evolutions. Our minds have reached the end of their development. So, in their present form, have yours. Yet you can make the jump to the next stage, and therein lies the difference between us."

> "We are your guardians — no more. Often you must have wondered what position my race held in the hierarchy of the universe. As we are above you, so there is something above us, using us for its own purposes. We have never discovered what it is, though we have been its tool for ages and dare not disobey it.

Again and again we have received our orders, have gone to some world in the early flower of its civilization, and have guided it along the road that we can never follow — the road that you are traveling now."

"Again and again we had studied the process we have been sent to foster, hoping that we might learn to escape form our limitations. But we have glimpsed only the vague outlines of the truth. You called us the Overlords, not knowing the irony of that title. [...] Let us say that above us is the Overmind, using us as the potter uses his wheel."

"And your race is the clay that is being shaped on that wheel."

An interesting aspect of the evolutionary model presented in *Childhood's End* is that intelligence is not the decisive factor catalyzing the evolutionary event horizon. The Overlords are well aware of this and recognize that it is parapsychological abilities that are more essential to the metamorphosis. Karellan makes this explicit in his final speech:

"Your mystics, though they were lost in their own delusions, had seen part of the truth. There are powers of the mind, and powers beyond the mind, which your science could never have brought within its framework without shattering it entirely. All down the ages there have been countless reports of strange phenomena — poltergeists, telepathy, precognition — which you had named but never explained. At first science ignored them, even denied their existence, despite the testimony of five thousand years. But they exist, and, if it is to be complete, any theory of the universe must account for them."

"During the first half of the twentieth century, a few of your scientists began to investigate these matters. They did not know it, but they were tampering with the lock of Pandora's box. The forces they might have unleashed transcended any perils that the atom could have brought. For the physicists could only have ruined the earth: the paraphysicists could have spread havoc to the stars" (178-182).

The reference to Pandora's box here will be very relevant when we look at the world of Pandora in *Avatar*, a world where paraphysics trumps technological physics.

On earth, in addition to keeping human beings from destroying each other, the Overlords have a secret task, to search for an extraordinary individual who will be the first human being to exhibit these evolutionary changes. This individual is referred to as "Subject Zero," and the concept seems close to a naturalistic version of searching for the Messiah.

As part of this search, Rasheverak pays a visit to an American man who has one of the largest privately owned collections of books on parapsychology and the occult. Rasheverak is interested in this library because he is looking for any examples of extraordinary functioning that might indicate the emergence of Subject Zero. Like any intelligent, skeptical reader of such material, Rasheverak finds that it is often difficult to sift the truth from the abundant nonsense.

After reading half of the library, Rashaverak reports to his supervisor that he has found, "eleven cases of partial breakthrough and twenty-seven probables. The material is so selective, however that one cannot use it for sampling purposes. And the evidence is confused with mysticism — perhaps the chief aberration of the human mind."

Rashaverak also reports that Rupert, "pretends to be open-minded and skeptical, but it's clear that he would never have spent so much time and effort in this field unless he has some unconscious faith" (99).

During Rashaverak's stay at his home, Rupert has a party for friends apparently drawn by the celebrity name-dropping opportunity of meeting an Overlord. The guests, like the owner, seem to be narcissistic individuals with a gullible appetite for occult and parapsychological entertainments. In many ways they seem a prophetic anticipation of stereotyped New Agers. At one point, as part of the entertainment, Rupert invites his guests to have a session with the Ouija board. Rashaverak does not participate, but he does observe. Rupert asks the board to identify itself and it replies "IAMALL," a statement very suggestive of a collective unconscious. The board delivers some more ambiguous messages, such as, "BELIEVEINMANNATUREISWITH YOU" and "REMBERMANISNOTALONENEARMANISCOUNTRY OFOTHER." Finally one skeptic among the group asks, "Which star is the Overlord's sun?" a piece of information which the Overlords have kept from mankind. The board replies "NGS 546972," which turns out to be the correct coordinates.

Rashaverak later explains that the information came from a young woman participating in the séance:

> "Miss Morrel's mind was the channel that, if only for a moment, let through the knowledge which no one alive at that time could possess. It could only come from another mind, intimately linked to hers. The fact that it was a mind not yet born was of no consequence, for Time is very much stranger than you think" (99).

Rasheverak is also aware that, "All through history there have been people with inexplicable powers which seem to transcend space and time" (172).

Rashaverak explains these powers in terms that clearly imply a collective unconscious:

> "But there is one analogy which is — well suggestive and helpful. It occurs over and over again in your literature. Imagine that every man's mind is an island, surrounded by ocean. Each seems isolated, yet in reality all are linked by the bedrock from which they spring. If the ocean were to vanish, that would be the end of the islands. They would all be part of one continent, but their individuality would be gone" (178).

There are no obvious signs within man himself that he is evolving and we are reminded that intellect wouldn't have much to do with it. We are told that, "there was no evidence that the intelligence of the human race had improved…" The child that the Overlords suspect of being the first sample of the new breed, Miss Morrell's son, seems perfectly average: "I was able to see the school records of subject Zero, without arousing curiosity. The relevant statistics are attached, and it will be seen that there are still no signs of any unusual development. Yet, as we know, breakthrough seldom gives much prior warning" (99).

Subject Zero begins to have strange visions of other worlds. The Overlord's knowledge of the universe indicates that the dreams are accurate visions, and that each dream describes a world further from the center of the universe. The subject's infant sister, meanwhile, is developing telekinesis and non-physical senses. She is progressing more rapidly, we are told, because "she had so much less to unlearn."

Karellan tries to prepare mankind for the shocking metamorphosis in his final speech:

> "All the earlier changes your race has known took countless ages. But this is a transformation of the mind, not of the body. By the standards of evolution, it will be cataclysmic — instantaneous. It has already begun. You must face the fact that yours is the last generation of Homo sapiens.
>
> "As to the nature of that change, we can tell you very little. We do not know how it is produced — what trigger impulse the Overmind employs when it judges that the time is ripe. All we have discovered is that it starts with a single individual — always a child — and then spreads explosively, like the formation of crystals round the first nucleus in a saturated solution. Adults will not be affected for their minds are already set in an unalterable mold.

"In a few years, it will all be over, and the human race will have divided in twain. There is no way back, and no future for the world you know. All the hopes and dreams of your race are ended now. You have given birth to your successors, and it is your tragedy that you will never understand them — will never even be able to communicate with their minds. Indeed they will not possess minds as you know them. They will be a single entity, as you yourselves are the sums of your myriad cells. You will not think them human, and you will be right" (178-182).

All the children born after a certain point are of this new type and exhibit parapsychological powers. Once a critical number of them are born, all human beings of the older type become sterile. This is the literal part of the meaning of the title, *Childhood's End*. The new children evolve quickly and become more powerful as their psyches merge to form a collective consciousness. At a certain point the children materialize themselves on one continent and join hands forming a giant moving configuration the Overlords call "The Long Dance." Older, pre-Subject Zero human beings are not destroyed, but having given birth to their successors they become literally sterile and are utterly demoralized by their irrelevance and inevitable extinction.

When the children manifest their ultimate evolution and are able to merge energetically with the Overmind, they appear to the last human being left alive as an aurora borealis, a spiral of light in the sky also described as a glittering network of lights.

Childhood's End uncannily parallels the three dreams we have considered. In the young man's dream, darkness and earthquake transform into a spiraling white eagle bearing a golden egg. Similarly, the dark wing of Satan descends in the dream of a simple Protestant woman, only to be later revealed as the cloak of God. And all three manifestations envision a white spiral of light in the sky as the interdimensional, evolutionary portal of the species. A central, emergent theme is that what seems apocalyptic from the earthbound ego point of view is revealed from a cosmic point of view to be a transcendent evolutionary metamorphosis.

I have recorded and studied numerous other examples of this Singularity Archetype and found the essential pattern repeated with all sorts of interesting variations. We'll take a look at some of them later, but if you keep your eyes open I think you'll find many examples for yourself. The world of contemporary culture is intensely mythological; it is only a question of recognizing it. Tune into the right frequencies and you will notice that archetypal information about this approaching Singularity permeates our environment as ubiquitously as radio and television waves. If you remember that the same tools of symbolic analysis employed in dream interpretation may be employed in understanding all sorts of cultural manifestations, you will find yourself provided with endless messages about the approaching event horizon.

II. Logos Beheld

Stone plaque I bought in a Boulder thrift store. An eye with a spiral is the ideal symbol of the singularity archetype. It's signed [approximately] B. Guannano 7/95 — a play on Bat Guano?

This life's dim windows of the soul
Distorts the heavens from pole to pole
And lead you to believe a lie
When you see with, not through, the eye.

— William Blake[12]

Uncanny Eyes

FROM my earliest encounters with the Singularity Archetype in the Seventies, it was apparent that uncanny eyes, visual languages and telepathies were consistent motifs. If you wanted to reduce the Singularity Archetype to an icon, you would probably end up with an eye at the center of a spiral.

---

[12] From *The Everlasting Gospel* (c.1818).

The earliest instance that I've found of the uncanny eye motif in an expression of the Singularity Archetype is in the Bible, Revelation 4:6: "And before the throne there was a sea of glass like unto crystal and in the midst of the throne, and round about the throne, were four beasts full of eyes before and behind." The four beasts are covered with eyes and before them is the most optically pure and light-conductive material, — "glass like unto crystal."

Uncanny eyes also feature prominently in modern apocalyptic visions. For example, a Japanese man dreamed the following on August 24th, 1945, about three weeks after experiencing the nuclear bombing of Hiroshima:

> "I was in Tokyo after the great earthquake and around me were decomposing bodies heaped in piles, all of whom were looking right at me. I saw an eye sitting in the palm of a girl's hand. Suddenly it turned and leaped into the sky and then came flying back toward me, so that looking up I could see a great bare eyeball, bigger than life hovering over my head, staring point-blank at me. I was powerless to move. I awakened short of breath and my heart pounding."[13]

My very first encounter with the Singularity Archetype was watching the movie *The Village of the Damned,* which featured mutant children with light-transmitting eyes and telepathic communication. In the novel by John Wyndham on which the movie was based, *The Midwich Cuckoos,* the new children's eyes are described as follows: "The eyes, however, were even more remarkable than he had been led to expect. He had been told of the curious golden color of their irises, but no one had succeeded in conveying to him their striking lambency, their strange effect of being softly lit from within" (103).

In Issac Asimov's *Foundation* series, The Mule is a powerful mutant whose telepathic powers allow him to manipulate the emotions of entire planetary populations. The Mule, incognito as Magnifico Giganticus the clown, is described:

> "'He is a man of overpowering might, respected sir, and cruel in the use of his power — and his eyes, respected sir, no one sees.'
>
> 'What's that? What's that last?'
>
> 'He wears spectacles, respected sir, of a curious nature. It is said that they are opaque and that he sees by a powerful magic that far transcends human powers. I have heard,' and his voice was

---

[13] Edinger, E. *Archetype of the Apocalypse: A Jungian Study of the Book of Revelation.* Chicago: Open Court Publishing Company, 1999. 49.

small and mysterious, 'that to see his eyes is to see death, that he kills with his eyes, respected sir.'"[14]

Magnifico is a virtuoso of the Visi-Sonor, an instrument that through radiation on the optic nerve produces musical images of pulsing color that people simultaneously perceive differently. The new mutants are almost always described as being able to transmit linguistic content through their eyes or some other visual medium. For example, consider this description from Theodore Sturgeon's 1953 science fiction novel, *More Than Human*:

> "Thompson took off his glasses. He had wide round eyes, just the color and luminescence of a black and white television screen. The irises showed the whites all the way around; they were perfectly round and they looked as if they were about to spin."[15]

What is most interesting about this description is that the eyes are compared to a television screen — a medium of visual communication.

In Frank Herbert's classic 1965 science fiction novel, *Dune*, there are frequent descriptions of uncanny eyes. People who take the visionary spice mélange, the most precious substance in the universe and a catalyst for parapsychological abilities, develop eyes that are all irises. It is said of Alia, a young mutant girl, that "her eyes kill our enemies and torment the unbelievers."[16] When Alia's brother Paul, a messianic being also called the Kwisatz Haderach, has his eyes destroyed by a "stone burner," a type of nuclear device, he retains his ability to see through prescience.

The Visual Transcends the Verbal

In the *Medusa Touch*, Peter Van Greenaway's novel about a man with the ability to create catastrophes with his mind, the main character's eyes are continually emphasized:

> "eyes — extraordinary — luminous eyes, like dice flung into a plate of cold porridge. Features defying one to look twice, but even in a poor photograph those eyes were of such an incredible intensity…" (16).

> "I cannot describe the ultimate transformation of those features. Discomposing flesh set with diamonds.

> "It was as if I gazed through a Dadaist exterior at a crystal skull; as if I saw, physically saw, through him — into him — nothing

[14] Asimov, I. *Foundation and Empire*. New York: Avon, 1974.
[15] Sturgeon, T. *More Than Human. A Science Fiction Argosy*. Ed. Damon Knight. New York: Simon and Schuster, 1972.
[16] The Medusa Touch, Van Greenaway, P.

alive beyond the transparency except eyes fired by preternatural intent" (211).

"Quite the most intense, almost mesmeric eyes I've ever seen. Best looked at through smoked glass kind of a thing. Twin seals of absolute authority. It creates difficulties of course, trying to separate visual fascination from verbal statements — influenced by one you're bound to accept the other" (43).

The last sentence of this final quote reveals something of great interest: "trying to separate visual fascination from verbal statements — influenced by one you're bound to accept the other." Essentially it implies that visual communication trumps verbal communication, and that principle is implicit in so many versions of the Singularity Archetype. Visual, telepathic communication transcends ordinary communication. In *More Than Human*: "The probe that passes invisibly from his brain through his eyes into mine."[17]

Two characters who have never met in any conventional way are already aware of each other through silent, radiant communication: "She had been aware of him for days and he of her, and now their silent radiations reached out to each other, mixed and mingled and meshed" (652).

In Stephen King's 1977 horror novel, *The Shining*, "shining" is a modality of visual telepathy. Danny, a five-year-old boy, is a sensitive, and his intuitions and perceptions of his parents' unexpressed thoughts are described in terms of colors. Adult thoughts beyond his limited experience to comprehend and interpret come to him "only as colors and moods." His father's divorce thoughts are described as "more complex, colored dark violet and shot through with frightening veins of pure black."

Hallorann, a caretaker of the Overlook Hotel in Colorado, is in Florida when he hears Danny's telepathic call for help. King describes their bond:

"He knew the boy. They had shared each other the way good friends can't even after forty years of it. He knew the boy and the boy knew him, because they each had a kind of searchlight in their heads, something they hadn't asked for, something that had just been given. (No, you got a flashlight, he the one with the searchlight.) And sometimes that light, that shine, seemed like a pretty good thing."[18]

[17] Sturgeon, Theodore. "More Than Human". *A Science Fiction Argosy*. Ed. Damon Knight. New York: Simon and Schuster, 1972. 684.

[18] King, Stephen. *The Shining*. New York: Doubleday, 1977. 80.

Haunting the Overlook is a collectivized entity of negative light. It is described alternately as "a huge, obscene manta," and a whirling blackness, "dancing like negative motes of light."

The Eye as Evolution's Star Gate?

In Arthur C. Clarke's 1968 science fiction novel, *2001*, the "Star Gate" through which the protagonist, Bowman, crosses the evolutionary event horizon is compared to an eye. Bowman looks out at the white surface of the moon, Japetus, and for no visual reason feels,

> "The satellite was a huge, empty eye, staring at him as he approached. It was an eye without a pupil, for nowhere could he see anything to mar its perfect blankness.

> Not until the ship was only fifty thousands miles out... did he notice the tiny black dot at the exact center of the ellipse."[19]

The pupil of the eye turns out to be a monolith. Early in the book another monolith appears that is described as having a "pulsing aura of light." This monolith uses rhythmic light to reprogram a group of missing-link man-apes in an evolutionary intervention that leads to Homo sapiens and eventually space travel. Bowman attempts to land on the giant monolith on Japetus and discovers it to be a "Star Gate," an infinitely receding corridor where he is bombarded with mind-blowing images. On the other side of the evolutionary event horizon, Bowman has become the "Star Child," an infant "with eyes that already held more than human intentness." In the 1968 film, *2001*, the Star Child looks like a fetal version of a classic grey alien — the large-eyed beings universally reported to communicate telepathically with abductees and other experiencers.

The Eye, the Cambrian Explosion, and the Light Switch Theory

That eyes should be associated with future, quantum evolutionary change seems strangely appropriate, as the development of eyes may have been the catalyst for quantum evolutionary change in the distant past. Andrew Parker, an Oxford University zoologist, in his book, *In the Blink of an Eye*, has developed the "Light Switch" theory to explain the Cambrian explosion — one of paleontology's greatest mysteries.

Approximately 543 million years ago there was an explosion of new life forms. As Parker puts it, "544 million years ago there were indeed three animal phyla with their variety of external forms, but at 538 million

---

[19] Clarke, Arthur C. *2001*. New York: New American Library, 1968. 181.

years ago there were thirty-eight, the same number that exists today" (9). According to the Light Switch theory, the relatively sudden evolution of vision made active predation possible, and this created tremendous pressure on prey to adapt novel ways of avoiding detection. With the dawn of vision new habitats opened up, inter and intra species relations became more complex, and organisms specialized and differentiated to deal with this quantum evolutionary shift.

The Alphabet versus the Goddess, The Chalice and the Blade

As we will discuss in greater depth later, the current phase of human evolution is being catalyzed by an explosion of visual technologies and an environment ever more saturated with visual information. The blossoming of visual novelty is causing a shift in hemispheric dominance of the brain from the left to the right, as well as vast changes in perception and communication.

Vascular surgeon Leonard Shlain in his flawed but intriguing and paradigm-shifting book, *The Alphabet Versus the Goddess*, presents a theory of cultural and social transformation based on hemispheric dominance. Shlain's theory grows out of Riane Eisler's seminal work, *The Chalice and the Blade*, a book that anthropologist Ashley Montagu praised as "the most important book since Darwin's Origin of the Species."

The Chalice and the Blade presents the theory that a Partnership model of social organization characterized Neolithic Europe and lasted up till the time of the Bronze Age civilization of Minoan Crete. Partnership societies were characterized by egalitarian relations between the sexes, goddess worship and life-affirming values. The emblematic object of this era was the chalice, which symbolized abundance, feminine values and the goddess. The end of the Partnership era came with the invasion of patriarchal tribes built on the Dominator model, which is characterized by strict hierarchies, men dominating women, and death-centered values represented by the sword — the new iconic, emblematic object. Joseph Campbell mapped out this transformation in a parallel way, according to Carolyn G. Heilbrun in her book, *Toward a Recognition of Androgyny*:

> "Joseph Campbell's five-volume study of mythology, published under the general title of *The Masks of God*, contains in each of its volumes an extraordinary record of the ancient shift from matriarchy to patriarchy. The shift is schematized by Campbell in four steps as follows:
>
> The world born of a goddess without consort,
> The world born of a goddess fecundated by a consort,
> The world fashioned from the body of a goddess by a male

warrior-god,
The world created by the unaided power of a male god alone"
(5).

Hemispheric Lateralization:

Essentially, *The Alphabet Versus the Goddess* is an attempt to explain this enormous shift from Partnership societies and feminine values to Dominator societies with patriarchal values. According to Shlain, the switch over to dominator culture was always preceded by the adoption of a written alphabet. Written alphabets, as objects of perception, cause a shift in hemispheric dominance emphasizing the left hemisphere. Homo sapiens have a "hemispheric lateralization"[20] — a specialization of brain lobes greater than that of any other animal (17).

The right hemisphere develops before the left and has more in common with the way other animals process reality. The right hemisphere is intuitive, holistic, it integrates feelings and appreciates music and images. The right hemisphere is nonverbal, but it recognizes faces and body language. The left hemisphere has specialized to deal with abstracted language, with word and number, and is associated with linear thinking and the ability to categorize. It is the hierarchical left hemisphere that carries the powerful will to build a dominator society. As Shlain illustrates, quickly following the adoption of a written alphabet goddesses are eliminated, women are forbidden to preside over religious rituals, or even to participate at all, and in general become second-class citizens or disposable property. A text of some sort becomes the ruling principle ("In the beginning was the word…"), and that text could be religious (the Bible, the Koran) or secular (the Communist Manifesto, the "rule of law"). Clerics would even come to prefer garments of black and white, the colors of ink and paper.

Thou Shalt Not Have Images

Shlain points out, for example, that the Second of the Ten Commandments is about not having images, while we have to drop down to the Sixth Commandment before we find a prohibition against murder. From Exodus 20:4, the Second Commandment reads:

"Thou shalt not make unto thee any graven images, or any likeness of any thing that is in heaven above, or that is in the water under the earth."

---

[20] Hemispheric differences are much more complex than I will be making them out to be here. I am drawing a "rough and ready" distinction so as not to overwhelm the text with complicated neuroscience.

The Second Commandment is popularly interpreted as being against idol worship, but it is actually a ban on all representational art. This taboo is repeated throughout the Torah. For example, from Deuteronomy 4:15-18:

Take ye therefore good heed unto yourselves [...]
Lest ye corrupt yourselves, and make you a graven image, the
Similitude of any figure, the likeness of male or female
The likeness of any beast that is on the earth, the likeness of any
Winged fowl that flieth in the air.

The likeness of any thing that creepeth on the ground, the
likeness of
Any fish that is in the waters beneath the earth.

Clearly, the Second Commandment is not just a ban on idols. However, the etymology of the word "idol" is interesting and relevant. "Idol" derives from the Latin word "idolum," and idolum derives from "eidolon," — the Greek word for image.

Yahweh's first instruction to Adam in Genesis is to attach word labels to things, to name things. It is Adam's left hemisphere ability to name things that gives him dominion over them. Shlain finds a hemispheric bias in the Abrahamic faiths Judaism, Christianity and Islam: "Each is an exemplar of patriarchy. Each monotheistic religion features an imageless Father deity whose authority shines through His revealed Word, sanctified in its written form."

Eve's Choice and Punishment

The Abrahamic faiths, unless heavily reformed and reinterpreted, show a profound bias against women, and this bias seems to run strangely parallel to the bias against image in favor of word. The punishment of Eve, the very first woman according to the Bible, is about as excessive and over-the-top as can be imagined. Eve makes a choice before she ate the fruit and learned the difference between good and evil. Any reasonable person morally excuses the actions of animals, small children, etc. who have not had the opportunity to learn the difference between good and evil. Eve is in a state of innocence and unconsciousness. Furthermore, she makes the correct choice! Of course we have to eat from the tree of the knowledge of good and evil, why else did we leave the womb! And yet Yahweh not only punishes her, but curses all women into the indefinite future for this one innocent and correct choice. As Genesis 3:16 tells us: "Unto the woman he said, I will greatly multiply thy sorrow and thy conception, in sorrow thou shalt bring forth children and thy desire shall be to thy husband and he shall rule over thee."

What is especially ironic here is that it is true that human females have greater sorrow in conception than other mammals for a reason that we now know very clearly: evolution! What makes human conception so perilous is the increased size of a cranium to make way for a larger brain. Women suffer in childbirth to allow us to have a complex enough brain so that we are able to learn the difference between good and evil and a great many other things.

A Strange Convergence

Correlation does not mean causation, but it does seem striking how much worship of the written word and hatred of images and women seem to converge. Let's take a quick tour of examples of this convergence from a variety of cultures, courtesy of *The Alphabet and the Goddess*. Many examples will emphasize a single point of the triad (word worship, anti-image, misogyny), sometimes two points, rarely all three, so it is reasonable to question how much the aggregation of examples really demonstrates convergence.

A Crusade Against Images

"In the 8th century a sect arose [...] that so despised images that its members declared and all-out war against statues and paintings. They called themselves the Iconoclasts, which means image-destroyers. Leo III ordered all church murals covered with plaster and all likenesses of the Virgin effaced. Their targets also included painters, sculptors and craftsmen. Monks who resisted were blinded and had their tongues torn out" (275-6).

The Face Closet

Islam, to this day, is filled with prohibitions against images. Just a few years ago there was an explosion of Islamic rage toward Sweden because of a few cartoons. More than a hundred people died as a result. The repressive custom of the burqa erases women visually. No other animal has a face that compares with the expressiveness of the human face. We have more muscles in our faces than any other animal allowing us a complex medium of visual communication with facial expressions that change in microseconds. Even when an infant is unable to focus her eyes, she can recognize faces and her brain lights up differently than for any other object. To block a woman's ability to have this sort of communication is an inexcusable form of repression that is perhaps even more profound than genital mutilation. It is fundamentally wrong to use moral relativism to rationalize such repression as a cultural difference when it is clearly an amputation of human potential. Shlain points out that the face-covering taboo is so strong among some Muslim women that if surprised in the bath they will cover their faces before their bodies.

In 2002, a fire in a school in the holy city of Mecca, Saudi Arabia was attended by morality police, who are known as "The Commission for the Promotion of Virtue and Prevention of Vice." The morality police fatally interfered with firemen and others trying to help. They kept girls inside the burning building because they were not wearing headscarves and abayas (black robes) as required by the kingdom's strict interpretation of Islam. A witness saw three morality policemen "beating young girls to prevent them from leaving the school because they were not wearing the abaya." The morality police also stopped men trying to help the girls, warning that "it is sinful to approach them." Fifteen girls died in the blaze.[21]

Women are Sinful, but Reading is Fundamental

While women and images are often treated as radioactive, a text, the Koran, is considered divine, perfect, and supreme. The great miracle of Mohammed's encounter with the angel Gabriel is that he instantaneously acquired literacy. As Shlain puts it, Allah tells Mohammed that "reading is fundamental." From the Koran, Surah 96:

> *Read in the name of thy Lord who created!*
> *Read: and thy lord is the most Bountiful*
> *He who hath taught by the pen*
> *Taught man what he knew not.*

Many other patriarchal cultures have combined misogyny with a worship of texts. Hinduism provides some dramatic examples. For instance, in the Manu Code (ca. 300 B.C.) it is written: "A faithful wife must serve [...] her lord as if he were a god, and never do ought to pain him, whatsoever be his state, and even though he is devoid of any virtue."

Shlain points out: "Brahmins gained precedence over other castes in India and allowed no one else to be literate. Should a member of the Shudra class be convicted of reciting the Vedas, he would have his tongue split; if he possessed a written text, he would be cut in two. [...] One edict proclaims, 'All that exists in this universe is the Brahmin's property'" (*AVG* 164).

The Law of Manu states: "The source of dishonor is woman; the source of strife is woman; the source of earthly existence is woman,

---

[21] http://news.bbc.co.uk/2/hi/1874471.stm

therefore avoid woman." Wives were expected to commit suicide at the funeral of their husbands.

Socrates, Plato, Aristotle and the Transition to Literacy

Another interesting example Shlain provides involves the early Greek philosophers Socrates, Plato and Aristotle. Socrates preferred the bihemispheric mode of the oral tradition and philosophical dialogue. Socrates, like Jesus, never committed his philosophy to writing. The written accounts of Socrates' thought all come from his student, Plato. Socrates viewed writing as a mechanical prop that merely served "to remind him who knows (about) the things that have been written" (153). Socrates felt that philosophy was better pursued by the back-and-forth of philosophical debate rather than reading or writing a static document. In *Protagoras,* Socrates disparages some of his contemporaries: "They are just like papyrus rolls, being able neither to answer your questions nor to ask themselves" (153). Socrates also made many feminists statements. For example, after watching the performance of a skilled young female acrobat, he remarked: "Not only from this girl, my friends, but from other things, too, we may infer that a woman's talent is not at all inferior to a man's" (154).

Plato was the transitional figure between the oral tradition of Socrates and literacy. Plato remained suspicious of writing even as he immersed himself in it. His attitude toward women was condescending. He also, very peculiar for an Athenian, developed an antipathy toward images. Writing in Book 10 of *The Republic* about his theory of art, Plato disparaged those who created representational images as "charlatans":

> "The art of representation is therefore a long way removed from truth, and it is able to reproduce everything because it has little grasp of anything, and that little is of a mere phenomenal appearance. For example, a painter can paint a portrait of a shoemaker or a carpenter or any other craftsman without understanding any of their crafts; yet, if he is skillful enough, his portrait of a carpenter may, at a distance, deceive children or simple people into thinking it is a real carpenter" (155).

When we move from Plato to his student Aristotle we find the full expression of both literacy and also of hierarchical, dominator thinking. Aristotle was a champion of inequality and justified both slavery and the domination of women: "The male is, by nature, superior and the female inferior; and the one rules and the other is ruled; this principle, of necessity, extends to all mankind" (156).

The Anti-Feminine Bias of Buddhism

Buddhism, as Shlain points out, also has an anti-feminine bias at its core: "Buddha's disciples excluded women and his monks took vows of celibacy. The message [was] that women were connected with craving and ignorance... His syllogism equating the end of suffering with the negation of birth eviscerates the very essence of womanhood" (174).

Shlain also makes an intriguing, speculative connection between the death of the Buddha's mother in childbirth and Buddhism's negative and anti-feminine stance toward birth as the cause of all human suffering. Buddha's mother was named "Maya," the Sanskrit word for illusion. (175)

Taoism and the Right Hemisphere

In dramatic contrast to the patriarchal bias of most religion stands Taoism. As Shlain points out, the Tao Te Ching is almost like the voice of the right hemisphere. The opening couplet of the Tao Te Ching states Lao-tzu's key principle that language, the naming of things that Yahweh commands Adam to do, is exactly what keeps us from finding the Way:

"The Tao that can be spoken is not the real Tao.
The Name that can be named is not the Eternal Name."

Lao-tzu adds: "He who knows does not speak and he who speaks does not know." "Therefore the sage goes about doing nothing, teaching no talking." The Tao can only be grasped intuitively and holistically.

Confucianism, which came slightly later, seems like a patriarchal correction of Taoism. Obedience to strict and rigid hierarchies is a central virtue in Confucianism. Any modern user of the classic Wilhelm I Ching experiences the tension between Taoism and Confucianism. The I Ching precedes and inspires both Taoism and Confucianism. Confucius wrote many of the commentaries and there is a dissonance at times between Taoist principles and the patriarchal, hierarchical principles, models and metaphors of Confucius.

Shlain points out that Confucianism surged past Taoism at the same moment when the printing press began to dominate. This moment also coincided with the first effective code of universal written laws. At the very same moment of history the bizarre and repressive practice of binding women's feet began: "The first mention of foot-binding is in the annals of the court of the Sung emperor Li Hou-chu in the year A.D. 970 — virtually coincident with the precise moment in China's five-thousand-year history when the printing press began to dominate the structure of society" (196). The practice was so disabling that many upper class women were unable to walk and had to be carried by servants. Chinese men found the sight of these hobbled and deformed women sexually exciting. Interestingly, the strips of linen used to bind the feet of young girls were the same strips of linen used to make paper. (196-97)

The aforementioned are some of the stronger examples of the often-converging triad of worship of text, misogyny and anti-image bias. There are a number of other cases where Shlain, with a touch of left hemispheric monomania, contorts history to fit the theory. In an epilogue, Shlain more or less admits this tendency. Nevertheless this is an extremely important book everyone should read and evaluate for themselves. The communication media that predominate in our lives profoundly affect our consciousness and every other core attribute. As Marshal McLuhan famously put it, "The medium is the message." *The Alphabet Versus the Goddess* would encourage us to add, "and especially neurologically." Shlain has correctly identified an enormous factor affecting human history and culture and can perhaps be forgiven for at times overstating the case.

Terence McKenna, A Logos Beheld Visionary

The late Terence McKenna was a visionary genius I encountered in the Nineties who had many crucial insights related to the Singularity Archetype.[22] From my first contact with Terence's ideas, I was astounded by the parallels between the conclusions I had reached in the Seventies and those that Terence had arrived at traveling a very different path. One of the strongest areas of convergence was the prediction of visual telepathy as we approached the evolutionary event horizon. The title of this section, "Logos Beheld," comes from comments Terence made in his book, *The Archaic Revival,* about Philo Judaeus, an Alexandrian Jewish philosopher who was a contemporary of Christ:

> "I always think of Philo Judaeus writing on the Logos. He posed to himself the question: 'What would be a more perfect logos?' and then he answered, saying it would be a Logos that is not heard but beheld. And he imagined a communication where the ears would not be the primary receptors but the eyes would be. A language where meaning was not constructed through a dictionary of spoken words, but where three-dimensional objects were actually generated with a kind of hyperlanguage so that there was perfect understanding between people. This may sound bizarre in ordinary reality, but these forms of synesthesia and

---

[22] For an account of my discourse with Terence, see "A Mutant Convergence — How John Major Jenkins, Jonathan Zap and Terence McKenna Met During a Weekend of High Strangeness in 1996" at ZapOracle.com

synesthesic glossolalia are commonplace in psychedelic states" (162).

A Telepathic Synesthesia

A possible early Biblical example of the sort of synesthesia Terence is referring to can be found in Exodus 20:18: "And all the people were seeing the sounds." Terence also made reference to the tribal hallucinogen Ayahusca as a catalyst for a kind of telepathic synesthesia. Anthropologists once called Ayahusca "telepethine" because of persistent reports that it produced telepathic states. Reportedly, individuals in a group Ayahusca experience can sing nonverbal songs that will be experienced by the entire group as changing colored forms. Musical intentionality occurs as both sound and imagery, and

A T-shirt Andy Young found in 2010

afterwards different individuals in the group will describe the visual symphony using the same adjectives of color and shape. Terence reports from first-hand experience:

"My experiences with shamanic hallucinogens, especially ayahuasca used in the Upper Amazon Basin, had shown me the reality of vocal performances that are experienced as visual. The magical songs of the ayahuasqueros, the folk medicos of the Indians and mestizos of the jungle back rivers, are not song as we understand the term. Rather they are intended to be seen and to be judged primarily as visual works of art. To those intoxicated and adrift upon the visionary reveries unleashed by the brew, the singing voice of the shaman has become a magical airbrush of color and organized imagery that is breathtaking in its alien and cosmic grandeur" (234).

Terence makes the case that a visually beheld language would be far superior to a verbal/auditory language. He was in an interesting position to make such a claim because he was the most articulate and witty speaker of the English language that I have ever encountered. Terence had certainly pushed to the edge of the spoken-language performance envelope. Since Terence is so uniquely articulate I won't try to paraphrase him. What follows is an excerpt from a talk he gave in LA in 1987 entitled, "Understanding and Imagination in the Light of Nature":

"What we need is to see what we mean. It's not without consequence or implication, that when we try to communicate the notion of clarity of speech, we always shift into visual metaphors: I see what you mean; he painted a picture; his description was very colorful. It means that when we intend to indicate a lack of ambiguity and communication, we shift to visual analogies. This can in fact be actualized. And in fact, this is what is happening in the psychedelic experience. There we discover, just under the surface of human biological organization, the next level in the organization of language: the ability to generate some kind of acoustical hologram that is manipulated by linguistic intent.

"Now don't ask me how this happens, because nobody knows how it happens. At this point it's magic. Nevertheless, the fact is it does happen — you can have this experience. It represents a synesthesia in the presence of ongoing communication. It is, in fact, telepathy. It is not what we thought telepathy would be, which I suppose if you're like me, you imagine telepathy would be hearing what other people think. It isn't that. It's seeing what other people mean. And them also seeing what they mean. So that once something has been communicated, both parties can walk around it and look at it, the way you study a Brancusi, or a Henry Moore in an art gallery.

"By eliminating the ambiguity of the audio signal, and substituting the concreteness of the visual image, the membrane of separation that allows the fiction of our individuality, can be temporarily overcome. And the temporary overcoming of the illusion of individuality is a much richer notion of ego-death than the kind of white-light, null-states that it has [been] imagined to be. Because the overcoming of the illusion of individuality has political consequences. The political consequences are that one can love one's neighbor, because the commonalty of being is felt.

Not reasoned toward, or propagandized into, or reinforced, but felt."[23]

Cephalopods and Becoming Your Linguistic Intent

Terence turns to nature to illustrate how such a visually beheld language can work and uses the example of cephalopods:

"I was drawn to look, strangely enough, at cephalopods, octopi. Because I felt, first of all, they are extremely alien. The break between our line of development in the phylogenetic tree, and the mollusca, which is what a cephalopod is, is about 700 million years ago. Nevertheless, and many of you who are students of evolution know, that when evolutionists talk about parallel evolution, they always bring out the example of the optical system of the octopi. Because, isn't this astonishing? — it's very much like the human eye, and yet it developed entirely independently. This shows how the same set of external factors impinging on a raw gene pool will inevitably sculpt the same organs or attain the same end, and so forth and so on.

"Well, the optical capacity of octopi is one thing. What interested me was their linguistic organization. They are virtually entirely nervous system. First of all, they have eight arms in the case of the octopods, and ten arms in the case of the squid, the decapods. So coordinating all these organs of manipulation has given them a very capable nervous system as well as a highly evolved ocular system.

"But what is really interesting about them is that they communicate with each other by changing the color and texture of their skin and their physical shape. You may know that octopi could change colors, but you may have thought it was camouflage or something very passive like that. It isn't that at all. They have a vast repertoire of traveling bars, dots, blushes, merging pastels, herringbone patterns, tweeds, mottled this-and-thats, can blush from apricot through teal into dove Grey and on to olive — do all of these things communicating to each other. That is what their large optical system is for. It is to be able to see each other.

"The other thing which octopi can do — besides having these chromatophores on the surface of their skin — they can change the texture of the skin surface: can make it rugose, papillaed, smooth, lobed, rubbery, runneled, so forth and so on. And then,

[23] http://www.ratical.org/many_worlds/UILN.html

of course, being shell-less mollusks, they can hide arms, and display certain parts of themselves and carry on a dance.

"When you analyze what is going on here, what at first seems like merely fascinating facts from natural history, begins to take on a more profound aspect. Because it is an ontological transformation of language that is going on in front of you. Note that by being able to communicate *visually*, they have no need of a conventionalized culturally reinforced dictionary. Rather, they experience pure intent of each other without ambiguity because each octopus can *see* what is meant — this is very important — can *see* what is meant. And I think that this heralds, or could be made to herald, a transformation in our own definitions of language and communication."

In *The Archaic Revival* Terence adds:

"An octopus does not communicate with spoken words as we do, even though water is a good medium for acoustical signaling; rather the octopus becomes its own linguistic intent. The octopus is like a naked nervous system, say rather a naked mind: the inner states, the thoughts, if you will, of the octopus are directly reflected in its outward appearance. It is as though the octopus were wearing its mind on its exterior. This is in fact the case. The Octopus literally dances its thoughts through expression of a series of color changes and position changes that require no local linguistic conventions for understanding as do our words and sentences. In the world of the octopus to behold is to understand. The octopus does not transmit its linguistic intent, it *becomes* its linguistic intent. The mind and the body of the octopus are the same and are equally visible. This means that the octopus wears its language like a kind of second skin; it appears to be and becomes what it seeks to mean" (*AR* 231).

A parallel example to Terence's understanding of cephalopods as creatures that can wear their language on their skin is Ray Bradbury's 1951 science fiction classic, *The Illustrated Man*. In 1951, being covered with tattoos was unusual, and very likely meant that you were a circus freak. The Illustrated Man is covered with living, linguistically dense tattoos:

"For he was a riot of rockets and fountains and people, in such intricate detail and color that you could hear the voices murmuring small and muted, from the crowds that inhabited his body. [...] Each illustration is a little story. If you watch them, in a few minutes they tell you a tale. In three hours of looking you could see 18 or 20 stories acted right on my body, you could hear voices and think thoughts" (3-4). The Illustrated Man got the tattoos from "a little old witch from the future, a changeling, one moment she looked a 1000 years old and the next 20 years old" (231-32). In other words he got his illustrated skin from a shape-shifter, the body type most appropriate to Logos Beheld.

Presently, being covered with tattoos has become commonplace. Although tattoos are painful and expensive, people are very motivated to acquire them in order to be able to externalize linguistic intent onto their skin. The tattoos that people get usually come out of their most personal mythologies and can be seen as consciously created dream fragments or image stories that are worn on the skin in what amounts to a low-tech form of shape-shifting. Tattooing and other forms of body modification are motivated by what I call "the will toward the glorified body."[24]

The high-technology way to become our linguistic intent is virtual reality. As Terence speculates,

> "Like the octopus, our destiny is to become what we think, to have our thoughts become our bodies and our bodies become our thoughts. This is the essence of a more perfect Logos, a Logos not heard or beheld. VR can help here, for electronics can change vocal utterance into visually beheld colored output in the virtual reality [...] The ambiguity of invisible meanings that attend audio speech is replaced by the unambiguous topology of meanings beheld. At last we will truly see what we mean. And we will see what others means too, for cyberspace will be a dimension where anything that can be imagined can be made to seem real" (*AR* 231).

Of course, Terence is hardly alone in imagining a virtual-reality future for the species. In his 1984 pioneer cyberpunk novel, *Neuromancer*, William Gibson introduces the concept of cyberspace:

> "[A] consensual hallucination experienced daily by billions of legitimate operators, in every nation [...] A graphic representation of data abstracted from the banks of every computer in the human system. Unthinkable complexity. Lines of light ranged in the nonspace of the mind, clusters and constellations of data. Like city lights, receding" (3).

In the future of virtual reality, as Terence and others have imagined it, VR is not merely a new environment but something we become, a new medium for being. In a 1989 interview, Terence remarked,

> "When the world's being run by machines, we'll all be at the movies. Oh boy."
> Interviewer: "Or making movies."
> Terence: "Or being movies" (*AR* 213).

---

[24] See chapter IV on the "The Glorified Body".

As Terence sees it: "In the not-too-distant future men and women may shed the monkey body to become virtual octopi swimming in a silicon sea" (*AR* 231).

Although Terence's metaphor sounds exotic and far off, much of the transformation he is talking about is not only underway, it has been ongoing for more than a century. Everyone reading this has spent his or her lifetime being transformed by an intensifying vortex of technological change. Consider the change experienced in just three generations. My maternal grandfather grew up in a Latvian village that had no electricity. OK, maybe Latvia is a bit of a backwater, but my father was born in New York City in 1919. In 1919, even in New York City, there were no commercial radio stations and wouldn't be for a few more years. When my father was born the most high tech medium available was the silent film. Early viewers of silent films almost couldn't process what they were seeing. When the zoom lens was first introduced, and there was a zoom in on a woman's face, people in the audience gasped. This woman's face was getting bigger! But nowadays, the opening credits of a movie might involve a series of rapidly unfolding surreal montages, and yet even children comprehend them. When *The Wizard of Oz* came out in 1939, audiences saw Dorothy pulled out of the black and white world of Kansas by the spiraling vortex of a tornado. The technological tornado acted as an interdimensional portal for both Dorothy and the audience when it delivered them into the Technicolor world of Oz. Everyone reading this has been born inside of this tornado and can reflect with amazement at the technological innovations occurring within his own lifespan.

From my present vantage in 2011, I can foresee a couple of upcoming breakthroughs that will greatly empower the Logos Beheld function of technology. The closest one will be when we perfect relatively inexpensive widescreen, high-definition video-display glasses that will allow a much more immersive visual experience. Another breakthrough is further out, but seems a reasonable extrapolation of present technology. Currently, advanced CGI movies like *Avatar* use technology that can record live actors and convert them into CGI avatars in real-time. Some day there will be enough distributed processing power that the webcam on your laptop, for example, can take a live, moving image of you and convert it in real-time into an avatar. At the cutting edge, something like this is already available. On the set of *Avatar*, director James Cameron was able to look through a camera and see actors converted into their Pandoran avatars in real-time. Presently, the social experience people are having in networked computer games like *World of Warcraft* and in primitive virtual-reality environments like *Second Life* is limited by a lack of complex facial expressions. As we've discussed earlier, human beings employ a subtle visual language of facial expressions as a major part of our social experience. When we can put on a pair of video display glasses and enter a world of avatars that are conveying the real-time fluctuations of other users' facial expressions, we will cross a major threshold where the virtual social experience will have far greater power.

We do not, however, have to wait for the future to experience virtual realities or Logos Beheld languages. As Terence pointed out, language and culture were the first virtual realities. Also, we have created visually beheld languages. While it may not have all the complexities of a fully realized language, the international language of icons is not just in airports anymore. It is increasingly become how we navigate the internet and our personal computers. American Sign Language is a fully realized, visually beheld language with great power of evocation, inflection and style possible in every gesture. ASL poetry, poems that do not start as words but as visually beheld sequences of gestures, is a growing artistic movement. Deaf children in Nicaragua who had not been taught ASL created their own visually beheld language — Nicaraguan Sign Language.

We also don't have to wait for greater computer processing power to experience fully engrossing virtual reality; we just have to go to sleep. Dreaming is a spontaneous, organic virtual reality where meaning is often beheld as scene, spectacle or phantasmagoria.

Nature's Virtual Reality

"In James Joyce's Ulysses, Stephen Dedalus tells us, 'History is the nightmare from which I am trying to awaken.' I would turn this around and say that history is what we are trying to escape from into dream." — Terence McKenna[25]

The dreamtime can be seen as a virtual-reality environment where the expression of meaning transcends verbal language. Transcendence includes that which is transcended, so dreams don't need to exclude verbal language. Dreams often make very sophisticated use of language, employing double and triple entendres to create multiple layers of meaning in a single phrase. But dreams can also convey linguistic intent without any verbal content.

The dreamtime environment can parallel, and dreamtime characters can personify, meaningful content. The fluctuations of the dreamtime not only parallel the dynamism of inner process, they are inner process — psyche and universe become one. Matter in dreams is spiritualized and

---

[25] From *The Archaic Revival.* p.90.

can come into being, disappear or mutate in perfect accord with psychic need.

T.S. Elliot popularized the term "objective correlative" to describe externalizations of inner states in literary texts. An objective correlative could be any object, scene, event or situation that stands for or evokes a particular mood, emotion or inner state. For example, a wilted rose in a poem may be the objective correlative of a disappointment in love. The dreamtime is a universe composed mostly of objective correlatives, a cauldron of objects, events, people, entities and situations that evoke emotions and inner meanings and often without the intercession of words.

The language of dreams is not exclusively self-referential. There are numerous well-documented cases of mutual or shared dreaming where two or more persons share a common dream. In my many years of doing dream interpretation for people I have heard a few reports of mutual dreaming and experienced one possible case of it myself. From William James' principle that one white crow is sufficient to disprove the notion that all crows are black, a single valid case of mutual dreaming in all of human history indicates that the human species has the ability to use organic virtual reality as a language medium. However rare, the ultimate Logos Beheld language already exists. One way that a quantum evolutionary change can take place is that the potential for a new means of consciousness/communication slowly develops and after a certain point it begins to emerge episodically, in fits and starts. These episodes may gradually increase in frequency and/or some great shock to the system may catalyze them into greater manifestation. Whether through technology, organic evolution, or some combination thereof, shared virtual realities, where we become our meanings, are likely the most potent way for us to transcend verbal language. Perhaps Terence is right, one day we may awaken from the nightmare of history into a mutual dreamtime.

Logos Beheld Cuts Both Ways

Where I disagree with Terence is in his assertion that Logos Beheld communication will eliminate deception and other forms of darkness. I think that some people will wake up from the nightmare of history into the nightmares of the dreamtime or into nightmarish realms of virtual reality. When novelty intensifies, when there is a time of great transformation, the outer edges of both light and dark tend to intensify. As Sophocles said, "Nothing vast enters the life of mortals without a curse."

When I discussed my theories with Ram Dass a few years ago, he expressed a POV almost identical to Terence's. Ram also believes that on the other side of the shift to the new means of conscious and communication it will be impossible to do evil. "You would be aware that you were doing it to yourself, that there was only one of you," he told me. I would like to believe that Terence and Ram are right, but I think they are only half right. I'll let Terence make his case in his own words:

> "We are going to go from a linguistic mode that is heard to a linguistic mode that is beheld. When this transition is complete, the ambiguity, the uncertainty, and the subterfuge that haunt our efforts at communication will be obsolete. And it will be in this environment of beheld communication that the new world of the Logos will be realized" (*AR* 37).

> "The shared beholding of the same linguistic intention in an objectified manifold is a true union. We become as one mind with this style of communication. Language beheld could perhaps serve as the basis for a deeper web of interlocking understandings between human beings that would represent a kind of technically aided evolutionary forward leap of the species."[26]

Both Terence and Ram have had the same crucial insight. A fully realized Logos Beheld language would, in some cases at least, fundamentally alter the separation of subject and object and move things from what Martin Buber called the I-it relationship to the I-Thou relationship. Indeed, the Singularity Archetype, as we will discuss later, contains within its core a shock to the ego and a metamorphosis that the ego may interpret as apocalypse.

On the other hand, egoism, will to power, deceptive intentions, etc. are very resilient forces that can adapt themselves to a new means of communication and use visually beheld language in diabolical ways. This is not conjecture, everyday we are bombarded with myriad examples of visually beheld deceptions called advertisements. What is that sexy, air-brushed person in the glossy cigarette ad if not the devil that hath the power to assuming a pleasing shape? Ruthless advertisers, power hungry politicians, and sexual vampires are among the types that already use visually beheld linguistic deception to manipulate people. I am reminded of a skit I saw a few years ago on *The Daily Show with John Stewart*. A conglomerate of the big oil companies agrees to be interviewed by a *Daily Show* correspondent but only if they can be represented by a nine-year-old girl. The interview takes place and the

---

[26] From "Understanding and the Imagination in the Light of Nature".

nine-year-old girl, who has long blonde hair and is impossibly cute and charming, talks about how sad she feels when people say bad things about the oil companies, etc. Similarly, the gorgeous female avatar you meet at a disco in *Second Life* is very likely an obese guy masturbating in front of his computer monitor.

I have also heard that in the near future of political propaganda, a politician could could have his face in a pre-recorded video shifted slightly to reflect the demographics of particular regions. For example, stations broadcasting to Hispanic precincts would get an image of the politician's face that had been subtly merged with some hispanic faces. I've heard that there are studies that show that we tend to vote for politicians who look more like us. With enough computer power, a politician could merge his face slightly to resemble that of an individual viewer.

Shelia's Dream: Heaven and Demon Ride

A few years ago, a highly intelligent young woman we'll call Shelia asked me to interpret an extraordinary dream she had that has extreme relevance to the potential for darkness in virtual reality. The following is a very slightly edited version of a transcript I made of a recording of the dream interpretation session. In the interview, I merely asked clarifying questions because the dream largely spoke for itself without the aid of interpretation.

S: The dream begins and I'm at a friend's house, sort of a party house. A guy approaches me. He's not anyone I recognized from real life, a dream character, but someone I feel I can trust and that I have a connection with. He comes up to me and says,

"There's this new stuff, you've got to try it!"

"Well, what is it?" I asked.

"It's Heaven," he said, but in a way that told me that there was no implication of anything religious. Heaven was just the name of some sort of drug. My friend is at a computer and he's going to make this drug for me. It's extremely difficult to make — you have to make it on a computer and you have to know physics and computer programming to make this drug.

J: So how did you make a drug on a computer? Is it made out of zeros and ones? What is the computer doing to make it?

S: The computer program has access to a whole repertoire of chemicals. It's not a purely informational thing. It's spit out as a mixture of all these chemicals, molecules in a small capsule, very, very small, a little bit smaller than one centimeter squared.

J: And so the computer makes just one capsule at a given time?

S: It could make several capsules, but with every particular program there's only one, each one is unique…

I could tell that my friend was putting a lot of effort into making my capsule. He finishes it and I swallow the capsule.

The trip was pretty indescribable. I went to some sort of alien world and it was very, very beautiful. The colors were so vivid, almost too vivid. There were strange iridescent colors I have never seen before. Another very unique thing is that everything I saw was in frames of about one and a half feet. In every direction I would see everything repeated to infinity in frames of about one and half feet. So when I looked at my arm I would see it repeated in these artificial frames extending out to infinity. I know how absurd it sounds, but this was just beautiful.

J: So everything you looked at had this telescoping effect as if it were an infinite chain of dominos? But what is it that you are seeing in this environment?

S: Yeah, I saw plants that looked like belladonnas. They were very inviting and the overall feeling I had was one of total euphoria. The sun was shining — or a star of some sort — and every sensation was really articulate. This trip, within the dream, lasted somewhere between ten and thirty minutes.

When it was over I wanted to know more, how the capsule was made and how it did this to me. My friend began describing to me what it takes to start making your own. The duration of the trip could be anywhere between two minutes and eighteen hours. He was also adamant about one point — how incredibly dangerous it was to design your own capsule if you didn't know what you are doing. He wouldn't let me even touch the computer. He told me what it would take to run the trip and it was pretty intensive. You couldn't just put in a bunch of lines and dots and squiggles and be like: 'There you go.'

J: So when he's designing a trip, he's not just designing what chemicals go in, he's also designing the visual parameters, he's designing a whole virtual reality environment.

S: Correct. So I'm talking further with my friend because I want to know more and keep in mind I'm still feeling some euphoria from having just had this trip. I asked him: "How many different kinds of this stuff are there?"

And then my friend got quiet because he didn't want to say anything more, but eventually answered: "There's only three." He was fine to tell me about the first two — the first was called Heaven, the one that I took, and the second was called Earth and the third was called Demon Ride. Demon Ride was made for the sort of person who liked horror films. And then I thought to myself: Wait a minute, this can last for up to eighteen hours, what if someone gave it to you without your knowing about it or against your will? I was thinking about the implications of all this. I was still euphoric from my experience with Heaven, but I wanted to know the full implications of this Pandora's Box. As I went deeper into it I became more disturbed. I realized that this was an odorless, colorless, tasteless substance that dissolves instantly in water, can last up to eighteen hours and there's no antidote, once you've taken it you have no choice but to let it run its entire course. Some people who like horror films could get together and design this H.P. Lovecraft/H.R. Gieger/ Hellraiser-type trip with demons coming after you and things that can't actually physically harm you but that could be very psychologically traumatizing. And I'm thinking to myself that if it were up to me, considering the benefits and the risks, I couldn't approve this drug. I was realizing what a Pandora's Box this was because on the one hand people could have these great experiences, as I had, and heal psychological trauma, and I was only thinking about all the benefits until my friend told me about Demon Ride. Also, I realized that there was no way you could just outlaw this stuff. Once the program exists it can be abused. It does take quite a level of skill with chemistry and computer programming to make these capsules, but someone who did have these skills could sit there at a computer making pill after pill of these utter horror shows.

J: So you've discussed what Heaven is like, the one you actually experienced, and you've also discussed Demon Ride, but what was the one called 'Earth' like?

S: Earth was a so-so, nothing bad would happen, probably nothing good would happen, low-intensity, mass-market one that took very little skill to make, low potency, doesn't last that long — half an hour at most — and it's sold in conventional places where alcohol would be sold, though people still charged an arm and a leg for it. But whichever of the three kinds you take you are no longer experiencing this world; they all replace that with a different experience. What everyone was trying to work on was a way for you to still process the real, physical world while you were on the substance. When you are having the experience it is not like your motor skills are paralyzed, you can still move your body, but you can't orient yourself to the real world. Also, a unique aspect of these capsules is that if you were to take two instead of one, those trips would run parallel to each other.

J: So instead of magnifying each other or running consecutively you have two individual trips running at the same time?

S: Correct, and I tried that one time. My friend said, "I'm going to give you a two-minute trip of that because I don't want you to freak out. I'm going to give you something really straightforward." He gave me a two-minute trip of skydiving plus a two-minute trip of going to an ancient library.

J: And which of the three types were these two capsules?

S: They were both Heaven capsules. That's the only kind my friend would make. They are the highest quality. Heaven had the most clarity, the most purity, the most clean sort of experience you could have with no traumatic after effects.

J: And so what was this simultaneous experience like? What did you see in the ancient library, for example?

S: There were all these Flower of Life symbols all over the place, as if the whole thing were woven.

J: What whole thing was woven?

S: The library itself, not the books.

J: The library itself was woven? Can you explain that?

S: The library was woven with the Symbol of Life.

J: So was the library a physical building with a marble floor, for example, and so forth?

S: Yes.

J: So, in other words, the pattern of the tiles on the floor would be the Flower of Life and the pattern of the drapes would be the Flower of Life and so forth?

S: Yes.

J: So it was woven in the sense that it was a decorative motif that was repeated everywhere but it wasn't literally woven out of this symbol?

S: Yes.

J: Did you see any particular books or was it just endlessly receding bookcases or what?

S: Actually there weren't books. There were scrolls — that's what I meant by an ancient library. And I never actually opened up any scrolls or tried to read them or anything. I was just dazzled by this old place that had the smell of old parchment. My hands were steady, and I would have been able to handle the scrolls, but my hair was just going everywhere because of the skydiving.

J: So when you were seeing the ancient library you were simultaneously having the kinesthetic sensations of skydiving?

S: Yep.

J: But were you only seeing the library or were you also seeing the skydiving?

S: Seeing both, both superimposed on each other.

J: So you are able to have two completely encompassing visual experiences at the same time?

S: Sometimes it seemed like the library was less present, the floor seemed semi-transparent and it would fade in and out.

J: So it was as if you were experiencing two holograms at the same time that were bleeding into each other and sometimes one or the other would be more vivid?

S: Yes... When I woke up, the implications of Demon Ride were so intense that I was sweating and I was beside myself because it seemed like something that was very feasible, that would be possible at some point. What if someone gave an eighteen-hour version of Demon Ride to a child? What sort of psychological scars would that leave?

III. Near-Death Experience and the Singularity Archetype

"And Death, which alike levels all, alike impresses all with a last revelation, which only an author from the dead could adequately tell."[27]

Near-Death Experiences (NDEs) are not a new phenomenon. They have been experienced by people throughout the ages, but documented occurrences have increased dramatically since we have become much better at resuscitating the clinically dead. Based on Gallup polling done in the Eighties and a German study in 1999, approximately 4.2 percent of the population will report having an NDE[28]. Modern, popular awareness of NDEs began only very recently with the publication in 1975 of *Life after Life* by Raymond Moody, M.D., Ph.D.

Hieronymus Bosch, *Ascent of the Blessed*

[27] Melville, H. *Moby Dick*. New York: Harper & Brothers Publishers, 1851. 530.
[28] Van Lommel, Pim. *Consciousness Beyond Life: The Science of the Near-Death Experience*. New York: HarperOne, 2011. 9.

We can find many references to NDEs in both the near and distant past. Certainly it is easy to find references to the idea that consciousness can live on past the death of the body. For example the Roman poet Ovid wrote in *Metamorphoses*:

> "Then, death, so call'd, is but old matter dress'd
> In some new figure, and a vary'd vest:
> Thus all things are but alter'd, nothing dies;
> And here, and there the' unbody'd spirit flies" (*CBL* 83).

In ancient India it was said, "Coming and going is all pure delusion; the soul never comes nor goes. Where is the place to which it shall go when all space is in the soul? When shall be the time for the entering and departing when all time is in the soul?" (*CBL* 83).

NDE as Benign Virus

Extensive research has shown that near-death experiences have classic, universal elements and that near-death experiencers are usually profoundly and positively transformed as a result.   Research   also shows that parallel positive effects can occur in people just by reading about NDEs. As Dr. Kenneth Ring (professor emeritus of psychology at the University of Connecticut) put it:

> "In general, then the overall pattern of our data here gives us a strong suggestion that merely acquiring knowledge about NDEs can act like a 'benign virus'; that is, by exposing yourself to NDE-related information, you can 'catch it,' because the NDE appears to be contagious" (*LL* 203).

Although much of the testimony of experiencers that follows will be spiritual in nature, I want to assure you that I have no religious agenda. The NDE material resonates with me because of parallel OBEs (out-of-body experiences) I've had and not because of any religious orientation. In fact, one consistent research finding is that experiencers become more spiritual, but significantly less identified with formal, institutional religion after their NDEs. Eight years after their NDEs, the church attendance of experiencers decreased 42%, but a control group of people, who had cardiac arrest but no NDE, increased their church attendance by 25%. (*CBL* 68)

A woman in her forties who was raised in the South describes the change in her religious orientation:

> "I was brought up in the Bible Belt and when I was a child I was very religious... I mean I was taught certain things and I believed them as a child and adhered to them... just out of rote. But after this [her NDE], it made me less religious formally but

probably more religious inwardly... I don't think I was in a church one time since [my NDE], but I think I'm spiritually stronger than I ever was before" (*HTO* 154).

Another woman, a Baptist living in Texas, found that after her NDE "she could no longer relate to what she describes as 'traditional Christian dogma'" (*LL* 45).

Parallel Journeys, my first collage, with apologies to my friend Alex Grey — I cut up my copy of his book *Sacred Mirrors* to appropriate some of his images. One way of interpreting the image is a dying person crossing the event horizon of death and having a life review or merging with the dreamtime.

A Simulated NDE

Before we delve into the ways people are transformed by NDEs, I would like to put this in context by offering a brief simulation of a classic NDE. NDEs usually involve a well-defined series of classic stages, though as Raymond Moody points out in *Life after Life*, no two experiences are identical. What follows will be a hypothetical composite version of an NDE containing all the classic elements and closely based on actual accounts. I am going to present it in the second person singular to better allow the reader to visualize the experience:

After suffering a life-threatening injury or other sort of medical emergency, you find that suddenly all physical pain is gone and you are feeling a deep sense of peace and well-being. There is a whistling, almost wind-like sound. You feel delightfully weightless and below you there is an injured body that looks just like you. The realization dawns on you that you are seeing your former body lying below you and that you must now be dead. The realization is not upsetting at all because you also realize that you are very much alive and aware. Around your former body there are frantic medical personnel and you wonder what all the fuss and anxiety is about since you are perfectly fine. You can hear every word being spoken and can also sense people's thoughts and feelings. Your vision is panoramic and spherical and you can see everything with dazzling clarity. You can count the dust particles on the top of the surgical lights and see every tiny crack in the floor. You lose interest in this scene and find yourself rising above it, above the roof of the hospital where you notice an old sneaker lying on a window ledge.

You are delighted to find that you can fly and just by thinking of a place you can journey there. Above the earth you find you are drawn toward a dark space and as you approach it seems to form into a kind of spiraling tunnel, and then you find yourself being drawn rapidly through the tunnel at a speed that feels like it must be faster than the speed of light. Ahead of you is the most brilliant light, brighter than the sun and yet it doesn't hurt your eyes, it seems to be bathing you in warmth, love and complete acceptance. You hear glorious music and it feels like a homecoming, like you are coming back to where you were always from.

An androgynous being steps out of the light and you feel a deep sense of familiarity with this being, that you have always known each other, and you feel completely seen, recognized, understood and loved.

The being communicates with you telepathically and asks if you would like to review your life. You assent and begin to observe your entire life play out chronologically. You see every detail, and so much more than you were able to see at the time the events played out. You are aware of the thoughts and feelings of everyone present and sometimes it is quite difficult when you observe how every little action you have taken has had significant effects on others. The being of light comforts you during the review, assures you that no one is judging your deeds but that it is of great value to witness them and learn from them. As you experience your life unfolding you see how so much of what you thought was important at the time was a sham and a sideshow. You find that many small moments of compassion, a kind gesture to a stranger, for example, were of far greater significance. You become aware of a depth of meaning in even the smallest moments and become aware of the reasons for everything. There was a great purpose in your life you had never recognized before.

After the review, you find yourself with your guide in a beautiful field of wild flowers. Some of the flowers have colors you have never seen before and seem as if they are lit from within. There is a stream running through the field and you are told that you have a choice, if you go across the stream you will be able to stay in this beautiful world that feels like home, but will also miss out on many years you could have had in your former life. You don't want to leave this place of peace and love but you also feel a deep responsibility to those you left behind. You indicate your choice to return and find yourself hurtling back through the tunnel and into your wounded body and its painful sensations. Despite the confinement of the body you feel a deepened sense of purpose in life, a deeper appreciation of the meaningfulness of life and a will to fulfill your mission.

The Pamela Reynolds Case:

Since the above is a simulated case, let's take a detailed look at an actual case that is particularly well-evidenced. Pamela Reynolds, aged thirty-five, a working mother of three, received a grim diagnosis following a CAT scan in 1991. She had a giant aneurysm in a cerebral artery close to her brain stem. It was only a matter of time before the aneurysm burst with an immediately fatal outcome. There was no conventional way to operate on an aneurysm so deep in the brain. Pamela's one slight chance for survival was a high-risk surgery that could only be performed at the Barrow Neurological Institute in Phoenix, Arizona, two thousand miles from her hometown of Atlanta.

Neurosurgeon Dr. Robert Spetzler had pioneered a high-risk and daring surgical procedure known as "hypothermic cardiac arrest," or less formally as "standstill." Pamela's body temperature would be lowered to 60 degrees, her heart beat and breathing would be arrested, and all blood would be drained from her head. She would be flatlined, in a state that would be consistent with all clinical definitions of death. As doctor Spetzler explained to the BBC, "What we want to do is we want to bring that brain to a halt. We don't just want the brain to be asleep. We want the metabolism of the brain to stop. Every measurable output that the body puts out really disappears completely so that you have no neuronal activity whatsoever."

As cardiologist Michael Sabom, M.D. put it: "During 'standstill,' Pam's brain was found 'dead' by all three clinical tests — her electroencephalogram was silent, her brain-stem response was absent, and no blood flowed through her brain."

What is also exceptional about this case is that Pamela, who was being worked on by a number of medical teams, was heavily instrumented and under continual state-of-the-art monitoring including EEGs of both her cerebral cortex and brain stem. No brain activity was measured even though her brain stem was being tested via "evoked potentials" in the form of 100-decibel clicks emitted continuously by small molded speakers inserted in her ears.

Despite the lack of brain activity, Pamela had a detailed NDE. Here are some excerpts from her testimony to the BBC and another account recorded by Dr. Sabom:

> "I remember seeing several things in the operating room when I was looking down. It was the most aware that I think that I have ever been in my entire life... I was metaphorically sitting on Dr. Spetzler's shoulder. It was not like normal vision... There was so much in the operating room that I didn't recognize, and so many people.

> "I thought the way they had my head shaved was very peculiar. I expected them to take all of the hair, but they did not. [...] I heard the term "saw," but what I saw looked more like a drill than a saw.

> "The saw thing that I hated the sound of looked like an electric toothbrush and it had a dent in it, a groove at the top where the saw appeared to go into the handle, but it didn't... And the saw had interchangeable blades, too, but these blades were in what looked like a socket wrench case... I heard the saw crank up... It was humming at a relatively high pitch and then all of a sudden it went Brrrrrrrrr! like that."

Pamela provides a highly accurate layman's description of the pneumatically-powered Midas Rex whirlwind bone saw, which was spinning at 73,000 rpm and did indeed look more like an electric toothbrush or dentist's drill than a conventional saw. The box of drill bits looked exactly like a socket wrench case. Yet her eyes had been lubricated and were taped shut and she had been under general anesthesia for 90 minutes before the procedure.

Pamela continues:

> "Someone said something about my veins and arteries being very small... I distinctly remember a female voice saying: 'We have a problem. Her arteries are too small.' And then a male voice: 'Try the other side.' It seemed to come from further down

on the table. I do remember wondering what are they doing there [laughs] because this is brain surgery!"

While the bone saw was opening Pamela's head, a female cardiac surgeon had located the femoral artery and vein in the right side of Pamela's groin. These blood vessels turned out to be too small because a large flow of blood would be needed to feed the cardiopulmonary bypass machine. Pamela's left femoral artery and vein were prepped to be used instead.

As the surgery progressed, Pamela was brought to cardiac arrest, her core body temperature was 60 degrees Fahrenheit (15.5 celsius). The 100-decibel clicks from the ear speakers elicited no response and both EEGs were completely flat. At that point came one of the most radical medical procedures ever performed. The cardiopulmonary bypass machine was shut off, the head of the operating table was tilted up, and the blood was drained from Pamela's brain and body like the oil from a car.

At some point during this time, Pamela's NDE intensified. As Pamela narrates,

"I felt a presence. I sort of turned around to look at it. And that's when I saw the very tiny pinpoint of light. And the light started to pull me, but not against my will. I was going of my own accord because I wanted to go. And there was a physical sensation to the point... rather like going over a hill real fast. It was like the *Wizard of Oz* — being taken up in a tornado vortex, only you're not spinning around. The feeling was like going up in an elevator real fast. It was like a tunnel, but it wasn't a tunnel. And I went toward the light. The closer I got to the light, I began to discern different figures, different people, and I distinctly heard my grandmother calling me. She has a very distinct voice. But I didn't hear her call me with my ears... It was a clearer hearing than with my ears... I trust that sense more than I trust my ears... The feeling was that she wanted me to come to her, so I continued with no fear down the shaft. It's a dark shaft that I went through, and at the very end there was this very little tiny pinpoint of light that kept getting bigger and bigger and bigger.

"The light was incredibly bright, like sitting in the middle of a lightbulb. I noticed that as I began to discern different figures in the light — and they were all covered with light, they were light, and had light permeating all around them — and they began to form shapes I could recognize and understand. And I saw many, many people I knew and many, many I didn't know, but I knew that I was somehow connected to them. And it felt... great!

Everyone I saw, looking back on it, fit perfectly into my understanding of what that person looked like at their best during their lives.

"I recognized a lot of people. And one of them was my grandmother. And I saw my uncle Gene, who passed away when he was only thirty-nine years old. He taught me a lot; he taught me to play my first guitar. So was my great-great aunt Maggie. On Papa's side of the family, my grandfather was there... They were specifically taking care of me, looking after me.

"They would not permit me to go further... It was communicated to me — that's the best way I know how to say it, because they didn't speak like I'm speaking — that if I went all the way into the light something would happen to me physically. They would be unable to put this me back into the body me, like I had gone too far and they couldn't reconnect. So they wouldn't let me go anywhere or do anything.

"I wanted to go into the light, but I also wanted to come back. I had children to be reared...

"Then they [the deceased relatives] were feeding me. They were not doing this through my mouth, like with food, but they were nourishing me with something — the only way I know how to put it is something sparkly. Sparkles is the image that I get. I definitely recall the sensation of being nurtured and being fed and being made strong.

"I asked if God was the light, and the answer was: 'No, God is not the light, the light is what happens when God breathes.' And I distinctly remember thinking: I'm standing in the breath of God...

"At some point in time I was reminded that it was time to go back. Of course I had made my decision to go back before I ever laid down on that table. But, you know, the more I was there, the better I like it [laughs]. My grandmother didn't take me back through the tunnel or even send me back or ask me to go. She just looked up at me. I expected to go with her, but it was communicated to me that she just didn't think she would do that. My uncle said that he would do it. He's the one who took me back through the end of the tunnel. Everything was fine. I did want to go.

"But then when I got to the end of it and saw the thing, my body, I didn't want to get into it... It looked terrible, like a train wreck... It looked pretty much like what it was: void of life. I believe it was covered. It scared me and I didn't want to look at it. And I knew it would hurt, so I didn't want to get in. But he kept reasoning with me. He says: 'Like diving into a swimming pool, just jump in.' No. 'What about the children?' You know what, the children will be fine [laughs]. And he goes: 'Honey, you got to go.'... I didn't want to, but I guess I was late or something because he pushed me... he gave me a little help there. It's taken a long time, but I think I'm ready to forgive him for that [laughs]... I felt a definite repelling and at the same time a pulling from the body. The body was pulling and the tunnel was pushing... I felt it chill me inside. I returned to my body. It was like diving into a pool of ice water... It hurt!"

The coldness that Pamela experienced was probably her perception of her chilled body, which was in a state of deep hypothermia. Pamela continues:

"When I came back, and I was still under general anesthesia in the operating theater, they were playing 'Hotel California,' and the line was 'You can check out anytime you like, but you can never leave.' I mentioned [later] to Dr. Brown that that was incredibly insensitive, and he told me that I needed to sleep more [laughter]. When I regained consciousness, I was still on the respirator."

Pamela concludes: "I think death is an illusion. I think death is a really nasty bad lie."

Neurosurgeon Spetzler observes about Pam's NDE:

"I don't think that the observations that she made were based on what she experienced as she went into the operating theater. They were just not available to her. For example, the drill and so on, those things are all covered up. They aren't visible, they were inside their packages. You really don't begin to open up until the patient is completely asleep so that you maintain a sterile environment... At that stage in the operation nobody can observe, hear in that state. And... I find it inconceivable that the normal senses, such as hearing, let alone the fact that she had clicking devices in each ear, that there was any way for her to hear those through normal auditory pathways."[29]

---

[29] All accounts of Pamela's NDE are taken from the following three sources: Pim Van Lommel's *Consciousness Beyond Life: The Science of the Near-Death Experience*; Dr. Michael Sabom's *Light and Death: One Doctor's Fascinating Account of Near Death Experiences*; The BBC Documentary, *The Day I Died*.

Life Lessons from the Living Dead

The lessons that people derive from their NDEs have a high consistency. They reflect the way values change or are deepened after an encounter with the Singularity Archetype. The multilayered connections between NDE and the Singularity Archetype, however, will become much more apparent later. Dr. Ring enumerates the value shifts and realizations that occur to experiences as follows:

1. There is nothing whatever to fear about death.
2. Dying is peaceful and beautiful.
3. Life does not begin with birth nor end with death.
4. Life is precious — live it to the fullest.
5. The body and its senses are tremendous gifts — appreciate them.
6. What matters most in life is love.
7. Living a life oriented toward materialistic acquisition is missing the point.
8. Cooperation rather than competition makes for a better world.
9. Being a success in life is not all it is cracked up to be.
10. Seeking knowledge is important — you take that with you. (LL 19)

It is common to find that all ten of these points will come up in the testimony of an experiencer regardless of what culture or religious orientation (if any) they come from. For example, a young man named Neev summarizes what he learned from his NDE:

"My outlook on life was no longer bleak and dismal. I felt like I now had a purpose, which was to help people and share my positive perspective. My dependence on time seemed to stop. I no longer felt pressured by the clock — there was always time to do something else or more. I tried to fit in as much as possible into every day. I experienced everything for what it was — not for what it could do or give to me. I was no longer interested in what "society" had to say about how I lived my life. I was no longer interested in what people thought or how they felt about me, or if I looked good or not. I learned that I am much more than my body" (*LL* 24).

The above is just an excerpt from Neev's extensive account of his experience. Summarizing the major points of Neev's outlook, Dr. Ring provides a list with many parallels to the universal list quoted above:

1. There is a reason for everything that happens.
2. Find your own purpose in life.
3. Do not be a slave to time.
4. Appreciate things for what they are — not for what they can give you.
5. Do not allow yourself to be dominated by the thoughts and expectations of others.

6. Do not be concerned with what others think of you, either.
7. Remember, you are not your body.
8. Fear not — even pain and certainly not death.
9. Be open to life, and live it to its fullest.
10. Money and material things are not particularly important in the scheme of things.
11. Helping others is what counts in life.
12. Do not trouble yourself with competition — just enjoy the show. (LL 26)

NDE as Encounter with the Singularity Archetype

Most NDEs seem to create metamorphosis in the experiencer in ways that are consistent with an encounter with the Singularity Archetype. As we'll discuss in depth later, parapsychological elements are involved, and often catalyze the long-term manifestation of parapsychological abilities in the experiencer. An "end of time" and rupture-of-plane singularity is experienced which transforms all core values. The baseline ego is shattered and transformed by the experience.

The NDE usually causes profound, lasting spiritual and psychological evolution for the experiencer. According to the prospective Dutch study reported in the journal *Lancet,* these effects only intensify through time. (*CBL* 66-68) A control group that experienced cardiac arrest but no NDE had dramatically different outcomes and did not, as a group, exhibit this metamorphosis. The research on NDEs, and especially on the long-term changes they produce, gives us the best-documented evidence of what effects an encounter with the Singularity Archetype has on the human psyche. Before we analyze these effects I would like to present some first-hand testimony from the experiencers on what they learned from the encounter and how they were transformed by it.

One reason for alternating analysis with some of the more raw material is that it provides, in document form, an encounter with the Singularity Archetype for the reader. Reading may seem an abstracted form of encounter compared to some of the more overwhelming ways some people have encountered the Singularity Archetype. It is very easy, however, to underestimate the power of such second and third-hand encounters. Since archetypes live inside of us, we are not merely importing information from the outside. Words may create inner resonance and evoke recognition and awareness lying just below the surface of our personalities.

Scientific Studies of NDE Metamorphosis

The testimonies of experiencers imply how they have been changed by crossing the event horizon, but these changes have also been studied with scientific methodology. However, most studies of near-death experiencers have been retrospective.

Dr. van Lommel's study deserves some preeminence because he and his colleagues did the first large-scale study to use prospective methodology. His study group was comprised of all individuals in ten Dutch hospitals who experienced cardiac arrest between 1988-1992. This group was divided into those who survived cardiac arrest but had no NDE (the control group) and those who had NDEs. A longitudinal study was conducted with follow-up interviews at two and eight years after cardiac arrest. What follows will be a brief tour of some of the study results and other studies that van Lommel summarizes and analyzes. Those interested in the details of how the study was conducted and all the findings should read Dr. van Lommel's book, *Consciousness Beyond Life* or at least the findings published in *Lancet*. We will also be looking at studies by Dr. Ring and some of his general analysis.

Homo gestalt and the NDE

Many of the findings are consistent with what we would expect from an encounter with the Singularity Archetype: isolated, egoistic consciousness gives way to a Homo gestalt-like sense of unity and connectedness to others. Dr. van Lommel summarizes: "The new found insight [...] pertains to insight into connectedness: everything and everybody is connected. Because of this sense of connectedness, some people describe the NDE as an experience of unity" (*CBL* 46).

The sense of unity with others is more than a philosophical notion, it is a profound I-Thou empathy that lessens the boundary of subject/object and will often have parapsychological aspects. Neev, the young male experiencer, comments:

> "These instincts also allow me to empathize with almost anyone. I feel that when I talk to people, I can physically and emotionally feel what they are going through at that time. It is as if I become them for an instant. [...] The gift of insight allows me to help many people with their problems, but sometimes [it] gets to the point where there are so many that I lose myself in other people" (*LL* 25).

This greater sense of unity with others is combined with a more robust form of individuality. Dr. van Lommel points out that "people become less dependent on the approval of others" (*CBL* 52). Deep spiritual changes occur and "people's religious sentiment increases after an NDE while their interest in organized religion declines sharply" (*CBL* 56). "By contrast, cardiac survivors without an NDE display a marked decline in interest in spirituality" (*CBL* 58).

Individuation

Paradoxically, at the same time that their sense of unity with others becomes exponentially greater, there is also a great strengthening of individuality and what Jung called "individuation." The NDE, consistent with an encounter with the Singularity Archetype, explodes the conditioned, false personality and allows the experiencer to return to his or her essence.

Barbara, a middle-class mother of three from the Midwest, was the sort of woman who "before her NDE lived to please others" (*HTO* 104). Her experience triggered a process of individuation. As Barbara describes it:

> "That experience made me whole and that experience wiped away all the scars that I collected and that experience gave me all the tools to struggle through these seven years and get to the feeling now that I'm always here. You know, it took me a long time to recapture that person because everybody around me, I felt, was restricting me from becoming that person because of who they were. So the experience itself gave me the spirituality that I need and the tools that I needed to be who I am now" (*HTO* 108).

Dr. Ring's study found that while experiencers "may feel a greater sense of self-worth following their experience, that change is not typically accompanied by an increase in self-inflation. Indeed, in my experience, NDErs do not tend to regard themselves as anyone special." As evidence, Dr. Ring points out that experiencers responding to his questionnaire showed a decline in the valuation of making a good impression, desiring to become well-known, and concern about what others think of them. (*HTO* 129-130)

Self vs. False Ego

In Jungian terms we could say that their connection to the Self has been strengthened while the domination of false ego concerns has been dramatically lessened. This is exactly what we should expect from a successful encounter with the Singularity Archetype. As we'll discuss in depth later, a central meaning of apocalypse is the encounter of the false ego with the Self. This is the central premise of leading Jungian analyst

Edward Edinger's study of the Book of Revelation, *Archetype of the Apocalypse.*

I want to make a clear distinction here between "ego" and "false ego." Although the ego is villainized in some New Age and Eastern circles, it is actually a crucial psychic function. What gets destroyed by many NDEs and other transcendent experiences is not the ego, but certain aspects of the false ego, which is sometimes referred to as the "false self" or "conditioned self." Dr. Ring describes this transformation:

> "I have talked about this authentic or true self as something that is the Light's function to disclose to the individual. How does it do that? The answer is, often by first showing the NDEr his or her false or socially conditioned self. In some cases, the mechanism by which this is effected is the life review...

> "In other instances, however, the NDEr is given a direct perception into the nature of the false self and is thereby allowed intuitively to understand that the person one has identified with and habitually thought of as one's essential self was nothing more than a fiction" (*LL* 51).

Peggy describes this exact realization and transformative separation from the false self:

> "[At one point] my consciousness must have pulled away from my body because I suddenly observed it from a short distance as it sobbed. I was completely unemotional as I observed my body. As I watched, I saw some shiny, clear object lift away from my body. It was obvious to me it was my ego. The moment my ego started lifting, my consciousness went back into my body and I felt distress, thinking, 'It's my ego, it's my ego!' not wanting it to leave me. I felt like I had to have it or I wouldn't be alive. It pulled away from me anyway, and in it I saw all the things that I had done wrong in my life. I was stunned because I thought all that was part of me and simply couldn't be separated from me. I can't tell you how happy I was when it dawned on me that 'that was never me.' That identity was never the real me.

> "I began to realize I was okay without it and was, in fact, better off. It was sort of like taking a dusty, old, clogged-up, used filter off an air-conditioner vent and letting the air go through unhindered. Only, in this case, it was pure, undiluted love going through me. I decide to relax and let the light pour all this magnificent energy into me. [...] If there is such a thing as 'restoring a soul,' then that's exactly what happened to me" (*LL* 52).

You can see from Peggy's testimony why the ego fears confrontation with the Singularity Archetype and views it as apocalypse. For the false self, the Singularity is experienced as a catastrophic shock leading to extinction. From the larger vantage of the Self, however, the very same shock is the catalyst preceding rebirth, a transcendent evolutionary event.

The NDE clears out the false self and provides room for the development of an authentic self that is more compassionate and concerned about the collective welfare. Dr. Ring describes the transformation: "Egocentric agendas diminish, and concern for the good of the collective increases. 80% of experiencers report an increase in concern for the planetary welfare (*OP* 181). As one experiencer put it, being of service to others is 'more real than this world'" (*LL* 125).

NDE as Living Archetype

Studies by Dr. Ring and Dr. van Lommel indicate that the power of NDEs seems to increase for experiencers as the years pass. In the following conclusion from Dr. Ring, we hear a description that exactly matches what we should expect from an encounter with an archetype that continues to live inside of an experiencer:

"Thus we see that it appears not merely that core experiencers have an overpowering experience of the energy of the light but also that the light projects its energy into them and fills them with its love. It's for this reason that the core experience — and NDEs in general — can never remain, as I have already said, simply 'a beautiful memory.' It is an experience that continues to pulsate within and, when the circumstances are right, to shine without afterward" (*HTO* 89).

NDE and Intimations of a Transcendent Evolutionary Event

In the closest connection to the Singularity Archetype, Dr. Ring finds that experiencers agree that "these experiences reflect a purposive intelligence and that they are part of an accelerating evolutionary current that is propelling the human race toward higher consciousness and heightened spirituality" (*OP* 190).

The future evolutionary aspects of the Singularity Archetype, like Logos Beheld visual/telepathic communication, are not just notions that occur to experiencers, in many cases they encounter them as actualities. NDEs often involve paranormal vision and telepathic/visual communication.

NDE and Parapsychological Metamorphosis

After their NDEs experiencers often undergo a parapsychological metamorphosis with an array of reported effects. Dr. Ring summarizes the transformation:

> "Although a number of recent investigations have confirmed this, it has been known for some time that having an NDE seems to accelerate the development of a whole range of psychic sensitivities. It has been found, for example, that following an NDE, there is a marked increase in reports of the incidence of such paranormal phenomena as telepathy, clairvoyance, and precognition. In addition, NDErs claim to have more instances of spontaneous OBEs and unusual perceptions, such as seeing energy fields (or "auras") around the bodies of others" (*LL* 128).

Dr. van Lommel adds, "Without really wanting to, many NDErs feel inundated with information from or via another dimension" (*CBL* 60).

The parapsychological changes are often threatening to the experiencer's pre-NDE sense of self-identity: "All of a sudden these people have a very acute sense of the emotions of others. Heightened intuition can cause major problems. Clairvoyance, enhanced sensitivity, and precognition can feel extremely threatening" (*CBL* 60).

In general, "NDErs often experience enhanced intuitive sensitivity, such as clairvoyance, clairsentience, clairaudience, or prognostic dreams about events that have yet to take place, as we have seen. The NDE seems to permanently enhance their reception capacity" (*CBL* 319). Dr. van Lommel substantiates his findings with the following table:

Experience	Before NDE	After NDE	General Population
Clairvoyance	38 %	71 %	38 %
Telepathy	42 %	86 %	58 %
Precognition	49 %	86 %	NA
Déjà vu	73 %	85 %	NA
Enhanced Intuition	54 %	92 %	NA
Dream Awareness	44 %	79 %	42 %
OBE	8 %	49 %	14 %
Spirits	22 %	65 %	27 %
Healing ability	8 %	65 %	NA
Perception of auras	13 %	47 %	5 %
Psychic phenomena	55 %	98 %	39 % (Sweden)

(*CBL* 61)

Paranormal Vision, Especially Autoscopic

One of the most universal elements of NDEs is paranormal vision. Experiencers typically report that once they leave their bodies, their senses, especially vision, develop a dazzling acuity. Panoramic, 360-degree and even spherical vision are often reported. Even more remarkable, as we will examine later, experiencers who have been blind since birth will report highly visual experiences.

Craig, one of Dr. Ring's students who is in his late twenties, describes the intensification of sensory acuity he experienced during an NDE that occurred when he was eighteen. The NDE involved a rafting accident in which he was nearly drowned. Craig's visual acuity included infinite depth of field, an optical impossibility with conventional vision:

> "I was shocked to find that I was floating upwards into the open air above the river. I remember vividly the scene of the water level passing before my eyes. Suddenly I could see and hear as never before. The sound of the waterfall was so crisp and clear that it just cannot be explained by words. Earlier that year, my right ear had been injured when somebody threw an M-80 into a bar where I was listening to a band, and it exploded right next to my head. But now I could hear perfectly clearly, better than I ever had before. My sight was even more beautiful. Sights that were close in distance were as clear as those far away, and this was at the same moment, which astounded me. There was no blurriness in my vision whatsoever. I felt as if I had been limited by my physical senses all these years, and that I had been looking at a distorted picture of reality" (*LL* 15-16).

An audiologist who is extremely myopic, wears thick glasses, and describes himself as blind as a bat six inches from his nose, describes an NDE that happened to him in a Japanese hospital during the Korean War:

> "I sensed something turning sour in my system and literally yelled in my mind, 'Hey guys, you're losing me!' [Then] I just floated upward to the top of the canvas tent and looked down at the scene. (Here is where I emphasize the word *look* [he says].) In finite detail, I saw the dust on the supposedly clean and sterile OR lights, someone just outside smoking a cigarette, the near-panic of the medical staff, and the expression of the big, black Air Force corpsman who was called to come in to forklift me in his arms to get me on my back. He had a clearly discernible scar on the top of his closely cropped head, in the form of a small cross. He was the only one not wearing a face mask, having been summoned on the spur of the moment" (*LL* 61).

A Canadian anthropologist, in a letter to Dr. Ring, describes the extraordinary vision she experienced:

> "I was hovering over a stretcher in one of the emergency rooms at the hospital. I glanced down at the stretcher, knew the body wrapped in blankets was mine, and really didn't care. The room was much more interesting than my body. And what a neat perspective. I could see everything. And I do mean everything! I could see the top of the light on the ceiling, and the underside of the stretcher. I could see the tiles on the ceiling and the tiles on the floor, simultaneously: three hundred degree spherical vision. And not just spherical. Detailed! I could see every single hair and the follicle out of which it grew on the head of the nurse standing beside the stretcher. At the time, I knew exactly how many hairs there were to look at. But I shifted focus. She was wearing glittery white nylons. Every single shimmer and sheen stood out in glowing detail, and once again, I knew exactly how many sparkles there were" (*LL* 62-63).

Perceiving Unknown Colors

Another classic element of NDEs is the perception of uncannily intense or previously unknown colors. Typically these perceptions occur when the experiencer has crossed through the tunnel and gotten to the other side. For example, Howard Storm, an atheistic art professor prior to his NDE, observes:

> "We traversed an enormous distance, although very little time seemed to elapse. Then, off in the distance, I saw a vast area of illumination that looked like a galaxy. In the center, there was an enormously bright concentration. Outside the center, countless millions of spheres of light were flying about, entering and leaving what was a great Beingness at the center.

> "The radiance emanating from the luminous spheres contained exquisite colors of a range and intensity that far exceeded anything I as an artist had ever experienced. It was similar to looking at the opalescence one experiences looking into a white pearl or the brilliance of a diamond" (*LL* 292).

Joseph, a forty-six-year-old author, publisher and businessman: "At first I became aware of beautiful colors which were all the colors of the rainbow. They were magnified in crystalized light and beamed with a brilliance in every direction. It was as if all this light was coming at me through a prism made by a most beautiful and purified diamond, and yet at the same time it was as if I were the center" (*HTO* 64).

Stella, a forty-one-year-old woman whose NDE was caused my massive hemorrhaging following surgery: "The flowers and the flower buds by that street — the intensity, the vibrant colors, like pebbles that have been polished in a running stream, but they were all like precious stones, rubies and diamonds and sapphires" (*HTO* 73).

Mindsight to the Blind

Even more remarkable are highly visual NDEs occurring to people who have been blind since birth. The pioneering work in this field has been done by Drs. Kenneth Ring and Sharon Cooper, and is available in their book, *Mindsight — Near-Death and Out-of-Body Experiences in the Blind*. One of the most interesting cases in *Mindsight* is Vicki Umipeg, a forty-three-year-old woman who lives in the state of Washington.

> "Vicki was born very premature at twenty-two weeks and the optic nerves to both of her eyes were destroyed while she was still in the incubator. Until her NDE, she never had any sort of visual experience. When asked by an interviewer if she could see anything she replied: 'Nothing, never. No light, no shadows, no nothing, ever... I've never been able to understand even the concept of light'" (14).

Vicki's classic NDE involved many visual elements. She had the typical autoscopic experience of seeing her own body from the POV of the ceiling. Initially she didn't recognize herself because she had never seen her body before. She felt herself ascend above the roof of the hospital and got a panoramic view of her surroundings. She emerged from a tunnel to find herself lying on grass in a place filled with light. Dr. Ring describes her account: "She was surrounded by trees and flowers and a vast number of people. She was in a place of tremendous light, and the light, Vicki said, was something you could feel as well as see. Even the people she saw were bright" (16).

In Vicki's own words: "Everybody there was made of light. And I was made of light. What the light conveyed was love. There was love everywhere. It was like love came from the grass, love came from the birds, love came from the trees" (26).

Vicki, who had two NDEs, both of them involving vision, tells us that, "Those two experiences were the only time I could ever relate to seeing and to what light was, because I experienced it" (26). Vicki describes what it was like to see for the first time: "I was shocked. I was totally in awe. I mean, I can't even describe it because I thought, 'So that's what it's like!' But then I thought, 'Well, it's even better [...] than what I could have imagined" (26).

The experience was so novel that it was disorienting and hard to cope with:

> "I had a hard time relating to it [i.e., seeing]. I had a real difficult time relating to it because I've never experienced it. And it was something very foreign to me... Let's see how can I put it into words? It was like hearing words and not being able to understand them, but knowing that they were words. And before you'd never heard anything. But it was something new, something you'd not been able to previously attach any meaning to" (27).

Not only do some blind people report visual NDEs, they also report many of the same visual anomalies reported by sighted experiencers. As we've heard before, novel and unusually brilliant colors, often in the form of flowers, are classic aspects of descriptions of the other side. Joyce, a woman blind since birth, describes the flowers she encountered this way: "The only thing that I can remember about the flowers is that they were, like, larger than normal, softer than normal. I don't know how I know this, but more brilliant — the colors [more] magnified than they would be on Earth" (*LL* 52-53).

Another interesting case is that of a woman Dr. Ring refers to as "Debbie," who lost her sight at birth but still has some light perception, allowing her to distinguish light from dark without any detail, color or distance vision. For example, she might be able to perceive if a person were standing right in front of her, but would not be able to tell visually if it was a person. She also describes the unusual colors encountered in her NDE: "I saw, like in stereo, colors that were indescribable, colors that we don't have words for" (*MS* 53). Debbie was also able to see some of her relatives whom she had never been able to see before. The descriptions were later confirmed. In an interesting exchange with an interviewer Debbie describes what it was like to see for the first time:

> Interviewer: Was this the first time that you recall having sight?
> Debbie: Yeah.
> Interviewer: Did that surprise you?
> Debbie: Yeah, I didn't want to be back in this little body because I wouldn't be able to see in it.
> Interviewer: Was there a period you needed to adjust visually or was it immediate that you knew what was going on?
> Debbie: It was immediate. I knew it was, I was my soul. I knew.
> (MS 54)

Drs. Ring and Cooper summarize their findings:

> "Overall, 80% of our respondents reported these claims, most of them in the language of unhesitating declaration, even when they

may have been surprised, or even stunned, by the unexpected discovery that they could in fact see. Like sighted experiencers, our blind respondents described to us both perceptions of this world as well as other-worldly scenes, often in fulsome, fine-grained detail, and sometimes with a sense of extremely sharp, even subjectively perfect, acuity."

However, Drs. Ring and Cooper are careful to point out that we cannot assume that what the blind perceive in these experiences is analogous to retinal vision. It is clearly some form of perception, and many experiencers report verifiable visual details, but it is not necessarily identical to the visual perception of the sighted.

That NDEs can bring mindsight to the blind is a powerful example of the enhanced visual perception that so often comes with crossing the evolutionary event horizon associated with the Singularity Archetype.

NDEs and Logos Beheld Telepathic Communication

As I've mentioned before, some of the aspects of NDEs seem like actualizations of the evolutionary potential revealed by the Singularity Archetype. One of the most striking actualizations is Logos Beheld telepathic communication and consciousness. The guiding entity or entities that experiencers encounter is universally described as communicating telepathically. As Dr. van Lommel puts it: "People always report direct communication with this being, as if it reads their mind and responds through the mind" (*CBL* 33-34). This type of communication, which is especially striking during the life review, often has the anticipated effect of dissolving egoism and the boundary between subject and object. Many experiencers will report how superior this form of communication seems compared to ordinary verbal communication.

Tom, a thirty-three-year-old man whose chest was crushed when a truck he was working on fell off its supports: "Then the light immediately communicates to you... This communication is what you might call telepathic. It's absolutely instant, absolutely clear. It wouldn't even matter if a different language was being spoken... whatever you thought and attempted to speak, it would be instant and absolutely clear. There would never be a doubtful statement made" (*HTO* 58).

Janis, a forty-one-year-old woman who nearly died in an automobile accident and was comatose for a long time: "When I communicated [...] with the light, there wasn't a transfer of words. I mean, no words were spoken. It's like thinking a thought and having them know it and answer it immediately. I mean, it's transference of thoughts. It was instantaneous" (*HTO* 60).

Dr. Ring describes the testimony of a five-year-old experiencer named Mark, who related his experience before the publication of Raymond Moody's *Life After Life*, before the term "near-death experience" had even been coined:

> "'You know I died... It was really, really dark, daddy, and then it was really, really bright. And I ran and ran, and it didn't hurt anymore... Oh, daddy, I was running up there [pointing upward].'And he said he didn't hurt anymore, and the man talked to him. And his dad said, 'What kind of words did he say?' And Mark said, 'He didn't talk like this [pointing to his mouth], he talked like this [pointing to his head]'" (*LL* 109).

Life Review often Logos Beheld

The life review is often described as a visually beheld revelation comparable to movies. A young man who nearly drowned in a boating accident narrates his experience of the life review:

> "It was amazing. I could see in the back of my head an array, just an innumerable array of thoughts, memories, things I had dreamt, just in general thoughts and recollections of the past, just raced in front of me, in less than thirty seconds. All these things about my mother and grandmother and my brothers and these dreams I've had. I felt like this frame, millions of frames, just flashed through. It was thoughts and images of people. And a lot of thoughts just raced [snaps his fingers several times] in split seconds. I had my eyes closed under water, but I could still see those images...'" (*LL* 145).

A man who miraculously survived a skydiving accident in which his parachute failed to open at 3,500 feet makes some parallel observations:

> "It's like a picture runs in front of your eyes, like from the time you can remember up to the time, you know, what was happening [that is, the present moment]... It seems like pictures of your life just flow in front of your eyes, the things you used to do when you were small and stuff: stupid things... It was like a picture, it was like a movie camera running across your eyes. In a matter of a second or two. Just boom, boom [snaps his fingers]. It was clear as day, clear as day. It was very fast and you could see everything" (*LL* 146).

The life reviews, however, are not merely cinematic, but typically involve Logos Beheld revelations of deeper meanings. Vision will typically include perspectives of both participant and observer, and the vision is not merely optical but comes with telepathic/empathic overlays of what people are feeling and thinking. For example, Dr. Ring discusses a woman who "said she beheld her life in an array of 'tiny points of light and patterns of light'" (*LL* 152). He also points out that highly visual life reviews are not passive but interactive:

> "But you should not think that this process is purely mechanical, with the images flashing by at an unvarying rate of incredible speed. On the contrary, what NDErs say is that they can, as a matter of will, slow down these images and even dilate them so as to reach a deeper understanding of their significance. [...] One woman — one who had reviewed her life in an array of bubbles — told me: 'Whenever I wanted to, I could sort of zoom in on different huge events in my life...'" (*LL* 152-153).

The life review will often involve a dissolution of the ego's sharp division of subject and object. Neev describes it this way:

> "Like, if you were going to have a life review, and we were going to have a play of it, I would be in the play, but I'd also be watching the play from the audience. And I would feel all the emotions, pain and suffering of all the characters around me in the play. And I'd feel it as an actor in the play, and I'd experience it as the viewer of the play. So I'd have both perspectives" (*LL* 155).

A woman experiencer in Raymond Moody's *The Light Beyond*: "When I was there in that review there was no covering up. I was the very people that I hurt, and I was the very people I helped to feel good..." (*LL* 159).

Subject/Object Breakdown and Homo gestalt

The breakdown in subject/object, the dissolved boundaries and telepathic communication can lead to a Homo gestalt realization, a realization that our individual identities are integrated parts of a larger whole. Mellen-Thomas Benedict describes what the light showed him during his NDE:

> "And at that time, the Light revealed itself to me on a level that I had never been to before. I can't say it's words; it was a telepathic understanding more than anything else, very vivid. I could feel it, I could feel this light. And the Light just reacted and revealed itself on another level, and the message was 'Yes, [for] most people, depending on where you are coming from, it could be Jesus, it could be Buddha, it could be Krishna, whatever.'

> "But I said, 'But what is it really?' And the Light then changed into — the only thing I can tell you [is that] it turned into a matrix, a mandala of human souls, and what I saw was that what

we call our higher self in each of us is a matrix. It's also a conduit to the source; each one of us comes directly, as a direct experience [from] the source. And it became very clear to me that all the higher selves are connected as one being, all humans are connected as one being, we are actually the same being, different aspects of the same being. And I saw this mandala of human souls. It was the most beautiful thing I have ever seen..." (*LL* 287-288).

The boundary-dissolving effects of the NDE seem to expand consciousness on multiple levels. Egocentrism dissolves into a profound Homo gestalt awareness of being part of a species and a living matrix. Another great boundary dissolution involves time, and the linear time boundaries of ordinary consciousness that wall off past and future. It seems that with the disassociation from the physical body, an organism that is so embedded in linear time, the experiencer is also able to disassociate from linear time. We have already discussed the life review that unlocks the past in infinite detail. Somewhat less common, but still a widely reported feature of NDEs, is the "personal flash forward" — a kind of memory of the future.

The Personal Flash Forward

An example of a personal flash forward, that Dr. Ring documents, involves a British man who had an NDE in 1941 when he was ten-years-old. While he was recovering from the appendicitis surgery that caused the NDE, "memories" of future events arose in his mind. In each case, when he reached the age associated with the memories, he found that he was living out the exact memories. For example, a future memory told him flatly, "You will be married at age twenty-eight." This occurred, even though on his twenty-eighth birthday he had not yet met his future wife. He also had a memory of a very specific scene wherein he is married and two children are playing on the floor. In this scene there was a strange detail: "And I was also aware that behind the wall... there was something very strange that I did not understand at all." The memory is not merely a picture of the event, but a living occurrence. In the experiencer's own words:

"I had a vivid memory of sitting in a chair, from which I could see two children playing on the floor in front of me. And I knew that I was married, although in this vision there was no indication of who it was that I was married to. Now, a married person knows what it's like to be single, because he or she was once single, and he or she knows what it's like to be married because he or she is married. But it is not possible for a single person to know what it feels like to be married; in particular, it is not possible for a ten-year-old boy to know what it feels like to be married! It is this strange, impossible feeling that I remember so clearly and why this incident remained in my mind. I had a 'memory' of something that was not to happen for almost twenty-five years hence! But it was not seeing the future in the conventional sense; it was experiencing the future. In this incident the future was now...

"This 'memory' suddenly became present one day in 1968, when I was sitting in the chair, reading a book, and happened to glance over at the children. [...] I realized that this was the 'memory' from 1941! After that I began to realize that there was something to these strange recollections. And the strange object behind the wall was a forced-air heater. These heating units were not — and to the best of my knowledge, are still not — used in England. This was why I could not grasp what it was; it was not in my sphere of knowledge in 1941" (*HTO* 187).

Transcending Linear Time

Many encounters with the Singularity Archetype involve a transcendence of linear time that allows one to perceive a future event horizon — death, eschaton — as though it is happening now. For example, one near-death experiencer had a life review that included both a past and a future portion. The past events were presented to her in black and white. When she came to future events the life "review" switched to color. (*HTO* 187) As in the dreamtime, and some other transcendent events, linear time is suspended. In the ordinary waking life we are closely bound up with our corporeal bodies, which are closely bound to linear time. Your body tells you that you are between breakfast and lunch, that you have only so many hours left until sleep will be necessary. When a newspaper article introduces a person, it usually puts a linear time marker right after their name: "Johnny Jones, 22, said — " When we encounter the Singularity Archetype, individually or collectively, we cross an event horizon where linear time is irrealized.

Formed and Unformed Futures and Free Will

From my present (and very tentative) model of time, the future contains both formed and unformed elements. A formed element, for example, is death as an inevitable event horizon for the individual. The time and manner of the death, however, may not be fully formed. It is the unformed aspects of the future that allow for free will. In some cases, for example, the dietary choices a person makes, the risks he chooses to take, etc. may determine the timing and manner of his death. In other cases, however, the timing of death does not seem to have anything to do with personal choices — for example, the death of a child living in 79 AD Pompeii when Vesuvius erupted.

Free will, in my current model, operates on the unformed elements to generate a particular timeline. Visions of the future, therefore, may be visions of possible timelines, and free will and other wild-card variables determine the timeline actually traveled. Dr. Ring's view seems to be similar: "Since quantum physics is rooted in a purely probabilistic conception of the universe, where nothing can be fixed or known with certainty, precognitive perceptions are held to be previews of possible futures" (*HTO* 208). Dr. Ring quotes physicist Danah Zohar from her book, *Through the Time Barrier*: "It does not imply that the future is already fixed, but rather suggests that there are a range of possible futures and that in some way we may be able to perceive these possibilities" (*HTO* 209).

This is a key aspect of the Singularity Archetype — death and eschaton may be inevitable, but visions of the singularity may be metaphorical or visions of possible futures. In some cases, possible futures become actual futures, in many other cases they do not. For example, in the early Eighties there were quite a number of both UFO abduction and near-death experiencers who had visions of the world ending in the late Eighties. (*HTO* 187-209) In many of these cases, the cause of the vision is probably more psychological than the result of a temporal anomaly. As I'll discuss in greater depth later in the section on apocalypticism, the human psyche frequently blurs inner and outer. Someone encountering the imminence of their individual death may project that recognition outward and envision an end-of-the-world scenario.

The Many Worlds Interpretation

From the temporal range of possibilities, an alternative to the possible-futures model is the "many-worlds interpretation" first introduced by physicist Hugh Everett in 1957. There are many variations of this interpretation, but essentially it would suggest that possible futures are actually alternative futures and that all alternative futures happen. Although the many-worlds interpretation was originally conceived as accounting for events on the scale of quantum mechanics, its implication for macro events is also accepted by many physicists. It is beyond the scope of this book, however, to try to sort through the many different models of possible and alternative futures.

Experiencers do sometimes report being shown possible or alternative personal futures and this is usually in the context of their having a choice about which timeline they are going to live out.

NDEs as Evolutionary Catalyst

Finally, in both *Heading Toward Omega* and *The Omega Project*, Dr. Ring overlaps NDE and the Singularity Archetype by wondering if near-death experiencers might be "the prototype of a new, more advanced strain of the human species striving to come into manifestation? No longer Homo sapiens perhaps. [...] Could NDErs be, then, an evolutionary bridge to the next step in our destiny as a species, a 'missing link' in our midst?" (*HTO* 255).

According to Dr Ring, "NDEs are a kind of experiential catalyst for human evolution, that potentially, at least, these experiences that we know have occurred to many millions of persons across the globe are serving the purpose of jump-stepping the human race to a higher level of spiritual awareness and pscyhophysical functioning" (*OP* 11-12).

From my perspective, NDEs are individual encounters with the Singularity Archetype. Possibly, their increased prevalence, and the exponentially increased awareness of them in the collective, may act as a catalyst for the species wide movement toward the evolutionary event horizon. NDEs are certainly not a new phenomenon, though advances in resuscitation technology are increasing their frequency. What is fairly new is the level of research and fascination with the phenomenon. One aspect of this fascination, which we will discuss in the next section, is an intensifying will in the human species to rebel from conventional corporeality. I call that intensifying drive "the will toward the Glorified Body." It is a key aspect of the Singularity Archetype.

IV. The Glorified Body: Metamorphosis of the Body and the Singularity Archetype

Glad Day of the Dance of Albion, c 1794, British Museum, London

THE ascending power of the Singularity Archetype is partly evidenced by our mutating relationship to being embodied. Body image disorders and some other cultural phenomenon related to body may be pathologized expressions of an evolutionary drive.

Suffering associated with body image has reached such epidemic proportions in our culture that it must be counted as one of the greatest spiritual plagues ever to be visited upon mankind. Media bombard us unceasingly with images of ever more idealized youth and beauty while vast portions of our population undergo voluntary starvation, grueling exercise regimens and surgery in an effort to control their body image. Attempts to control body image often result in collapsing self-esteem, intense suffering and premature death through self-imposed famine.

The temptation is to view body-image problems as an isolated illness, rather than as a phenomenon that points right to the core of our evolutionary predicament. What from one vantage seems an illness in need of eradication, from another is an evolutionary process in need of understanding and continued transformation. The purpose here is to explore body-image problems in their actual context — the spiritual/biological evolution of the species. Viewed from this depth, body-image disorders come to seem part of a difficult birthing process. This process involves risk and suffering, but may also result in the creation of new life.

The Primary Cause

From the illness point of view, body image is a problem neither hidden nor unstudied, and in the last twenty years there has been an explosion of studies, articles and books which have attempted to understand and ameliorate this collective illness. Eating disorders are the most lethal of psychiatric conditions. Much of the most profound and valuable work on body-image/eating disorders has been done by feminist historians and psychologists who have conducted incisive studies of how the oppressive force vectors of a patriarchal society, particularly the media, have distorted women's expectations of their bodies. This work is entirely valid as far as it goes, which, unfortunately, is not to the core of the problem. While the body-image epidemic is greatly exacerbated by media and patriarchal forces, it is not entirely reducible to those forces. What is often perceived by researchers as the cause of the illness is actually a set of pernicious symptoms created by a deeper, more primary cause. Hiding the primary cause of the collective illness are symptoms and secondary forces that are powerful, highly visible, and capable of acting as seemingly independent prime movers. At the true center of the epidemic and its vortex of symptoms is an absolutely primary human urge, which I have termed the will toward the Glorified Body. This primary cause, unlike the secondary forces mistaken as primary, is a force capable of creating growth and transformation. When we examine the actual core of this problem, we find both the reasons and the means for creating an unexpectedly positive outcome.

What is a Glorified Body?

To understand the will toward the Glorified Body we first need to define what I am referring to as "the Glorified Body." Many Christian writings describe the body of the resurrected Christ as being a "Glorified Body" — a radiant body free of mortal limitations. Although I am not working from a Christian point of view, I believe that this phrase captures a powerful archetype. We see images and hear stories of the Glorified Body in most or all cultures and periods. There are all sorts of variations and numerous gradations on the Glorified Body spectrum, but the defining characteristics are fairly apparent.

Although the Glorified Body occurs in endless variations, there are two very broad categories in which the term "Glorified Body" will be employed here. One use of Glorified Body refers to the inherent "energy body" that all human beings possess. Sometimes I will substitute "energy body" to make clear this first meaning of Glorified Body. The second and somewhat overlapping category of use for the term "Glorified Body" is to refer to human or nonhuman entities whose manifest bodies are closer to energy than conventional flesh and blood bodies. This type of Glorified Body hovers in the collective psyche of the human species as a highly charged image and expectation of our further evolution.

Energy Bodies

No mystical leap of faith or willing suspension of disbelief is required to accept the reality that we all possess an energy body. This type of Glorified Body has been recognized by secular and religious traditions throughout human history. Eastern models of the energy body from Chinese and Ayuvedic medicine, and Western scientific studies of human energy fields by psychologist and physiologist Valerie Hunt at UCLA, are examples of systematic studies of our energetic anatomy. The term "biofield" is officially recognized by the NIH (National Institues of Health).[30]

Although the intense materialism of our culture has caused us to lose touch with our real nature, in many other cultures and periods the existence of an energy body in parallel to the flesh and blood body was accepted as medical, everyday fact. Chinese medicine has for thousands of years recognized that we have a body made of "Chi," or life energy, and that it is composed of an intricate structure of energy meridians. Acupuncture works with "virtual points" located along these energy meridians that are not in any way discernible in the dense, physical body.

---

[30] The existence of biofields has been gaining mainstream acceptance:
   http://www.ncbi.nlm.nih.gov/pubmed/19856109

Western medicine has gradually come to recognize the validity of acupuncture, though it is as yet unable to explain how it works. In other Eastern traditions the Glorified Body is referred to as "Shakti" or "Kundalini." In Western occultism it is referred to variously as the "astral body," "subtle body," "light body," "dream body," "fine matter body," and "etheric body." Soul, psyche, self, mind, ego and consciousness can all be considered energy bodies or aspects of the Glorified Body, which materialist science has failed miserably to locate or explain in terms of the physical body.

Parapsychological phenomena are also difficult or impossible to explain in terms of a purely physical body. Materialist science tends to react to such phenomena with agitation and denial. But these supposedly anomalous phenomena become obvious and expected when we recognize that we have an energy body. William James once said that, "All that is necessary to disprove the notion that all crows are black is one white crow." A single occurrence in all of human history of a person, for example, being aware of another person while remote from sensory information, just one mother in all of human history being able to accurately visualize her child in trouble at a distant location, would be sufficient to disprove the notion that we are only physical bodies. And we've had whole flocks of such white crows pass over our heads. As discussed in the previous chapter, very large numbers of people in different cultures and periods report out-of-body and near-death experiences. OBEs and NDEs involve the experience of consciousness remote from the physical body. Increasingly, these phenomena have been subjected to serious, systematic study. As we've discussed, NDE researchers have found that people who are revived from states of arrested bodily function describe strikingly similar, life-changing experiences of departing their physical bodies and discovering their awareness existing as an energy body — a Glorified Body which many describe as possessed with extraordinary vitality, capable of seeing and hearing with dazzling acuity and sometimes able to travel anywhere in space or time at will.

Manifesting the Glorified Body

Although the Glorified Body may exist in all of us, some people are able to manifest it in different ways and degrees than others. A charismatic person, a person who seems radiant or has a powerful presence may be better able to manifest his Glorified Body. There are apparently rare cases of human beings who have shifted their energy body into the foreground of manifestation to such an extent that, for a period of time, they appear to be closer to light than flesh and blood.

The Glorified Body Mythologized

In mythologies, the Glorified Body appears free of some or all of the many limitations of mortality. The Glorified Body may be completely free of cosmetic blemishes, limited vitality, aging, pain, disease, and death. A Glorified Body may be able to transcend conventional limitations of space and time. For example, it may not need technology or an intermediary force of any sort to appear in any location it chooses. It may have transcendent clarity of vision and thought. Often it will transcend ordinary language and communicate through radiance or from the inside of another psyche. A being with a Glorified Body may live in a state of enlightenment and love. Or it could be evil and possess an incredibly potent array of diabolical powers. Visually, a Glorified Body may appear radiant and beautiful — awe inspiring, numinous — the body of an angel. But it could also choose to appear cloaked as a mundane physical body or as a hideous apparition or demon. The most evolved Glorified Bodies are infinitely plastic, able to take on whatever form is desired. This is the quality of the ideoplastic body, the shape shifter, the changeling — like the devil that "hath the power to assume a pleasing shape" or the liquid metal T-1000 terminator in the popular movie, *Terminator 2.*

In contemporary mythology, the Glorified Body appears in a spectrum of permutations ranging from an idealized human-material body to a state of omnipotent, omniscient godhood. In our materialistic culture, we have Superman, "the Man of Steel", who has a more industrialized version of the Glorified Body. Superman doesn't have special radiance, telepathy or most other divine attributes, but leaps tall buildings in a single bound, outruns locomotives and, most helpful in our culture, is bulletproof. At the other end of our cultural spectrum, the Glorified Body turns up as the shape-shifting UFO phenomenon perceived by human observers in endlessly varying forms.

An interesting mythological place to observe an evolving spectrum of Glorified Bodies in contemporary culture is in the rich fantasy world of Ann Rice's *Vampire Chronicles*. These novels also have much to say about the intensity of the modern will toward the Glorified Body. As Rice develops her vision, particular vampires grow more powerful and their bodies become more glorified. Fledgling vampires don't age, are stronger than mortals, more energetic, have superior mental clarity and memory, are superb mimics and have a number of telepathic abilities. But they are also dependent on living blood and can be destroyed by fire, sunlight and older, more powerful vampires. Vampire bodies go through a kind of reverse aging. They become stronger, more impervious, and develop an array of powers that seems to be evolving toward omnipotence. Significantly, the most advanced vampires are no longer fully dependent on drinking blood and become less and less constrained by the organic world. In Rice's mythology, the first vampire was created when a spirit, driven by jealous discontent at not having a body, was able to enter a human being and merge as a kind of symbiont with body and psyche. In other words, the vampire species began as a hybridization of a spirit, a purely energy body, merging with a physical body.

In the fourth book of the *Chronicles, The Body Thief,* the Vampire Lestat is tempted to trade his glorified vampire body for a mortal one by the "Body Thief," a man of dark psychic gifts who has learned how to transfer his psyche into the body of a vulnerable human being. Lestat agrees to a three-day exchange of his vampire body for the body of an exceptionally handsome, vital young man. This body was stolen by the body thief so that he could more effectively tempt the narcissistic Lestat. As soon as the exchange is made, Lestat is horrified by the clumsiness of the mortal body, its vulnerability, slowness, tendency toward fatigue, poor vision and lack of telepathic abilities. He feels the most extreme revulsion when he has to suffer through eating, indigestion, bowel movements and illness. It takes a desperate struggle for him to regain his Glorified Body from the duplicitous Body Thief and he is never again tempted by mortality.

In the *Chronicles,* you can feel the deep urge in Rice to have a Glorified Body herself, a body not limited by predetermined gender, unwanted body fat, limited beauty and power. Through her characters, Rice displays the gifts of a talented body thief in the imaginal realm as she projects her awareness into one Glorified Body after another. And of course there is her cult following — those folks who write her all the time begging to be made vampires so they can escape their mortal bodies.

The Will Toward the Glorified Body

The human will toward the Glorified Body is not a subtle urge. It is an iron fist pounding on both sides of the doors of perception. It is an urging of such terrible power that it will prompt some to go under the surgeon's knife, to starve themselves to death, to sell their souls in the hope of having a mortal body that will merely better resemble a Glorified Body for a brief time. The Glorified Body is not a casual, imaginative musing or an episodic blip on the radar screens of various cultures. It is a powerful, emergent archetype. It is one of our most ancient obsessions and one of the most explosively contemporary. It is related to the deepest sources of human suffering, an inextricable aspect of a thousand types of neurotic torment, a companion in some way to almost every form of personal hell. It is also a divine muse, one of the greatest sources of hope and inspiration we've ever known.

Messages about the will toward a Glorified Body are as ubiquitous in our culture as wi-fi and cellphone signals. Expression of this will can also be found deeply embedded in every religion and mythology, and yet it is rarely named, rarely seen as a highly defined, differentiated and absolutely integral aspect of human psychology. The will toward the Glorified Body is at the center of some of our most destructive and also some of our most creative impulses. This will is a primary urge which can inspire incredible athletic achievement, great art, and technology that blurs with magic.

The will toward the Glorified Body is what inspired Michelangelo to carve David. This same will has also inspired the technological magicians of the computer industry to provide us with "Avatars", animated characters that personify us in the once visually anonymous world of the Internet. Soon (and to some extent already) we will be able to boot up our virtual Glorified Bodies and revel in a digital garden of unearthly delights. Our bodies will be infinitely plastic and with a mouse click we can be leaner than Kate Moss or have cybernetically enhanced muscle definition that will make Mr. Universe look like the Pilsbury Dough Boy. It's interesting to note the term the computer industry has adopted for these new digital bodies: avatars. The first definition of "avatar" in the abridged Oxford dictionary is: "(in Hindu mythology) the descent of a deity or released soul to earth in bodily form."

But somewhere behind the ever more glowing computer monitor or virtual-reality goggles will be a human being, a digitally unenhanced mortal/corporeal version 1.0, who will very likely have bags under his eyes and a pot belly. The Wizard of Oz tells us not to look at the man behind the curtain. But we will look, and will be ever more horrified with the contrast between what we see behind the curtain and what's up there on the screen. The primary urge will remain agonizingly unfulfilled.

Technology and the Glorified Body

However unfulfilling it may be in some ways, technology is one of the central expressions of the will toward a Glorified Body. Technology actually does allow us to extend our physical bodies through time and space. The urge to become a celebrity, for example, is an urge toward a Glorified Body that modern technology can to some degree create. In her films, Marilyn Monroe still lives as a youthful beauty. Since she died young there is no aging, mortal body to provide an embarrassing contrast to her Glorified Body projected on the silver screen. Her life fulfills the Blondie song "Die Young Stay Pretty." Here are a few of the lyrics:

"Die young, stay pretty
Die young, stay pretty…

Love for youth, love for youth
So, die young and stay pretty"

Technology can actually allow you to die young and stay pretty. Marilyn has been dead for half a century but she remains a goddess. People in our culture perceive that someone like Marilyn Monroe has achieved a kind of technological Glorified Body and seek material, technological means to achieve immortality themselves.

Attempting to Glorify the Mortal Body

Projecting the image of a Glorified Body is much more difficult, however, for human beings who don't live on the silver screen and instead are subject to the embarrassment of having an organic mortal body visible to others in real time without airbrushing or digital enhancements. Most people don't possess unusual physical beauty, or, if they do presently, may have problems if they plan to live a normal life span. Many in our culture try to glorify their mortal bodies through dieting, cosmetic surgery and exercise regimens. But attempts to whip the mortal body into Glorified Body status can never result in a lasting feeling of success. There is always that person in the glossy magazine picture who looks better and seems to really have a Glorified Body. Projection of the Glorified Body onto the idealized other makes him or her light up like a god, a being impervious to the blemishes of mortality. Many people are secretly fascinated and delighted when a beautiful celebrity is revealed in a *People* magazine photo to have gained weight, aged or otherwise fallen from the projected glory of Mount Olympus to the mortal gutter. When many people see a glowingly beautiful person, they don't realize they are seeing a changing mortal body in a temporary condition of beauty. The glossy, airbrushed photo is relatively unchanging, but the super model is aging and hurtling toward death with the rest of us. For many, beautiful people, particularly celebrity beauties, are members of a fundamentally different caste than mortal appearing humans. These are the "hot" people that light up in our minds with the sacred fire of deep sexual longing. We behold them and we feel the stirrings of immortal, archetypal forces. It may seem as if there were a race of gods and a race of mortals inhabiting the same planet. Nietzche's Zarathustra said, "If there are gods, how can I stand it to be no god!" In our culture we say, "If there are beautiful people, how can I stand it to be no beautiful person!"

Mortal Body Identification and Meat Puppet Despair

One of the great causes of despair and suffering in modern society is our tendency to identify exclusively with the mortal body. The intense materialistic bias of our culture has caused many of us to forget that we also have a Glorified Body — an energy or spirit body that religious and secular traditions from all cultures and periods have recognized. Modern science has also begun to recognize that it is a fallacy to view a human being as an object. The mortal body is not a fixed object, but a process. Fifty trillion cellular animals, each of them changing nanosecond by nanosecond, work cooperatively to create a human body. The mortal body has been called "spiritualized tissue" and conventional materialist science has failed utterly to explain the connection between mind and brain. Quantum mechanics, meanwhile, has exploded the materialist bias of conventional science as an irrational prejudice definitively contradicted by experimental evidence. A number of open-minded physicists have confronted the replicable, empirical data which has exposed the materialist fallacy contaminating not only science, but every level of our culture. The so-called paradoxes of quantum mechanics: objects being in two places at the same time, the instantaneous parallelism of objects separated by any distance (nonlocality), the decisive need for consciousness to collapse the wave function and determine outside reality, etc, immediately cease to be paradoxes when we give up the obsolescent notion that the universe is composed of matter and that mind, body, and cosmos are separated. But does the materialist bias of science really affect, for example, a teenager with a body-image problem?

As a teacher in an Alternative School for troubled adolescents, I worked with a fifteen-year-old boy (we'll call him Adam) who was depressed, even suicidal. Adam was unhappy with his body and saw human existence as painful and futile. In talking about the source of his despair, he mentioned a television program he had seen a couple of years earlier. The program was a documentary that showed brain surgery being performed on someone suffering from epilepsy. During this operation, neurosurgeons would stimulate part of the patient's exposed brain, see what response they got, and label that portion. Adam was horrified by the television documentary. It seemed that being human was reducible to a brain that was nothing more than a circuit board. He felt that this show proved that he was nothing more than a "meat puppet", a term he borrowed from the name of a popular rock band. Adam's feelings about his own body, and human existence, were influenced by the briefest glimpse of the pseudoscientific position referred to as "neurological materialism" — the belief that human consciousness is nonexistent or is reducible to an epiphenomenal byproduct of chemical process in the brain.

But we are not "meat puppets." We are much more than our mortal bodies and we already possess a Glorified Body. For several hundred years the priests of science have influenced the rest of society toward the materialist fallacy. We have become much more focused on objects and our attention has been diverted from the realm of the spirit. Our present magic is technology, which we can buy at the store. The gods and goddesses we once saw in the heavens are now technology-wielding extraterrestrials who, like evil scientists, do medical tests on us inside of metal saucers. And, most significantly, we are focused on the body, our body and the body of the other, as an object. We've come to identify more strongly with the denser, mortal aspect of our being. That identification has become more and more exclusive, and our Glorified Body — the energy body that exists in parallel to the physical body — has been forgotten.

The Ghost in the Machine

Our Glorified Body has become the "ghost in the machine," an elusive, suspect dimension that can't be measured in grams, centimeters or amperes. Materialist science found that it was completely unable to explain mind, which is more a function of the Glorified Body than the physical body. Therefore, it literally and pervasively dismissed human consciousness as either nonexistent or, at best, as a byproduct of an automated neurological process. Once, the patriarchy declared man made in the image of God. More recently, however, the patriarchal dogma swung all the way to the other extreme and declared man made in the image of the machine. Consciousness and free will were disparaged as illusions, accidental subprograms of our "real" center — the brain misinterpreted as a tangled, wet, digital computer.

Ray Kurzweil is a neurological materialist and technology futurist who has written two influential books, *The Age of Spiritual Machines* and *The Singularity is Near*. The recent documentary film about him, *Transcendent Man*, confirmed my impression of him as a tragicomic figure, desperately trying to keep his aging body alive by taking 100 supplements a day so that he can be around for a kind of technological rapture he imagines. In a satirical piece[31] I wrote about aging a few years ago I describe his absurd predicament:

Ray Kurzweil — Transcendent Man?

Of course, if you are a fundamentalist materialist and a technological futurist, like Ray Kurzweil, then you may have some expectation of having your consciousness downloaded into a quantum computer housed in a titanium alloy exoskeleton with Zeiss Ikon optics and a shape-shifting dermal layer consisting of nanobots able to reconfigure

---

[31] "You are Only as Old as You Are: Six Noble Truths of the Zap Philosophy of Aging," available at ZapOracle.com.

themselves in any way that is consistent with the underlying titanium alloy exoskeleton. In other words, your expectation is the nerdy gadget version of being an immortal changeling. But no matter how many off-planet backups of yourself you have downloaded into quantum computers kept in super-cooled, fully hardened underground bunkers, there is always the possibility of a super wave or galaxy devouring black hole destroying all those backups. This is what Tolkien called premature immortality: the naïve confusion of immortality with being in a single, age-resistant body.

It's too bad that someone doesn't point Ray toward NDE research which ought to show him essential flaws in neurological materialism and allow him to realize that neither bodies nor machinery are necessary for the survival of consciousness.

Awakening from Materialism

To the great credit of progressive science there are now many scientists who have left the rather clueless paradigm of materialism behind. These scientists have begun to integrate the findings of quantum mechanics, and have stopped denying the existence of phenomena that materialist science finds impossible to explain. Still, we need to be cautious because although quantum mechanics does have profound implications, we can't be cavalier about applying them to the human reality. Quantum mechanics applies to the subatomic domain, and it is comprehensible in the language of mathematics, not English, so we need to be careful about applying our personal mythology of what quantum mechanics means to the human domain.

One of the best known findings of quantum mechanics is that point of view seems to change the physical reality of what is out there. A simple, replicable experiment illustrates this principle:

A photon emitter is set up to project one photon at a time at a metal plate. If the plate has one slit in it, the photon is a particle, and goes straight through the slit like a bullet. If the plate has two slits in it, however, the photon is a wave and a wave interference pattern results. The photon somehow "knows" what it is supposed to be even before it leaves the emitter. The result of this experiment was startling and agitating to the naive mind of the materialist. But almost anyone who pays open-minded attention to ordinary life sees all sorts of examples of inner psychic states having acausal parallelisms to outside reality. These are the strange, meaningful coincidences that Carl Jung termed "synchronicities."

The photon has been called a "wavicle" because it is either a particle or wave depending on what you expect it to be. Some physicists have suggested that human beings are like the wavicle: if you view a human being as an object, a particle, then you experience the mortal, physical body as all there is and will tend toward the "meat puppet" view of neurological materialism; if you view a human being as a soul, then you experience the wave-like spirit body and will tend toward a mystical, religious point of view. To see the full human being you must flip back and forth between these points of view until you are able to experience that human beings are both particle-like physical bodies and wave-like energy bodies.

The dualistic point of view formalized by Descartes at the dawn of science caused mind and body to be sundered into entirely separate realms. But that naive separation is failing both in science and society. Increasingly, a regained awareness is dawning in the West that body and mind are two sides of the same coin, that spirit and body have an inherent integration captured by the famous principle of alchemy, "As above, so below." The Glorified Body is an energy body that is still physical, but more difficult for our present instrumentation to measure. Classical Newtonian physics and the materialist paradigm fail to explain consciousness and other aspects of the Glorified Body. But contemporary physicists like Roger Penrose, Danah Zohar, Amit Goswami, Fred Alan Wolf and others are beginning to hypothesize quantum mechanical models of the human organism that account for both body and spirit. One problem is that a generation gap of sorts has opened up between those scientists who are aware of, and have struggled to integrate, new paradigms of reality that jive with the findings of quantum mechanics, and those who profess to do science but refuse to give up the obsolescent paradigm of materialism that fails to account for quantum mechanics, consciousness, parapsychological phenomena, etc. This generation gap is even wider in society, where many ordinary persons, like my fifteen-year-old former student Adam, believe that science has proven that we are "meat puppets" and that there is no spirit or energy body, and others who know the "facts of life" recognized by almost every other culture in history that we have both physical and energetic bodies.

Reflection vs. Radiance

A large part of our suffering is caused by our tendency to mistake "reflection" for "radiance." Our materialist bias causes us to equate ourselves and others with reflections. Mirrors, photographs, film, and video obviously present us with mere reflections of human beings. But directly gazing at a real-time human body passing us on the sidewalk can also be a case of seeing a mere reflection. What we actually see is the reflection of ambient light off the surface topography of skin, hair, and clothing. This reflection enters the simple convex lens of the cornea and emerges turned upside down on the back of the retina. The retina also has a large blind spot where the optic nerve connects. This imperfectly transmitted light must be turned right-side up, the blind spot must be filled in, and in numerous other ways the registered image must be interpreted by neurological processing. This doesn't happen instantaneously, so there exists a time buffer between environmental phenomena and our perception.

What we actually see is a neurological reconstruction of a past event. Fortunately, we don't perceive with just the conventional five bodily senses. Other persons have "radiance" — the direct transmission of self that allows us to feel their presence at a distance which precludes ordinary sense perception. What we actually perceive may be more like an overlay of reflection (a neurological construct) and radiance (direct perception of the self of the other). A person with the looks to create a beautiful topographical reflection might have a radiance that is sickening to behold. You see reflections; you behold radiance. We would ease a great deal of suffering if we could shift the ratio between seeing and beholding when we perceive ourselves and others. If we learn to behold others as radiance, to look beyond the blemishes of their reflections, to perceive the Glorified Body already present, then we will have gone a long way toward healing transformation. To accomplish that transformation we need to name and recognize the perception of radiance we already have. We also need to shift the ratio of reflection and radiance in our perception to favor radiance.

The Sixties and the Glorified Body

The Sixties rebellion from the dense, naive materialism of the Fifties was in many ways a reassertion of the Glorified Body. Consciousness-altering psychedelic experiences were sought as out-of-body experiences on demand. The fascination with Eastern religion, transcendental meditation, parapsychology and the occult was largely a rebellion from the patriarchal dogma that the material body was all that existed. For all the narcissistic goofiness, crass commercialism and gullibility often associated with the New Age, this movement grew out of the Sixties and further articulated the collective dissatisfaction with the reigning creed of materialism. Body-image and eating disorders are largely pernicious symptoms of this reigning materialism and its tendency to create an exclusive identification with the physical body that is both painful and highly disorienting. We need to heal that disorientation and expand our identification with the physical body to include recognition of our inherent Glorified Body.

A Primary Urge

The will toward a Glorified Body is a primary urge, the urge of our entire species and not just single individuals living in a particular culture. Organisms of all sorts seem to have the primary urge to reproduce, to genetically propagate. Among gendered organisms, there is an insistent urge to couple with other individuals of the same species. That urging may be intense enough to be described as "going into heat." Heat is a state of excitement and increased dynamism, whether it is the material heat of fire or the metabolic heat of a living organism. The organism in heat may appear agitated, even tormented, while in the grip of this urge. In the adolescent stage of development — the stage of recently acquired reproductive potential — there may be the particularly urgent will to achieve that first coupling. The unfulfilled urge is antecedent to the coupling event — an event that in chaos math would be a called an "attractor."[32] Very likely the organism will get to fulfill this urge. But it's not a sure thing. Some organisms may die before they fulfill the urge; but certainly some individuals of that species must succeed in fulfilling that urge or the species will become extinct. As far as I can tell, urges in nature are always fulfilled by a species, though not necessarily by every individual of that species. Only in human beings could we even imagine the existence of an urge that seems never to be fulfilled. My contention is that the human species has "gone into heat" — a state of heightened expectation, agitation and chaos. We are nearing the attractor, nearing the place where we can couple with the Glorified Body in a way that permanently releases us from the oppressive limits of corporeality and thereby fulfills a primary urge. Meanwhile, the findings of Near-Death Experience research, parapsychology and a number of other fields are quietly creating a new Copernican revolution. The disenchanting delusions of materialism, which put the wetware of a single corporeal body at the center of existence, is giving way to a recognition that we are much more than that. Instead of viewing consciousness as a byproduct or illusion generated by body, we are becoming aware that bodies are more like planets orbiting the radiance of psyche.

Evolutionary Crisis and the Glorified Body

The intensifying will toward the Glorified Body is happening at a time of evolutionary crisis when the metabolism of the whole species is heating up. Technological changes and scientific discoveries are fundamentally altering our experiences of self and outer reality. The biosphere that allows the existence of our physical bodies has undergone a global

---

[32] Roughly, an "attractor" is an event in the future that is so powerful that it warps causality and phenomenon in the present.

toxification, which is threatening the continuance of our species. To understand the body-image plague, we must view it in the context in which it occurs — a crisis phase of human evolution. Many attributes of the human psyche, from sexuality and body image to spirituality and our sense of relation to the universe, are rapidly mutating. We cannot comprehend symptoms without understanding the general condition of a species that is hurtling toward an evolutionary nexus charged with images of extinction and rebirth. Our intensifying will toward the Glorified Body is more than an urge to reconnect with the inherent, human energy body recognized by all human cultures. It is also a species-wide urge to make a quantum, evolutionary jump toward the Glorified Body as our embodied manifestation. We are experiencing an urge to massively redefine body, self and our relationship to physical reality.

Epilogue — We Finally Made It

The origins of this chapter on the Glorified Body are interesting and have something to add to the content:

On May 31 of 1996 (the exact date is easy to establish because it happened to be the day that Timothy Leary died), I woke up feeling somewhat downcast about certain neurotic aspects of my personality that I felt I had never made progress with. Feeling no particular inspiration, I decided to sit down with a notebook and a pen in front of me and take another try at understanding anyway. Suddenly, what felt energetically like a transmission occurred, and in a short period of time — this seems to be a pattern for me; the time interval always seems to be less than 40 minutes — an intense series of life-changing insights cascaded through my mind. Was this a last message from Timothy as he left his body? The insights I had, about the nature of body and consciousness, and a largely unrecognized will in the human species, did not merely change my thinking and philosophy, they profoundly shifted some of the most over-determined, stubbornly neurotic aspects of my personality, and I've been a different person ever since that morning. Just when I finished furiously scribbling down this compressed burst of insight, my pager went off. This could be the most mundane of events, but intuitively I was absolutely convinced that the pager was registering a parallel transmission, and that whoever was calling had something of immediate bearing to the burst of insight. I left my RV to look for a phone. There was a voice message from my friend Jordie saying he needed to talk to me, but the number left on the pager turned out to be that of a hospital in Louisiana. Another page came through from him, again with the number of the hospital in Louisiana, and I worried that there might be a medical emergency involving him or his partner, Sarah. I'll cut through the details here, suffice to say there were a series of telecommunication anomalies of different sorts, five inexplicable malfunctions of different systems making it impossible for us to communicate. It took more than twenty-four hours with both of us trying before we could have a live phone contact. Jordie had paged me immediately upon awakening from a dream of shocking intensity and import, in which I appeared as a dream character. The content of the dream had jaw-dropping parallelism to the transmission-like burst of insights I had received at the exact same time that Jordie was having his dream.

In the dream I am standing with Jordie and some of our other friends in the desert near Big Mountain, Arizona. In the waking life we had all been there doing volunteer work on a Navajo reservation, staying with the family of a medicine man. Our time there, in the Spring of 1996, corresponded with the appearance of Comet Hyakutake, the brightest comet in the last several hundred years. The reservation, which was in high desert with few electric lights, had ideal viewing conditions. We see some shooting stars. One of the shooting stars veers off its expected downward trajectory and comes shooting toward us. It appears before us as a glowing "impossibly geometric" (Jordie's phrase, he compared it to an M.C. Escher design) object. It seemed magical, merkaba-like, interdimensional and alchemical. I turn to Jordie and say, "We finally made it."

Upon interpretation, the dream seems to be about our coupling with the Glorified Body. The star that appears before us is a cosmic vessel, like the shape-shifting luminous craft of the UFO phenomenon. The key statement, "We finally made it," seems to have at least three levels of meaning. The first is the sense of victory, rescue, of accomplishment after long travail. The second is "made it" in the sense of manifestation, manufacture or creation — "We finally manifested it." And the third, from the American vernacular, is that we finally coupled with it. This third layer is interesting because of its sexual resonance, and implication of achieving sexual union that was a long time coming. For example, if a high school boy were speaking of his girlfriend and made the statement, "We finally made it." it would be understood to mean that after a long period of frustrated desire and working toward greater intimacy they finally had sexual intercourse. This layer resonates with the realization I had that morning that our will toward the Glorified Body was destined to be fulfilled, and that it was a core intentionality like sexual desire.

V. *Avatar* and the Singularity Archetype

THE most potent expressions of the Singularity Archetype continue to be science-fiction novels and films. More so than their counterparts in the genres of horror, action, comedy, drama, etc, science-fiction movies and texts are a forward-thinking species, extrapolatory of both modern technological trends and humanity's ultimate fate against the backdrop of space and time. James Cameron's *Avatar* is particularly charged with emergent archetypal messages from the collective unconscious that relate to an approaching evolutionary event horizon. Yet some of these most significant layers of meaning in *Avatar* have been overlooked. Most glaringly, they are not to  be found in the articles available on the web that discuss the film's underlying mythology (at least that I have been able to find). *Avatar*, as we'll see, has numerous points of connection with the Singularity Archetype and the Glorified Body.

The Will Toward the Glorified Body in *Avatar*

The will toward the Glorified Body is right at the center of *Avatar*. James Cameron seems to be aware of this. When Larry King asked him why he picked the name "Avatar," Cameron responded: "When I wrote it in 95' it just popped into my head that here you've got people projecting their consciousness into a fleshly body, a biological body, and that's what the Sanskrit word means, the taking of flesh, the incarnation of a divine being in the case of the Hindu religion. And although our characters aren't divine beings, obviously, the idea is that it's actually a fleshly incarnation."

As *Avatar* opens, our point of view is that of a Glorified Body, the flying dream body of the protagonist, Jake Sully, a young Marine who is a paraplegic. His character is perfectly designed to represent the will toward the Glorified Body. He is an athletic, vital young man with great physical courage and a warrior essence but whose body is half-paralyzed.

The next hauntingly numinous scene in the movie is when Jake first catches a glimpse of his avatar. As I pointed out in the previous chapter, "avatar," a term which has been adopted in the computer gaming world, comes from Hindu mythology and means a spirit form descended into the flesh. From that point of view, a human being is an avatar, a spirit bound to one body for the entire waking portion of an incarnation. We also have an intense will to break free of the one-body/one-psyche rule that dominates the waking mortal life. The movie *Avatar*, thanks to both content and the technological enhancements of its form, provides a powerful depiction of what it would be like to break the one-body/one-psyche rule. Jake cannot restrain his unbridled euphoria when he is able to enter his avatar, a far more powerful and glorified body than he had even before his paralysis. His new body is bioluminescent, idealized, more androgynous and suited to a world where gravity is less limiting than on the earth. In actuality, from the movie production standpoint, this is a virtual body that is a hybridization of the actor's body moving through space and time and a CGI avatar.

Breaking the One Body/One Psyche Rule

As I've already mentioned, we all get to break the one-body/one-psyche rule during the dreamtime, when we are able to merge our awareness with a variety of dream bodies. *Avatar* begins with the liberated feeling of Jake flying in his dream body. The process of merging with the avatars of the movie is very much like dreaming. Jake lies down in a coffin-like capsule and, analogous to falling asleep and dreaming, his connection to his waking body is submerged as he bonds to a different, enhanced body that lives in Pandora, a place analogous to the dreamtime. The dreamtime is a place of boundary dissolution. Everyone who has seriously studied the dreamtime, including both Freud and Jung, has noticed how telepathic it is compared to the waking time. Many of the reports of mutual dreaming illustrate this dramatically. Similarly, the bioluminescent world of Pandora is a massively telepathic network. I'll return to the concept of telepathic networks later in this essay.

Avatar and Near-Death Experience

The process of merging with the avatar also has many parallels to near-death experience. Jake dies to his waking life, passes through a tunnel of light and finds himself in a glorified body. Jake's life takes on a diurnal/nocturnal sort of cycling that undergoes a figure/ground reversal. The waking life of his paraplegic body recedes with the ghetto life of corporeal limitations, bureaucratic tensions, and intrusions from imperialistic patriarchy. His eros and enthusiasm for life become far more identified with his avatar/Pandoran life. He wants to more fully escape the inferior corporeal/waking life into the Glorified Body/dreamtime/afterlife.

Paradoxically, Cathy Lynn Pagano wrote an article entitled "Avatar: The Archetypal Message Is 'Get Back In Your Body!'" Pagano points out, quite insightfully, "The freedom and joy of the body moving, leaping, daring is a major component of this story, just as Pandora's beauty compliments the body's freedom. The corporate people live in metal boxes, without beauty or free movement; the walking which was such a big part of the game of golf is reduced to putting in the office."[33]

The paradox she does not recognize is that Jake gets back into 'the body,' or more correctly he becomes more vitally embodied by breaking free of the limitations of his damaged human body and merging with his avatar.

Subcreating Imaginal Worlds

"It's my world, you are all just living in it."
— James Cameron (referring to Pandora), on Larry King Live

While from the top layer of *Avatar's* mythology, Pandora is an exotic, extraterrestrial world, on both a more literal and deeper layer, Pandora is actually the world of the empowered human imagination. Pandora is an imaginal world created by James Cameron. Movies, as I've pointed out before, are essentially a dream delivery technology. Cameron, who unlike most of us can command a thousand technicians and a quarter-billion-dollar budget, is able to make his dream, his imaginal world, into a collective dream. His world is, of course, more an extrapolation of human psychology than anything extraterrestrial. For example, since like Cameron I am a baby boomer, I notice a common cultural influence that very likely inspired the bioluminescent world of Pandora. An early psychedelic experience for many baby boomers, including myself, was the backroom of various hippie shops where black lights illuminated black-light posters and created a little phosphorescent world reminiscent of the look of nocturnal Pandora. The avatar experience of the movie,

[33] http://www.opednews.com/articles/Avatar-The-Archetypal-Mes-by-Cathy-Lynn-Pagano-100121-11.html.

therefore, represents to me not so much extraterrestrial travel as intrapsychic imaginal travel, which has more to do with the dreamtime, the future of virtual reality, and a human evolutionary event horizon we are hurtling toward.

By my second viewing of the movie, much of the novelty was gone, and I found that what I really wanted was a 3D IMAX immersive visit to another exotic world, which would be much more exciting than a revisit to Pandora.

Naviblue Syndrome

Apparently there are quite a number of people, mostly young men, who are complaining on internet forums of depression because they can't live on Pandora, which seems so real to them while they are watching the film in 3D. For example, CNN, in an article entitled "Audiences experience 'Avatar' blues," reports:

> "A user named Mike wrote on the fan Web site 'Naviblue' that he contemplated suicide after seeing the movie.

> "'Ever since I went to see *Avatar* I have been depressed. Watching the wonderful world of Pandora and all the Na'vi made me want to be one of them. I can't stop thinking about all the things that happened in the film and all of the tears and shivers I got from it,' Mike posted. 'I even contemplate suicide thinking that if I do it I will be rebirthed in a world similar to Pandora and that everything is the same as in *Avatar*.'"[34]

The 'Naviblue' phenomenon is understandable because so many in our culture are magically disempowered. They want to live in someone else's dream because it doesn't occur to them that they are dreamers and potential subcreators who can create their own worlds. They have been conditioned to be passive consumers of the imaginal plane, not empowered creators.

Opening Pandora's Box

What is envisioned on the other side of the evolutionary event horizon is that the physics of the dreamtime will be the default, rather than the physics of the waking time, and we will have the ability to subcreate our own worlds without access to a thousand technicians and a quarter-billion dollars. I have also pointed out that unlike Terence McKenna and Ram Das, whom I have talked to a bit on the subject, I do not expect this evolutionary breakthrough to be a cure for human evils. When novelty

---

[34] http://www.cnn.com/2010/SHOWBIZ/Movies/01/11/avatar.movie.blues/index.html.

increases, the outer edge of light and dark both intensify, and I expect that there will be gifted black magicians making potent diabolical use of these enhanced abilities. I think the name "Pandora" suggests this with its connection to Pandora's Box. In the original myth, Pandora opened a jar, but a mistranslation has rendered it forever into a box. Now the word "Pandora" has been remythologized again and will forever be associated with the world of the Na'vi. *Avatar* represents an opening of Pandora's Box in the sense that it is a breakthrough in the technological magic of the movies, and now that the technology has been irretrievably loosed into the world, we can be sure that it will not always be used to deliver collective dreams as benign as *Avatar*.

Liminality and the Special Role of Hybrids in Evolution

The luminescent jellyfish-like envoys of Eywah, the divine intelligence of Pandora, recognize Jake as a key evolutionary catalyst. In many ways, to the practical intelligence of both human and Pandoran characters, he is the most unlikely of choices. He is severely handicapped in both the human and Pandoran realms, is not particularly bright and is woefully ignorant of Pandoran culture as well as foolish about human politics. What he does have, however, that makes him the ideal choice, is an enthusiastic beginner's mind. As the Pandoran shaman points out, "It's hard to fill a cup that is already full." His lack of knowledge, of course, is also ideal cinematically as we learn things for the first time as he does. Jake is a liminal figure, a person caught betwixt and between, who is not fully accepted in either realm. As is so often the case, that which is liminal and hybrid is the most alchemically charged and capable of metamorphosis.

Twins and Evolution

Another aspect of Jake that makes him an evolutionary catalyst is that he is a twin. His call to adventure comes because of the murder of his twin, who was trained to merge with a Na'vi avatar. Twins are very significant mythologically, but also from an evolutionary point of view. A new type of consciousness also means a new type of communication, and the new means of communication can easily be what creates the new type of consciousness. The last quantum evolutionary jump had to do with our ability to think and communicate in words. The breakthrough into a more sophisticated form of communication is very likely to happen (both in the past and the future) between identical twins. Identical twins sometimes invent their own languages. (Sometimes called idioglossia or cryptophasia or less technically as "twin talk" or "twin speech.") Identical twins are a maximal case of rapport that can exist between individuals, and with lessened barriers of difference and miscommunication, they seem like the most fertile ground for crossing the communication gap between individuals in novel ways.

In another 2009 CGI film, *9*, a masterpiece that unlike *Avatar* did not get the credit it deserved, we see a brilliant manifestation of the twin aspect of the Singularity Archetype. Amongst a group

of prototype rag-doll-like creatures there are a pair of twins. While the other prototypes have lens-like eyes that take in visual information, the twins have eyes that transmit information as light between them. They are also able to project moving images to others. As we've discussed, a visually-oriented telepathy is one of the most classic aspects of the Singularity Archetype. Also amazing is that *9* ends with some of the creatures in luminous spirit bodies merging with a moving spiral of light in the sky, another classic element of many of the permutations of the Singularity Archetype.

The mysterious "Norway Spiral" which appeared on December 9, 2009

The Ego and the Pandoran Telepathic Network

Jake, because of the murder of his human twin, is invited to merge with a new twin, his avatar, which has been grown to genetically match his murdered twin. When this twinned being (Jake in his avatar) travels to Pandora, he finds himself in a Logos Beheld kind of world where most or all of the life is bioluminescent, transmitting information about itself through the projection of light. It is also a world that has much in common with another key aspect of the Singularity Archetype — the telepathic network. All of Pandora seems to be a telepathic network. The human world of the movie, even though it is set in the future, is as ego-fractured as ever, with human psyches encapsulated by their own short-sighted egocentric perspectives.

Like the human characters of the imagined future in *Avatar*, we have reached an evolutionary cul-de-sac with the ego. Given the lethality of our present level of technology, we may no longer be able to survive the egocentric perspective. Unlike the Na'vi, the egocentric human is usually unaware, except in an abstracted way, of the living matrix of which he is a part. Encapsulated by technological exoskeletons — SUVs, gadget-filled homes, etc. — he may have no direct sense of how his lifestyle is impacting the rest of the living matrix. The problem of the insulated ego is already a very familiar theme, and the ego is all too easy to villainize, but the prejudice against the ego so often found in New Age and Eastern circles fails to notice that the ego served many powerful evolutionary purposes.

One of the great purposes of the ego was to encapsulate consciousness and create a firewall between psyches, greatly reducing the networked telepathy that I believe is more the norm in nature. We see what looks like networked telepathy, for example, in the amazing synchrony of schools of fish. Peter Thompson and Christopher Bird's *The Secret Life of Plants*, and some subsequent studies, seem to show that the vegetable kingdom is not only sentient, but aware of human thoughts and changes to living tissue (while remote from any sensory information). Tribal cultures do seem to be more aware and tapped into the networked intelligence of nature.

Pandora and the Pre/Trans Fallacy

The Na'vi resemble an idealized version of a terrestrial indigenous tribe, and that constitutes a subtle danger in the mythological resonance of the film. The danger is that the film encourages what Ken Wilber calls the "pre/trans" fallacy.

Essentially, the pre/trans fallacy notices a common tendency to confuse prerational states with transrational states, since both are non-rational. The "reductivist" version of this is the tendency of "scientism," which reduces all transrational mystical states to prerational infantilism, and dismisses authentic spiritual experience as "superstitious nonsense." Freud clearly fell for this half of the fallacy, especially in *The Future of an Illusion*. The "elevationist" version of the fallacy, ubiquitous in the New Age, is to elevate prerational states to the transcendent and to demonize rationality. From this side of the fallacy, babies are thought to be Buddhas, and anything tribal or aboriginal is romanticized and inflated as infinitely superior to anything modern or rational. Promiscuity is seen as a daring rebellion from antiquated taboos, even though it is usually in high conformity to what peers are doing. They recognize as conventional the older sexual morays of the past, but fail to recognize that their rebellion is part of a vast conventionalism of the present, and that this new conventionalism is actually based on a still more primitive level of development than the old conventionalism. Regressing to pre-rational hedonism, indulging every impulse and irrational notion is seen as enlightened, post-conventional and transcendent. This is the state of the typically goofy New Age person who never heard an urban legend or bit of mystical-sounding nonsense without adopting it wholesale. This type of person is fiercely anti-intellectual and anti-rational, so it is impossible to talk them down from their absurdities. Even the attempt to do so casts you, in their minds, as this clueless rationalist stuck in his ego. They believe they have transcended rationality, while forgetting that to transcend something you first have to achieve it![35]

The glorification of the Na'vi, especially since they appear not only exotic and tribal, but are also occurring in a futuristic sci-fi film, will encourage some people to believe that the answer to our present troubles would be a return to life as warriors in an indigenous rain-forest tribe. The Singularity Archetype, however, indicates that the answer has more to do with hybridization — of East and West, of aboriginal with high tech, of past and future. Jake, who appears amongst the Na'vi as a hybrid, is a better personification of the evolutionary message than the Na'vi themselves. Unfortunately, Jake's character is disappointingly ordinary, he has a good heart and physical courage, but little else to recommend him as the evolutionary catalyst he becomes in the film. From a marketing and story point of view, however, Jake's ordinariness makes him easier for young males to identify with. Also, in many traditional hero cycles the hero is a naïve young male who has to be initiated into a new world, and Jake fits very well into that tradition. In most of the more inspired versions of stories related to the Singularity

---

[35] For more on the pre/trans fallacy and the error of absolutisms, see my essay "Dynamic Paradoxicalism: The Anti-ism Ism" at ZapOracle.com.

Archetype, however, (*Dune*, *Akira*, many others) the evolutionary catalyst tends to be a young mutant with extraordinary parapsychological abilities.

Another way that *Avatar* seems to lean toward the preconventional rather than the transconventional is that a kind of hard-wired interspecies bond with various animals is emphasized over the intraspecies, nonlocal telepathic bond that we find in more inspired story versions of the Singularity Archetype. There seems to be a pantheistic networking with nature, but it is imagined in a very primitive, materialist way where the Na'vi have tails that seem to be the organic equivalent of Ethernet cables. Since Cameron first conceived of the Na'vi in 1995, before wifi networking existed, their rudimentary means of connection is understandable. Schools of fish, however, don't need to connect via nerve bundles to synchronize, so the networking model in the movie seems to have a bias toward the concrete, hard-wired connection. The imagined version of nature is actually more primitive than the already existing version of nature we find here on earth.

Avatar and Homo gestalt

In more sophisticated and inspired versions of the Singularity Archetype, the transcendence of ego-encapsulation is not imagined in such a materialist pre-conventional way. Collective consciousness turns up frequently in expressions of the Singularity Archetype and merits some examination. In Theodore Sturgeon's 1953 science-fiction novel, *More Than Human*, a group of mutants, who each have distinctly different strengths and weaknesses, form a collective consciousness while retaining some individuality and become, in many ways, a single entity where each mutant serves in a specialized role, as if they were organs of a single body. Sturgeon coined the term "Homo gestalt" to describe this new entity. Similarly, more recent abduction testimony has emphasized the "Greys" as having a hive-like collectivity, and this is experienced as another threatening aspect of their alien otherness.

There are a number of possible reasons for this collective consciousness motif appearing in so many permutations of this archetype. One is that it may be a fairly literal indicator of evolutionary change. If the ego ceases to dominate the human psyche, then perhaps the boundaries that it creates around the individual will dissipate and we will become more collectively aware. The shells of the oysters dissolve and the pearls lie together.

The Homo gestalt aspect of the Singularity Archetype reflects an evolutionary possibility. Encapsulated psyches become telepathically connected, but without a loss of individuality. For example, in the world of *Dune*, there is a sisterhood of highly conscious warriors known as the "Bene Gesserit." To become a Bene Gesserit Reverend Mother, one must survive a perilous rite called "The Water of Life." In this initiatory rite one imbibes a potent psychotropic, mutagenic poison. If the initiate survives and becomes a Reverend Mother, she will retain her individuality, but will also be aware of the memories and all the psyches of all other Reverend Mothers, living or dead, who have similarly survived this rite. The Reverend Mothers don't need cables or funny tails to be part of this network.

Parapsychological researchers such as Russell Targ (the laser physicist who cofounded the U.S. Government's remote viewing program) have long recognized that telepathy and many other parapsychological phenomena occur because our psyches exist in a nonlocal field. In other words, no signal needs to be sent anywhere because psyches do not need to be causally related. Early Soviet parapsychologists called telepathy "mental radio" because they imagined the psyche in the image of the current machine, the radio, and had a causal signal model. But the findings of many well-conducted experiments have shown that the telepathic effect is not lessened by distance (as any energetic signaling would be), nor is it diminished when the subject is in a Faraday Cage (which blocks all electromagnetic signals). More evolved visions of Homo gestalt are based on the emergence of encapsulated individuality into a nonlocal telepathic network.

In the final battle at the end of *Avatar*, the military/industrial/ patriarchal complex is personified by Colonel Quaritch, who is encapsulated in an exoskeleton. Jake is in his avatar, but ultimately is saved because of the telepathic bond with his Na'vi lover. He survives by transcending the technological connection to his avatar — done via something that looks like a cross between an MRI machine and a particle accelerator — and through an organic network permanently merges with his avatar.

Avatar as Cultural Milestone

Although I've been critical of what seem like failures of imagination in *Avatar*, I'd like to close this chapter with an appreciation of its immense significance for the collective. Earlier I speculated that technology would provide a potent catalyst for our evolution into the imaginal realm when there was enough distributed computer power to provide real-time mapping of human facial expressions onto CGI avatars. In other words, at our present level of technology, people from various parts of the world can interact in a networked computer game like *World of Warcraft* through their individualized digital avatars. The richness of this virtual social experience, however, is greatly lessened because the avatars are not capable of the complex visual communication enabled by the microsecond-by-microsecond changes of human facial expression. When we reach the point that your webcam can record your facial expressions and map them onto your real-time avatar, we will begin to approach the complexity of face-to-face social contacts in the virtual world. A*vatar* takes a crucial half step toward that because it advances the ability to give pre-rendered CGI avatars the complexity of the human form. In the making of *Avatar*, the actors each had a miniature camera with LED lights on a little boom in front of their face capturing minute changes of facial expression. The Na'vi avatars, especially since they were 3D, were a very significant advance from earlier live-action-into-CGI films like *Beowulf* (2007). With the well-handled bonding of Jake with his avatar, and the powerfully immersive medium of 3D IMAX, we had the best collective experience to date of what it would be like to merge with a different body in a different world. *Avatar* represents a huge cultural milestone though necessarily it is a mere phosphorescent shadow of what awaits us at the event horizon.

VI. UFOs — Harbingers of the Singularity?

Unknown photographer, unverified image

Jung on "Flying Saucers"

As with *Childhood's End*, many of the messages of an approaching Singularity involve UFOs. Jung, shortly before his death, wrote a book about UFOs entitled, *Flying Saucers, a Modern Myth of Things Seen in the Sky*. Jung believed that the relative spiritual vacuum and lack of a ruling myth characteristic of the Twentieth Century created a great tension in the collective unconscious, an uneasy tabula rasa on which almost anything might appear. Human beings have always looked toward the heavens for signs of God or other transcendent beings monitoring and altering human affairs. Jung was struck by the typically circular appearance of whatever was seen in the sky. To Jung this suggested the mandala, an archetypal circular pattern that represented God, Self and wholeness. Jung pointed out that the Sanskrit definition of God is a circle whose center is everywhere and whose circumference is nowhere. Jung gave the UFO field a much-needed examination from the point of view of depth psychology. He did not presume that UFOs were immaterial, and noted that they often seemed to reflect radar waves, but he wondered if they might not be physical exteriorizations of the collective unconscious. Like other archetypal manifestations, UFOs have the ability to appear in dreams and to haunt or inspire the imagination.

Holes in the Extraterrestrial Hypothesis and the Meaning of Skepticism

Since I originally wrote this section I have seen some slightly more substantial evidence favoring the extraterrestrial hypothesis, but I include it anyway because there are so many people who assume that UFOs must mean extraterrestrials in metal spacecraft. In dealing with anomalous phenomena and other areas of investigation that are at or beyond the boundaries of human comprehension, I recommend an avoidance of premature closure. Many people readily adopt some pet theory and then corral evidence and thinking to support it. I feel that it is wiser to learn to endure ambiguity, keep the mind open to multiple possibilities and delay the reaching of ultimate conclusions. That was essentially the philosophy of the Skeptics, Greek philosophers who believed that their observational powers would be improved by avoidance of conclusions. Ironically, people like Michael Shermer and others in the "skeptical community" practice the exact opposite of this philosophy because they are full of conclusions. They are true believers in a variety of negatives (UFOs aren't real, parapsychology is nonsense, etc.) and are therefore more properly called debunkers. During a conference call in 2010, I confronted Shermer about these issues and he didn't have much of a response. He had just spoken about what motivates people to believe untrue things and I questioned him about whether he had turned the analytical eye on himself. For example, now that his is the leading figure of the "skeptical" community, his income, ego identity and social status would all seem to be dependent on his maintaining his debunking stance. What immunizes him from the subjectivity of highly motivated thinking and observation? I found his answers to be glib, evasive and superficial.

When we investigate anomalous phenomena we need to always be wary about the human tendency to project expectations and needs onto the unknown that are generated by our own psyches. In a technological, materialistic era where the human ego seems to rule, fewer and fewer people have faith that there is a God watching over the human species who is ready to intervene miraculously. Speculations about UFOs, such as that they are the spacecraft of superior beings here to prevent us from destroying each other through nuclear war, create a secular equivalent of an absent Godhead. UFOs, as mysterious signs in the heavens, serve as extraordinary projection screens for people's needs, fears and archetypal visions. Since they are themselves singularities of a sort, they very naturally become associated with the Singularity Archetype.

This is not to imply, however, that they are purely psychological phantoms or that they do not have a relation to the approaching Singularity that is more than projection. Those who have taken an intelligent look at this phenomenon have recognized that underneath the hoaxes and manipulated stories, something of significance is occurring, but its ultimate nature may be beyond the present boundaries of human comprehension. Be forewarned, however, if you want to do research in this field. A great deal of the material available is highly unreliable. Many UFO buffs are gullible true believers, people utterly possessed by their need to believe a particular UFO mythology. Many others consciously perpetuate fraud and illusion.

One of the most insightful people to investigate this subject is the French astronomer, Jacque Valle. Valle, in his book *Messengers of Deception*, and elsewhere, has shown that exploring UFO lore means entering a trickster world, a carnival of warped mirrors where mental illness, fraud and government manipulation have layered illusion on top of illusion. Much of the warped thinking and conscious manipulation, including government manipulation, has the apparent aim of enforcing the extraterrestrial hypothesis as the ruling UFO creed. Most of the general public who take any interest at all in UFOs are convinced that they must be extraterrestrials.

Although no one can disprove the extraterrestrial hypothesis, the conventional version of it, that they are aliens in nuts and bolts metal space craft here to do scientific research or genetic manipulation, is filled with obvious holes. As Valle points out, there have been hundreds of thousands of sightings. If you assume that the supposed aliens are making efforts not to be detected, then presumably there must be millions of actual visitations. What program of scientific research or genetic manipulation could possibly require this much work? They must be dreadfully incompetent scientists to still be at it so often after all this time. Also, the idea that they are here in spacecraft, at least in a conventional sense, is inconsistent with the fact that UFOs are frequently reported to change shape or merge with one another. And wouldn't such an advanced technology that wanted to avoid detection have some sort of stealth capability? Would they really streak across the sky lit up like Christmas ornaments? The idea that they are technology-wielding imperialists, or well-meaning missionaries, may be a case of our recreating the unknown in our image.

Reality Transformers

The truth about UFOs is likely far more interesting and significant than some of the threadbare, conventional alien scenarios. Valle quotes a scientist who describes UFOs as *"reality transformers."* Reality transformers may well be the best and most accurate descriptive phrase that can be applied to UFOs at our present level of understanding. UFOs are apparently able to appear in a great variety of different forms to different people and, like an archetype, the variations seem to have much to do with the belief system and cultural conditioning of the perceiving psyche. Valle compares observing the UFO phenomenon to looking at a screen in a movie theater. You look at the screen and all sorts of fantastical images pass before your eyes. But to really understand what's going on you need to look over your shoulder back at the projector, the source of all the endlessly varying images.

UFOs seem more akin to projectors, capable of projecting all sorts of thoughts and images into the human psyche. The human mind, especially in our materialistic culture, is prone to take what it sees very literally. In the UFO world you can see an obvious inverse relationship between intelligence and how literal and specific a person's alleged knowledge of UFOs is. On one side of the spectrum, the most conscious observers acknowledge that UFOs are unknowns about which we can make some general speculations. And on the other side are those who know the names of everyone on the Pleiadian high council and who are channeling the most detailed information about superior beings who apparently live on worlds remarkably similar to those of grade B science-fiction movies from the 1950s.

Valle and others make a convincing case that the source of the UFO phenomenon is not new, that it has been involved with human culture throughout human history. Many of the miraculous experiences and visitations recorded from the past may well have been the same phenomenon viewed through psyches conditioned by differing sets of cultural values. We live in an age where magic takes the form of technology and where we launch crude metal spacecraft into the heavens. Unimaginative psyches will tend to view UFOs as an advanced extrapolation of present technology and human motivation. The manifestations of the phenomenon are probably not, however, reducible to the psychological expectations of the witnesses. The phenomenon seems to have an ability to actively, consciously form its own manifestations. Rather than merely reflecting cultural values, it may actually be adapting and manipulating them. Think again of the analogy of the movie projector. Movies both reflect and manipulate cultural values.

There is evidence that UFO phenomena, like dreams, are intelligently formed, and are both profoundly aware of the psyches to whom they communicate and capable of exerting powerful influence on them. Like dreams, the phenomenon is real and capable of leaving physical traces and effects. Dreaming is associated with profound energetic changes in the brain easily observed on an EEG. The supposedly solid world of the waking life, as we now know from physics, is actually composed of patterned energy and is comparable to a holographic projection. Dreams are also patterned energy, and in many ways it is merely cultural prejudice to view them as "less real" than the waking reality.

"They do not play by the rules of reality but of dream; they are not bound by the careful laws of physics, but by the wild ones of the imagination." — Close encounter experiencer, Whitley Strieber, writing in The Communion Letters.

UFOs seem to obey the physics of dreams far more than classical Newtonian physics, which we would expect solid, metal spacecraft to obey. The physics of dreams, where consciousness and reality are inextricable and the universe is infinitely plastic and mutable, is closer to the universe revealed by quantum mechanics, although both defy our conventional understanding of reality. As J.B.S. Haldane put it, "Reality is not only queerer than we suppose, but queerer than we can suppose."[36]

UFOs are powerful reminders of that inconceivable strangeness. It might be very comforting to our innate conservatism and limited imagination to view them as high-speed metal containers bearing "aliens" who stand upright and have two arms, legs and eyes, and familiar human motivations such as curiosity and conquest. But reality is not necessarily as limited as the imaginations of UFO buffs. The evidence seems more supportive of UFOs traveling interdimensionally rather than through long distances of space. They may be just as able to travel through inner psychic space as outer space. Far more likely than their being metal spacecraft, they may be organisms in a more energetic state than we are, or the projections of a consciousness of some sort.

(I am no longer quite as dismissive of the extraterrestrial hypothesis as I was in 1996 when I wrote the section above. There seems to be substantial evidence for both the reality-transformer aspect and more tangible, physical aspects.)

Strange Parallels — UFOs, Near Death Experiences, and Psychotropics

Dr. Kenneth Ring, the professor emeritus of psychology whom I referenced frequently in the chapter on Near-Death Experiences, has shown that there are striking similarities between NDEs and UFO experiences. Many of the stages and lasting effects of NDEs and abduction experiences have strong correspondences. For example, in both types of experience people often report seeing a vision of the earth

---

[36] Possible Worlds and Other Papers (1927), p. 286.

being destroyed and emerge from the episode with a new and lasting commitment to environmental work.

Many UFO experiences have aspects that strongly indicate that, whatever else might be happening, the experiencer has had an encounter with the Singularity Archetype. There are many connections to the Logos Beheld theme. Large-eyed aliens are almost universally described as communicating telepathically, sometimes using visual telepathy. Some encounters strongly suggest that they are capable of generating visions and surreal episodes in the minds of perceivers. Encounters often include explicit material about the evolutionary metamorphosis of Homo sapiens with extensive reports of matings between human and alien to produce hybrids. The Greys are increasingly described as having a "hive mind" and of being something like Homo gestalt. One of the strongest correspondences between the UFO experience and encounters with the Singularity Archetype is that both often pathologize into apocalypiticism.

Daniel Wojcik, Associate Professor of English and director of the Folklore Program at the University of Oregon, in his 1997 book, *The End of the World As We Know It — Faith, Fatalism, and Apocalypse*, provides several illuminated examples of UFO encounter-related apocalypticism.

The role of UFOs in the endtimes has also been noted by Louis Farrakhan, the leader of the Nation of Islam, who asserts that UFOs will be used to destroy the white man's world and the enemies of Allah in an apocalyptic battle. At a press conference on October 24, 1989, Farrakhan described his encounter with a UFO, during which he received messages from the founder of the Nation of Islam, Elijah Muhammad, who purportedly dwells in a mother ship, whence he orchestrates the downfall of the six-thousand-year reign of the white man. (*EWK* 177)

In Farrakhan's own words, "A beam of light came from the Wheel and I was carried up on this beam of light into the Wheel. [...] At the center of the ceiling was a speaker and through the speaker I heard the voice of the Honorable Elijah Muhammad speaking to me as clearly as you are hearing my voice this morning" (*EWK* 229).

Saucer cults[37] and some New Age writers will see UFOs and aliens as messianic, angelic entities here to act as catalysts of evolutionary metamorphosis. As Wojcik, puts it:

> "Human beings are usually viewed by these groups as an unenlightened, lower life form, and extraterrestrials are said to be helping humanity attain a higher form of consciousness that will lead to the next level of evolutionary development. This

---

[37] See the study of Heaven's Gate in Chapter XI

widely held belief is espoused by Brad Steiger, a leader in the UFO movement and author of more than one hundred books on UFOs. Steiger maintains that UFOs are multidimensional, higher entities that are guiding human beings into a new age of harmony and enlightenment, and that these godlike beings have always assisted humanity but that since the 1950s have accelerated the interactions in preparation for the imminent transformation of the planet. The transition, which has been predicted for centuries, will inevitably involve apocalyptic trauma: 'For generations our prophets and revelators have been referring to it as The Great Cleansing, Judgment Day, Armageddon. But we have been promised that, after a season of cataclysmic changes on the earth plane, a New Age consciousness will suffuse the planet. It is to this end that the gods have been utilizing the UFO as a transformative symbol'" (*EWK* 189).

As I also pointed out in my 1978 paper, "Archetypes of a New Evolution,"[38] some Evangelicals consider UFOs to be demonic manifestations related to apocalypse: "Several years ago a religious and sincere Seventh-Day Adventist, who believed Biblical prophecy indicated the imminent arrival of an Anti-Christ, related to me his belief that UFOs were a deceptive device of Satan's that might be used in the arrival of the Anti-Christ."

Wojcik came across similar interpretations:

"In his *Planet Earth — 2000 A.D.*, [Hal] Lindsey devotes an entire chapter to the prophetic importance of UFOs, stating at the outset:

"Since the publication of the *Late, Great Planet Earth*, I have become thoroughly convinced that the UFOs are real... And I believe they are operated by alien beings of great intelligence and power. Where I differ from most "ufologists" is in the question of origin. I believe these beings are not only extraterrestrial but supernatural in origin. To be blunt, I think they are demons. The Bible tells us that demons are spiritual beings at war with God. We are told that demons will be allowed to use their tremendous powers of deception in a grand way in the last days" (*EWK* 203).

In some cases at least, UFO experiences closely resemble other cases of people encountering the Singularity Archetype. The UFO experience strongly parallels many other states of nonordinary consciousness in which people encounter the Singularity Archetype.

---

[38] Available at ZapOracle.com.

William Buhlman, who has studied thousands of Out of Body Experiences (OBEs), has pointed out how much they resemble, and might be confused with, abductions. Terence McKenna, has shown connections between UFO experience and the experiences of people under the influence of hallucinogens. Terence refers to the effects of certain hallucinogens as *"UFO experiences on demand."* Although McKenna does have a tendency to overgeneralize from his particular experience, he does demonstrate convincingly that chemically altered mind states are valid access channels to the source of UFO phenomena.[39]

The so-called postmodern approach to UFOs is to study what effect they are having on us rather than what they are. Jacque Valle was the great pioneer of this approach and essentially said we should infer the intentionality of the phenomenon from its effects. The effect, Valle says, is that of a control system manipulating human beliefs, culture in general and even evolution. (*OP* 243) There is a certain validity to this approach because the nature of UFOs may be beyond human comprehension at this point.

Seen from that point of view, UFO phenomena could be considered cognitive singularities which have the effect of breaking down our collective over-confidence in how we perceive reality. In 1996, in a late night conversation with cattle mutilation expert David Perkins, I had the intuition that this might be the best perspective from which to view a number of anomalous phenomena. I wrote about this conversation in "A Mutant Convergence — How John Major Jenkins, Jonathan Zap and Terence McKenna met during a Weekend of High Strangeness in 1996":

> "It was late in the evening now, one or two o'clock in the morning, and having absorbed hours of cattle mutilation talk, my unconscious had suddenly begun to coalesce this information into an encompassing theory that linked cattle mutilations, crop circles and many anomalous aspects of ufology. What if these phenomena were crafted to be intriguing, anomalous, inexplicable — designed like Zen koans to defy rational comprehension, to awaken us to the realization that, as Terence so frequently quoted J.B.S. Haldane, 'Reality is not only queerer than you imagine; it is queerer than you can imagine."

A few years later I found a Terence McKenna talk in which he made a somewhat parallel point when he described UFO anomalies as "showing up like the cosmic giggle at the bachelor party of science." I found an even more striking case of mental parallelisms with my own conclusions

---

[39] For a detailed study of encountering the Singularity Archetype in the context of an ayahuasca experience, see "Andrew's Ayahuasca Journey — An Encounter with the Singularity Archetype" available at ZapOracle.com.

on ufology in Dr. Kenneth Ring's *The Omega Project — Near-Death Experiences, UFO Encounters, and Mind at Large.*

In *The Omega Project,* Dr. Ring references a Valle-influenced thinker, Carl Raschke, who has spoken of UFOs as "agents of cultural deconstruction." In Raschke's own words:

> "Such experiences tend to be convulsive, perplexing, and *outré* and to conflict strikingly with the habitual thought patterns of the subjects. A meeting with a UFO is apt to leave the witnesses' world in upheaval. One must remain curious therefore, whether the *purpose* of UFO sightings and contacts is mainly to undercut the ingrained human longing of secure knowledge and faith, rather than to gratify it.

> "Here then I shall advance a tentative assessment of what UFOs are in point of fact. [...] Our interest in them should center on how the spreading and deepening convictions about them subtly, yet irreversibly, remold not just peripheral religious or metaphysical ideas, but entire constellations of culture and social knowledge. In this connection, UFOs can be depicted as what I would call *ultraterrestrial agents of cultural deconstruction*" (*OP* 244).

Essentially, Raschke, Ring, Valle, and McKenna are all recognizing the UFO/alien phenomena as a cognitive singularity and are inferring that this might be the intent of the phenomena. A precedent for intended cognitive singularity, as I pointed out to David Perkins, is the Zen Koan, those paradoxical statements intended ("What is the sound of one hand clapping?") to shock the mind out of its rational categories. Dr. Ring makes almost the identical point: "Extraordinary encounters, UFOEs, NDEs, and others that disclose something of the mysteries of the transcendent universe, and of ourselves, are conundrums akin to a *koan*" (*OP* 246). In keeping with the trickster aspect of the phenomena, the UFO/alien doesn't even consistently play that role, however. As we see in the Farrakhan example above, thes phenomenon is also capable of working with and reinforcing the belief system of an experiencer.

Despite what I have just said about the UFO/alien as cognitive singularity, I think there is still value in our continued speculations about what "they" might be, keeping in mind that speculation may be an imaginative exercise while we struggle to understand something that is stranger than we can think. In that spirit, I'd like to offer some raw material from my own experience and provide a couple of possible "whats" in relation to UFOs. But before I do, I want to be absolutely clear that this is pure speculation and raw material. I don't regard the vision I am about to offer as "true," but rather present it as a psychological artifact open to interpretation.

Vision of a Multiply Incarnate Organism

Several years ago I had a vision of a roughly circular organism. The organism was composed of a series of highly differentiated connected organs. The awareness presented in the vision was that each of these organs was actually a separate incarnation or lifetime of this organism viewed outside of linear time. An analogy would be to viewing a human being outside of linear time. Rather than seeing a snapshot of a person at a particular age in a particular frozen moment, of time we might see the full lifecycle — a fertilized egg connected to a fetus connected to an infant, a child, an adolescent, a middle aged person, an aged person, a corpse. Yet this picture of the human lifecycle would still only represent that portion known to us, the interval between birth and death. We don't know that the human lifecycle is completely contained between a single birth and death, and there is much reason to think that it isn't.

The circular, manifold incarnate organism I saw presented itself to my mind as the full lifecycle of a being for whom human incarnation was one phase or organ. Outside of linear time all the incarnations or organs were perceived as connected and in a state of simultaneous interdependence and influence with all the other organs and incarnations. Human incarnation was an organ far closer to the "head" rather than the "tail" of this Ouroboros–like organism. In other words, human incarnation was a more conscious, differentiated organ of the body in much the same way that the brain is a more conscious, differentiated organ than the liver. Another analogy would be to the brain itself where we see a living manifestation of the principle, "ontogeny recapitulates phylogeny." More evolved structures, like the neocortex, are built on top of more primitive structures such as the hypothalamus. But in this manifold incarnate organism human beings were not the most advanced organ or incarnation. Ahead of us were the beings behind the UFOs. And this "alien" incarnation or organ is the most conscious and most aware of all the organs or incarnations.

Evolutionary Design Limitations

Since we're indulging the bizarre, let me push a bit further in that direction, however briefly. Michael Murphy, in his seminal book on human evolution, *The Future of the Body*, discusses the work of certain theorists in evolutionary biology. These theorists claim that some species have fundamental design limitations or flaws that will not allow them to ever evolve the degree of intelligence human beings have. Marsupial brains, for example, lack the corpus callosum, the dense bundle of nerve cells that connect the left and right hemispheres of the human brain. This neurological limitation means that the marsupial brain can never have the relatively excellent communication between hemispheres that the human brain usually enjoys. But, these theorists continue, the human brain may also have a fundamental design flaw limiting our further evolution or even survival. The structure of our brain is a kind of retrofit where a mammalian brain is superimposed on a reptile brain and the neocortex is retrofitted onto the mammalian brain. The neocortex, said to be the center of our self-reflective consciousness and ego, believes itself to be the head honcho, but unfortunately it has very poor communication with some of the earlier structures that control appetites and aggression and so forth. Anyone who goes on a diet discovers that the neocortex and its creation — the cognitive ego with all its powers — are not necessarily a match for the reptilian brain and its relentless will to defend body weight. Similarly, our sexuality seems largely beyond ego control, and for all our civilization and wisdom our ability to restrain territorial aggression has not prevented world wars and the possibility of our making ourselves extinct through technologically amplified territorial aggression. Poor communication between higher and lower brain structures may be a fundamental design flaw in the human species that may result in our eventual extinction.

One White Crow

On the other hand, I take the views of many evolutionary theorists, especially if they are neurological materialists, with many grains of salt. In fact, there's an obvious flaw in the aforementioned theory. As William James once said, "One white crow is all that is needed to disprove the notion that all crows are black." If we have even a single human being — Jesus, Buddha, whomever — who has overcome the problem of poor communication between brain structures, or whose consciousness transcends appetites and aggression, then there is the possibility that the species can also transcend this limitation. But, if the fatalistic conclusion of the theory is flawed, the problem it describes bears an interesting analogy to my vision of a manifold incarnate being.

In the way that I perceived the manifold incarnate organism, all the organs/incarnations are interdependent. Therefore, the health and fate of the "alien" incarnation is also dependent on the status of the human incarnation. I'll further speculate that the human incarnation is the adolescent phase of development, a crucial juncture on which the fate of the entire organism depends. The alien part of the organism recognizes that although there is interdependence, there is poor communication between organs or incarnations. It is capable of communication and is seeking to contact us through inner and outer space to make us aware of things crucial to our fate and that of the larger organism. It may also intend cognitive singularities to shock us out of constricted awareness and prepare us for crossing the event horizon of personal death/ species metamorphosis.

Consider another analogy to bodily organs. Normally, my waking consciousness is not very aware of what my liver is up to. But let's say my liver started to malfunction so seriously that it threatened the viability of my entire body. If I could somehow open up communication with my liver, perhaps shock it with my mind into functioning better, it would be in the interest of all my organs to do so. Perhaps the human species is like a malfunctioning organ right now. Certainly we have become a threat, not only to ourselves, but to many forms of life on the planet. If we are part of a much larger lifecycle than what we presently conceive, then perhaps there are unknown interdependent organisms concerned with what we are up to. For example, let's say I am an alcoholic man living during the Renaissance. The microbiological world has not yet been discovered, so I am in complete ignorance that I am a colony of fifty trillion interdependent cells, which I am poisoning with my alcoholism. If those cells could communicate with me and make an intervention they would have every reason to want to do so. More advanced communication skills, however, are more likely the province of more advanced parts of the lifecycle. Just as we, with our advanced medial technology have figured out some ways to make interventions with a malfunctioning liver, perhaps there is a part of the lifecycle, of which we are also a part, that is trying to intervene with us. Since the "aliens" are usually described as having a roughly human form, and since they seem to be so laboriously interested in us, perhaps it is more likely that they are us, rather than exotic extraterrestrials. For most of human existence we were clueless about the microbiological world. Surgeons used to wash their hands after surgery, but not before. Once the microscope was invented, we slowly began to catalogue millions of exotic species of microbiological life. The microbiological plane of life wasn't extraterrestrial, we didn't have to go anywhere to find it; it was us, it was a dimension of life that was both hidden and ubiquitous. So what if we, the culture of scientific materialism, are ignorant of another plane of life, a plane of energetic life forms? Every culture except scientific materialism has recognized energetic life forms — spirits, ancestors, ghosts, etc. We may be interpenetrated by a whole plane of life and just haven't yet discovered an instrument, like the microscope, that will allow us to see them on demand.

The "aliens" in this model may actually be us after we have crossed the event horizon of death. A part of the lifecycle of the human being about which we have much uncertainty is the post-death phase. As Terence McKenna has pointed out, if we wanted to look for an ecology of souls, an intelligent species that seems to be very interested in our evolution, by the principle of logic known as Ockham's Razor we seek the simplest hypothesis that accounts for all the facts. Our species is a source of several billion intelligent creatures that are very much interested in themselves and their evolution. Perhaps the "aliens" are merely us in an after-death phase of incarnation. When Terence showed pictures of grey aliens to tribal shamans in the Amazon they replied, "Oh, the ancestors." People who have abduction experiences frequently report seeing deceased relatives in the company of the grey aliens. A woman reported to Whitley Strieber an abduction experience where she saw her deceased mother as a Grey. I once had a dream where I saw what appeared to be a Grey emerging from a metallic saucer. As the grey approached I saw that the large almond-shaped eyes were actually the visors of a kind of astronaut helmet. Inside the helmet was a man I recognized from the neighborhood where I grew up in the Bronx. The neighbor was a mathematician and he passed away in the Eighties. In other words, inside what appeared to be an alien was a dead guy.

Once again, a warning to anyone tempted to quote any of the above out of context. What I have just presented is pure speculation. It is raw material of my psyche processing a rather inscrutable and paradoxical phenomena and I present it as more grist for the mill, available to be interpreted in many ways. It is not a conclusion I have reached, not something that I believe to be true or untrue, but merely the record of the thought process of one more puzzled human gazing at a singularity.

"They told me that they came from 'everywhere,' and their names, I suspect, are no more fixed than the wind. As far as why they came here, they said to me, 'We saw a glow.' At the time I thought that this referred to cities in the night, but now I feel that it was us they saw, our souls like embers, and they knew that we were trying to grow bright." — Whitley Strieber, from *The Communion Letters*

UFOs — Evolutionary Messages

In summary, UFOs seem to bear many messages related to our further evolution. In recent decades, the UFO beings that contactees experience frequently have a stereotyped appearance that UFO researchers used to call "the Delta type humanoid" and that is now more commonly known as "the Greys." What is perceived is an androgynous being with huge almond-shaped eyes, a somewhat ethereal, willowy body and a small, almost vestigial mouth. The beings typically communicate without spoken words. Increasingly, experiencers report that the Greys seem to have a hive mind. These reported qualities may be a message anticipating an evolutionary future where we have transcended ordinary language and gender limits, and our body is moving from matter toward a more ethereal, energetic state. As mentioned before, people who have UFO abduction experiences or NDEs are frequently shown images of the earth's destruction by manmade causes and are influenced by these visions toward a much greater awareness of our interdependence with the planet. Many will devote themselves to environmental causes after these deeply affecting experiences. Another typical theme of abduction experiences involves genetic manipulation, and particularly the cross-fertilization and hybridization of human and alien species. This is often presented as a symbiotic evolutionary step actually having greater benefit for the supposedly superior alien species. These experiments could be interpreted as metaphorical communication of our need to evolve and to merge with this other consciousness.

Whatever the source of UFOs, they do seem to be bearing a message that we are at a critical nexus and need to evolve. But once again, they remain, perhaps appropriately, in a realm of imaginative speculation. Their nature may not be understood until we have evolved further.

VII. The Future of the Ego — an Evolutionary Perspective

The author, seated in the Emperor's Chair, egoistically posing with Darth Vader

THE creation of the ego has obviously had some unpleasant consequences, but it was also an evolutionary development that allowed for a tremendous increase in complexity and consciousness.

The ego is a complex structure and difficult or impossible to define. The term itself is inevitably imprecise, as different people understand very different things by *ego*. From some vantage points the ego serves crucial functions in the human psyche. The ego has been called "the self-organizing principle of the organism" and necessary self-reference may not be possible without it. From other angles we see that the ego is often the carrier of will to power and destructive intentions. For all the novelty the human ego helped to create, and the invaluable role it plays in the human psyche, it has also become a very heavy albatross hanging around the neck of the species. It may now, in its present form at least, have exceeded its evolutionary purpose and be a type of psychic structure due for extinction/metamorphosis. But the ego, like all organisms, clings to life, and can act with a will of its own. Certainly the ego has a virulent will to power, and it is no more willing to quietly withdraw than Napoleon at his prime would be willing to accept life in a retirement home. This dark aspect of the ego, which is what I will sometimes be referring to when I use the loose term "ego," sees itself as God, as apart from the rest of the universe. It is driven by a will to bring external objects, animate and inanimate, under its control. This pathologized version of the ego doesn't see itself as part of a living matrix, but rather looks out at an abstracted chessboard consisting of real estate, technology and livestock waiting to be owned and exploited.

The power-oriented view of the ego is based on the illusion of separateness. Love may be considered the awareness that everything is connected. Let's consider two sentences that will illustrate this difference:

"We made love."

"I screwed Jane."

In the first example, subject and object are merged; there is an awareness of Eros, connection and mutuality. In the second example, we have an unerotic world of separated subject and object. The ego is the royal "I" enjoying conquests over beings that are merely objects to be dominated and controlled. The first sentence implies what Martin Buber called the "I-Thou" relationship, and the second sentence implies what he called the "I-It" relationship. An inflated ego will tend toward "I-It" perceptions and relationships.[40] Currently, we are suffering a highly contagious plague of this noxious type of ego that uses sex as a metaphor for power and views mother earth as real estate.

To frame this in dramatized, semi-mythological language for a paragraph:

For quite some time the ego has strutted triumphantly across our world consuming and poisoning its mother, the earth. Like many psychic forces, the ego is able to completely possess certain individuals. Of some of these, as it's done in the past, it will create Antichrist-like persons, malignant narcissists (many of them psychopaths) who will seek to prevent this evolutionary birth and will do whatever possible to destroy consciousness, love and life. If they sterilize the mother, then she cannot give birth to creatures that might take their place. The ego wants to be the only one sucking on the breast and would much rather see the mother dead than have her give birth to a more favored, usurping child. Very likely Antichrists — human puppets of the ego — and the herds of unconscious, fearful people eager to follow them, will create a good part of the dark events that will bring us to the edge of extinction. Like Napoleon or Hitler, the ego can be expected to win many costly battles before it gives up the ghost.

---

[40] http://en.wikipedia.org/wiki/I_and_Thou

Homo gestalt

Collective consciousness turns up frequently in expressions of the Singularity Archetype and merits some examination. A potent example we've already discussed is found in Theodore Sturgeon's science-fiction novel, *More than Human*, where a group of mutants, who each have distinctly different strengths and weaknesses, form a collective consciousness while retaining their individuality. Sturgeon coined the term "Homo gestalt" to describe this new entity. Similarly, in ufology the Greys are seen as possessing a hive-like connectivity and consciousness while still maintaining some very minimal degree of individualtiy. There are a number of possible reasons for this collective consciousness motif appearing in so many permutations of this archetype. One is that it may be a fairly literal indicator of evolutionary change. If the ego ceases to dominate the human psyche, then perhaps the boundaries that it creates around the individual will dissipate and we will become more collectively aware. The shells of the oysters dissolve and the pearls lie together. From the ego's point of view this would be a catastrophic loss of personal identity. This is also a typical ego view of that other attractor, death. From this pessimistic ego view, humans travel from dust to dust, and are simply returned to the undifferentiated source from which they are thought to emerge.

But if this were all that the evolutionary step amounted to it would be regressive and not evolutionary. Instead of expanding the immense novelty of individual identity, it would be contracting it into an homogenous mass with a great decrease in complexity. Certainly there are many cycles in nature that reverse themselves, that oscillate between extremes. Jung called this process of returning to the opposite, "*enantiodromia*," a term he borrowed from Heraclitus, the ancient Greek philosopher. The ego fears, somewhat reasonably, that the evolutionary process will be an enantiodromia, nature pressing the reset button and erasing all the individual differentiation it sacrificed so much to create. But the Singularity Archetype tells us that the pendulum of enantiodromia, viewed from the right perspective, is an evolutionary spiral. The evolutionary step may not be a loss of individuality, but rather an expansion of individual consciousness into collective awareness.

Another possible causation of the collective consciousness motif in these stories is that it is an expression of the boundary dissolution that occurred when the writer's imagination contacted the collective unconsciousness. This possibility is not mutually exclusive of the aforementioned one, and it is quite likely that both may be present and working in parallel with each other. A recurring motif in these visions, inextricably related to the collective consciousness, involves a new means of communication transcending speech. Conventionally, we think of telepathy as projecting a voice into someone's head. But conventional telepathy wouldn't be much of an improvement over speaking aloud, or calling someone on the telephone. More sophisticated visions of this new means of communication allow for a direct transmission of the self, and this becomes the medium through which individual and collective consciousness can merge.

The Singularity Seen through the Eyes of the Ego — *The Midwich Cuckoos*

Still image from the movie *Village of the Damned*

John Wyndham's 1957 novel, *The Midwich Cuckoos*, presents an interesting spin on this dissolution and transformation of the ego. In classic science-fiction fashion, the novel opens with the appearance of disc-shaped UFOs over the earth. These spacecraft shut down human consciousness. In a circular area with a very precise perimeter beneath each UFO, all higher animals, including humans, suddenly lapse into sleep. After twenty-four hours, everyone who wasn't at the wheel of a car, operating a power tool or otherwise in an unfortunate situation for nodding off, wakes up as if nothing happened. Everyone who didn't have an accident seems unchanged until some days pass and the village doctor, Zellaby, discovers that every woman of child bearing age, including young virgins and old maids, has become pregnant. Again, we are seeing an evolutionary change from the point of view of the ego. It sees itself in the helpless, unconscious *"little death"* of dreamless sleep. And while it is in this helpless, mortal state it is raped and inseminated by a hostile alien life form.

In the novel, the character who personifies the ego is the physician Zellaby. He is the man of science and reason trying to control this irrational, miraculous event. Zellaby sets out, like the Overlords, to be midwife to this evolutionary birth. Interestingly, the name "Midwich" sounds much like "midwife" but with the emphasis of "witch" modifying the second syllable. In this mutation of the word "midwife" we see the ego's xenophobic, witch-hunting view of the evolutionary birth. Rather than being a selfless midwife, it would rather burn the witches, the new children who possess the dangerous magic and represent change.

With inhuman speed the pregnancies come to term and all the women give birth to exceptionally large and healthy babies. But the prodigal infants seem to be racially different and unique; they have large golden eyes and platinum blonde hair. The infants grow and develop, physically and mentally, with unnatural speed. It becomes apparent that they have extraordinary powers. For example, after one mother accidentally pricks her daughter with a safety pin she is found compulsively stabbing herself with the pin. Apparently, the superior alien will of the child mind-pressured her into this self-violence.

Pseudospeciation

From the ego's point of view, the new children in *The Midwich Cuckoos* represent a hostile, alien, competing life form. Nature has played a trick, like the cuckoo bird leaving its young in another bird's nest. It is acknowledged that the children are superior, however, and since they are racially distinct they must be racially superior. In the classic 1960 film adaptation, *Village of the Damned,* the children look distinctly Aryan, as if they were cloned by Nazi scientists. Here we may have a case of shadow projection. The Nazis projected their shadow onto the Jews and claimed there was a Jewish conspiracy to take over the world, while the Nazis actively pursued world domination themselves. Here we have the British psyche of John Wyndham, born in 1903, creating imperialistic aliens determined to dominate a lesser species.

The fear that a new intelligent species will be bent on our destruction goes beyond the ego. Michael Murphy, in *The Future of the Body,* discusses a speculation about racism postulated by evolutionary biologists. These biologists use the term "pseudospeciation" to refer to the human tendency to view other racial groups as though they were a competing species. This pseudospeciation may have biological roots, as it's possible that Homo sapiens achieved evolutionary dominance by killing off other competing hominid species.

In *The Midwich Cuckoos* the children, although perfectly human in appearance and gestated in human mothers, are supposed to be a completely different species. Conversely, in Arthur C. Clarke's similarly-themed novel, *Childhood's End*, the new children are viewed as an evolutionary development of the human species. They would also have to be considered a new species, since a species is defined as a grouping of organisms that can mate and bear live young. Once the new children are born the old humans become sterile, and the soon-to-be extinct Homo sapiens species is demoted to the status of living fossils. But at least in *Childhood's End* the new children are acknowledged as descendants and not as completely other or alien. The older humans accept evolution and allow themselves to be supplanted.

In the world of the *The Midwich Cuckoos*, however, this evolutionary change is fought tooth and claw. Besides Midwich, there are other circular areas on the planet that have spawned alien children. But these other places are not as civilized as Britain and they treat their children more harshly. In the Irkutsk region near the borders of Outer Mongolia, for example, both the children and their mothers, who are presumed to have slept with devils, are killed. This is another interesting overlap with *Childhood's End* where the Overlords look like devils. One colony occurs in a Russian town. At first the Russians decide to cultivate what seem like a flock of potential geniuses, but when the children's uncanny powers start to manifest they use a nuclear projectile and wipe out the whole town where the children are growing.

Zellaby personifies an idealized face of the ego with all its civilized veneer. He's interested in the children for the sake of science and so forth, but ultimately he decides that his group of children must die too. His method of genocide is extremely interesting. He enters their classroom with a briefcase full of dynamite and then he visualizes a brick wall in his mind when the children try to probe his psyche. He shuts out communication by conjuring a wall in his mind. It's hard to imagine a more perfect symbol of repression! The ego feels it can only protect itself by putting up a psychic wall between itself and the collective awareness of the children. In contemporary mythology the wall represents patriarchal oppression, as in the Berlin Wall and Pink Floyd's *The Wall*.

Village of the Damned — a New Variation

Still from the 1995 John Carpenter remake of *Village of the Damned*

In the Spring of 1995, horror director John Carpenter released a remake of *Village of the Damned*. The new version was reasonably faithful to the original, but with some interesting variations. Since the new version occurs in the Nineties instead of the Fifties, the pregnant mothers face a decision on whether or not to bring their pregnancies to term. Simultaneously, they all have an archetypal dream, and apparently as a result of it they decide to keep the babies. When the new children are born, they all look human except for one. There is one female infant that looks completely alien and is apparently stillborn. As the infants become children it is observed that they always walk in male/female pairs, and that the pairs are constant as if the children were divided into a series of married couples. There is one boy, however, who walks at the end of the line alone, and appears to be the only one without a mate. This boy, whose name is David, is also unique in being empathic while the other children are impersonal and ruthless.

At one point in the story Zellaby finds David wandering alone in a cemetery. Asked what he is doing, the boy replies, "Looking for the baby. The one who was born with us. The one who died." Zellaby is astonished, because the children were never told about the baby. David reveals that the dead infant was meant to be his mate. Here we have an interesting variation on the human/alien-hybrid theme. This pairing is more polarized than the others, as this boy's intended mate was much closer to being an alien. Also this boy is much more human than the other new children as he exhibits an acute empathy for others. This empathy is heightened by the pain and suffering he feels as the one left behind without a mate. Ultimately, when the other children are destroyed, his life is spared and he is rescued by his mother. His survival makes him seem a kind of messianic Subject Zero, gifted in both psychic powers and empathy, and we are left with the hopeful feeling that evolution may somehow continue through him. This new variation is an improvement over the original ending where the ego, personified by Zellaby, destroys the children and itself with them.

A Troubling Synchronicity

But the new film version adds a strange unintentional piece to the story. To understand this additional piece will require a working understanding of a principle that Jung referred to as *"synchronicity."* Many of you are no doubt already familiar with the term. If you aren't, a brief explanation follows, but I would also recommend reading Jung's *Synchronicity: The Acausal Connecting Principle*.

Jung defined synchronicity as an "acausal connecting principle." In other words, synchronicity describes relationships that are not mediated by cause and effect, but instead by parallel, acausal relationships. Jung was searching for a way to account for those uncanny, completely improbable 'coincidences" (assumption of randomness) where something from the inner life and something from the outer world would "synch up." Jung developed this concept of synchronicity after some discussions with Albert Einstein and close collaboration with another Nobel prize-winning physicist, Wolfgang Pauli. At the time, Jung's theory of synchronicity was speculative, but we now know from the findings of quantum mechanics that parallel, acausal relationships do exist in the physical world.

A visual synchronicity? This photo was the first I ever attempted of someone tossing I Ching coins. The camera caught one of the coins landing exactly on its edge on top of a Wilhelm/Baynes I Ching which has an introduction by Carl Jung that discusses synchronicity. A few years later I took my second photo of someone tossing the I Ching coins and that image also caught a coin landing on its edge.

A classic illustration of synchronicity that Jung narrated concerned a female patient of his whose progress in analysis was blocked by her excessive rationalism. As Jung tells the story:

> "A young woman I was treating had, at a critical moment, a dream in which she was given a golden scarab. While she was telling me this dream, I sat with my back to the closed window. Suddenly I heard a noise behind me, like a gentle tapping. I turned round and saw a flying insect knocking against the window-pane from the outside. I opened the window and caught the creature in the air as it flew in. It was the nearest analogy to a golden scarab one finds in our latitudes, a scarabaeid beetle, the common rose-chafer (*Cetonia aurata*), which, contrary to its usual habits had evidently felt the urge to get into a dark room at this particular moment. I must admit that nothing like it ever happened to me before or since."

This dramatic synchronicity punctured the analysand's superficial rationalism, and she was able to progress with her analysis. Jung could find no causal agency that would explain why this insect would go against its natural instincts and demand admittance to a darkened room.

Most people reading this can no doubt provide personal examples of such striking synchronicities that are hard to dismiss as meaningless coincidence. They seem to become more frequent when one is exploring the psyche or involved in some creative enterprise, but can also happen when people are exploring dark paths, etc.

When Jung coined the term synchronicity it was a speculation. Since then, the findings of quantum mechanics (especially what is referred to as "nonlocality") demonstrate that acausal parallelisms are a key organizing principle of the universe. Synchronicities reveal that the inner microcosm of the psyche and the outer macrocosm of the external world have parallelisms. Inner and outer are not as separate as we have been conditioned to believe. Synchronicities show us that there is a connecting principle. It also seems that highly charged psychic contents are more likely to be paralleled by synchronicities. It should not be surprising, therefore, that highly charged collective visions of the Singularity Archetype may also have accompanying synchronicities. In the two film versions of *Village of the Damned* we see particularly interesting synchronicities involved with the casting of the character Dr. Zellaby (renamed "Dr. Alan Chaffee" in 1995), whom I've suggested is a personification of the ego.

In the original film Zellaby is played by George Sanders, who portrays the character as an urbane, dignified, sensitive and compassionate man. The ego is given the most sympathetic face possible and the audience is led to identify with Dr. Zellaby as a courageous, intelligent hero facing alien evil. Sanders pulls this off magnificently, but it is interesting to note that he himself was an almost archetypal personification of the dark side of the ego. Apparently he was egoistic and sadistic to a degree remarkable even for a film star gone bad. In 1960, the same year *Village of the Damned* was released, he published his autobiography, entitled: *Memoirs of a Professional Cad.*[41]

---

[41] Encarta Dictionary defines "cad": "An ungentlemanly man: a man who does not behave as a gentleman should, especially toward a woman (dated)."

A biography was written about Sanders posthumously. It was entitled, *A Perfectly Awful Man.* In 1972 he committed suicide and left behind a suicide note in which he listed boredom as the main reason for his suicide. Sander's dark side made him, in a mythological sense, an uncannily appropriate choice to play a character who is a personification of the ego, but an even more striking synchronicity involved the casting of Christopher Reeve as Dr. Chaffee in the remake.

George Sanders, photographer unknown

I feel some uncomfortable hesitation in pointing out this synchronicity because I don't want to trifle with the personal tragedy of a real human being. But the synchronicity involved seems so significant that I feel it must be pointed out. Christopher Reeve was an archetypally appropriate choice to represent the idealized face of the ego presented by the character Dr. Chaffee. He was, of course, the actor chosen to play Superman, and I hardly need to point out the relationship of Superman and an ego ideal. Reeve was highly intelligent, tall, graced with an Olympian physique, patrician good looks and aristocratic bearing. *Village of the Damned* opened on April 28, 1995. Twenty-nine days later, on May 27, 1995, Reeve suffered his tragic accident that left him a quadriplegic.

Many people were shocked at the irony of someone who portrayed Superman becoming a quadriplegic. This particular type of injury seems a far more powerful reminder of human mortality and frailty than someone actually dying, which in our culture is usually an off-stage, abstracted event. In fact, an early death for a movie or rock star usually results in their being romanticized and idealized. But for the ego, quadriplegia is one of the most frightening mortal scenarios, involving the fears of loss of control, loss of sexual functioning and completely dependent helplessness. That quadriplegia happened to a man who was identified in the popular culture as Superman was striking enough irony in itself, but for Reeve to also be playing in the movie theaters as Dr. Chaffee when the accident occurred seems like more than a coincidence.

Again, it may seem irresponsible and lacking in compassion to symbolically interpret someone's personal tragedy. But it really seems as though the collective were being sent a message — a profoundly disturbing message — of how the mighty ego is fallen. The ego strives arduously to be superman and to perfect the body and have control, fame and wealth. Rarely does someone like Christopher Reeve actually manage to achieve all those things. But fate can reverse all ego achievement in an instant. And to paraphrase Marshall McLuhan, the medium of this disturbing message is a message in itself. A terrible accident occurs with an acausal link to collective mythology. The archetypal realm reveals that it has shocking power in the "real" world. It was for exactly this reason that Jung was alarmed when his German patients started to dream about *Wotan,* a Germanic god of war and mayhem. Jung knew that what emerges in dreams emerges in the world. What emerges in films, which often manifest as technologically amplified collective dreams, also has a tendency to emerge into the "real" world. And the ego, for all its pretensions and efforts to deny mortality, may be fearfully aware that there is strange handwriting on the wall, and that its worst fears may well come true.

What is particularly disturbing in the case of Christopher Reeves is that, as Dr. Chaffee he is the character who ultimately destroys the children. Throughout the film, however, it is the children who bring punishment to those who harm them or whom they perceive as a threat. For example, the children force the woman scientist in charge of their colony to show them the preserved body of the infant girl that died. They observe a "T" shaped autopsy incision on the infant's body. Later in the film they telekinetically pressure this scientist to make a T-shaped incision on her own body. The children seem to be exacting an eye-for-an-eye version of karmic justice. The only character in the film on whom they are not able to exact this kind of justice is Dr. Chaffee. The synchronistic real-life accident makes it appear as if their power were able to reach beyond the realm of the film fantasy and into the external world.

An interesting approach to this disturbing synchronicity begins with considering how perceptual bias alters external reality. The effect of the observer on what is observed is most obvious in the case of one human psyche perceiving another. If an egoistic psyche perceives a particular child to be bad and dangerous, the child is likely to act that way. *Village of the Damned,* with its ego point of view personified by Zellaby/Chaffee, perceives the evolutionary change as bad. Both iterations of the doctor view the new human consciousness as a threat, a competing species bent on the domination and destruction of the older form. They are treated in kind by the children but ultimately succeed in destroying them. Their paranoid, fearful point of view constellates a paranoid world of fear, power and domination. The triumph of the ego over the new children in the film is bizarrely, disturbingly contradicted by the real life synchronicity of the actors who portray Zellaby/Chaffee. One way of interpreting this message is as a threatening warning to the ego. If you perceive this evolutionary change from your accustomed vantage of imperialistic dominator, be ready for a fall.

Promotional image for *Powder*

The Post-Singularity Ego in *Powder*

Other visions of the Singularity Archetype in popular culture view this evolutionary/ego shift more sympathetically. Take for example the 1995 film, *Powder*, about a male adolescent mutant.

Powder, like so many of the mutants portrayed in stories inspired by the Singularity Archetype, is a liminal figure in multiple senses. He is caught between being human and nonhuman, powerful and handicapped, male and female. Visually, Powder is entirely without body hair and looks quite androgynous. He has archetypal masculine qualities of will, courage and higher thinking, and archetypal feminine qualities of compassion, empathy, shyness, modesty, humility and healing ability. Most interestingly though, as a symbol of the metamorphosing ego, Powder exists between birth and death. His life, in fact, begins with death. Unlike *Village of the Damned*, Powder's mother is not impregnated by a UFO. However, in an equally cosmic birth scenario she is struck by lightning while pregnant, which sends her into labor. Lightning is a cosmic phenomenon that connects higher and lower when they become too polarized. She dies, but her unborn son lives and is transformed by this heavenly intervention. From an evolutionary perspective, Powder's birth blamelessly means the death of the old type of human (his mother). And like the children of Midwich, Powder is inherently feared by the society into which he is born. He is rejected by his father, and his grandparents raise him, but refuse to touch him.

Similarly, the children of *Village of the Damned* are born after women who go through a death-like sleep are impregnated in some unknown way by UFOs. Yet the orientation related to the ego and the collective is exactly reversed. Powder is a sympathetic, loving, unegoistic, Christ-like martyr persecuted by the old species. In *Village of the Damned*, the post-singularity children are portrayed as monsters and the ego, glorified as Dr. Zellaby/Chaffee, is the hero who must destroy them.

The Telepathic Empath

Powder is a post-singularity being. As a result of the divine lightning strike, he possesses both empathic and telepathic abilities. One of his few positive human relationships is with a sympathetic young woman named Lindsey. In conversation he asks her, "Ever listen to people from the inside?" He then reveals to her that he can locate what people are thinking and that this also includes their unconscious thoughts.

Powder as Symbol of Unification

The children of Village of the Damned are personifications of unresolvable difference. They are locked in a savage, zero-sum conflict with Homo sapiens where only one species can survive. Even their Homo gestalt collective awareness is split down the middle. What one child is taught is instantly known by others of their kind, but only of the same gender. As advanced as these children are, gender is seen as an absolute firewall that cannot be crossed, even by telepaths.

Powder, by contrast, is a profoundly unifying personification of the Singularity Archetype. He is strikingly androgynous in both appearance and personality. He unifies the gender split within himself. Powder also seems to be bisexual, another example of his liminality. Although bisexuality is an interpersonal orientation, and androgyny is an intrapsychic orientation, bisexuality can be a personified metaphor for androgyny. Although Powder's closest relationship in the movie is with Lindsey, a young woman, there is a very telling scene where Powder stares longingly at a half naked boy with long hair in the locker room. This causes John Box, Powder's chief antagonist, who is both homophobic and xenophobic in general, to accuse Powder of being gay and to intensify his campaign of persecution.

The name "Box" suggests that Powder's antagonist is emblematic of think-in-the-box, square-peg consciousness. Box is the homophobic alpha of a gang of male adolescents and so he represents atavistic, patriarchal, dominator consciousness. Box fears Powder's androgynous, telepathic eyes and tells him, "Don't look at me. I don't like your eyes."

Androgyny

Androgyny, at least a significant lessening of gender differentiation, if not its disappearance, surfaces again and again as an element of the evolutionary change. A good example is the "Greys." In addition to oversized eyes, telepathic ability and collective consciousness, they are also notably androgynous in appearance. Gender differentiation has not necessarily disappeared, however, as many who report contact with these creatures will say that they were able to sense gender in them even if they couldn't visually discern gender characteristics. There are also numerous cases of contactees who claim to have had sex with these creatures. In the *Dune* Books, the collective consciousness of a Reverend Mother is limited to other female Reverend Mothers. But the whole point of the Bene Gesserit Sisterhood's thousand-year-long plan of genetic manipulation is to create a messianic being they call the Kwitzaz Haderach, a male Reverend Mother whose consciousness will transcend the gender limits that constrain them. Themes and images of androgyny are deeply entwined in many manifestations of the Singularity Archetype. Androgyny is feared by the ego both for its connection to evolutionary change and because it is a state of dissolved boundaries. [42]

Powder Bridges Parapsychological Evolution and Near-Death Experience

Powder has a connection to both a more evolved, telepathic awareness and death. Powder's divine birth involves the death of his mother and his life begins at the edge of death in an incubator. He has a corpse-like pallor and his grandparents keep him hidden underground.

Powder has an affect on electromagnetic equipment, a phenomenon frequently reported by near-death experiencers. Many NDErs report that electrical devices will malfunction around them, especially if they are emotionally agitated. Computers, which operate on the quantum level and are therefore more susceptible to quantum fluctuations, seem to be the most effected (of course they are also the least reliable of appliances). Dr. van Lommel reports: "There are frequent reports of electrical

---

[42] For a discussion of androgyny and its significance to personal and collective evolution, see: "Casting Precious into the Cracks of Doom — Androgyny, Alchemy, Evolution and the One Ring" at ZapOracle.com.

phenomena: at emotionally charged moments in particular, the body can emit an electromagnetic field that interferes with electrical equipment — lights go out, the computer crashes, the car starter fails, or the supermarket checkout scanner refuses service" (*CBL* 59-60).

Dr. van Lommel quotes an experiencer: "Another strange thing was that after my NDE every piece of equipment I touched, such as lamps, dishwasher, kettle, the light in the cooker hood, it broke. I gave off energy everywhere" (*CBL* 60).

Dr. van Lommel continues, "Some people do not wear a watch because it stops as soon as they wear it on their wrist. Thinking that the watch is broken, they buy a new one, only to have the same thing happen" (*CBL* 60).

One of the instances of Powder causing electro-magnetic effects has an additional connection to NDEs. Donald Ripley, Powder's high school physics teacher sets up a Jacob's Ladder in class. A Jacob's Ladder is a high-voltage traveling arc device that uses a spark gap formed between two wires to create a continuous train of large sparks which travel upwards. We've all seen them in old sci-fi movies. What's especially interesting is that the Jacob's Ladder is named after the "ladder of heaven" that Jacob dreams about in the Bible.[43]

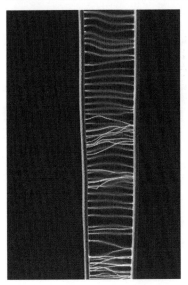 

Wikipedia image of a Jacob's Ladder   Jacob's Ladder as envisioned by William Blake

Because of its name, the device is the most appropriate machine to represent an NDE that I can think of. When the Jacob's Ladder is

---

[43] The Book of Genesis, 28:10-19.

activated, both Powder and the device are drastically effected resulting in havoc. Powder and the Jacob's ladder seem to amplify and intensify each other and this climaxes in one of a number of instances where we see Powder emerge as a glorified body. In the presence of the Jacob's Ladder, he is lifted off the ground and illuminated by blinding light and energy.

In his lecture before powering up the ladder, Ripley states that energy is "always transforming and never-ending." What Ripley is talking about has a direct connection to death and afterlife — the first law of thermodynamics that says that energy is neither created nor destroyed but is continually changing form. Many have attempted to use this physical principle to claim that consciousness is an energy and therefore it cannot be destroyed, but only changes form at death.

In one of the climatic episodes of the film, the gang of boys led by John Box that persecutes Powder is out hunting with an aggressive policeman who also doesn't like Powder. During the course of the hunt, the policeman shoots a deer. Powder, who comes upon the scene, is horrified and tries to put his hands on the dying animal to comfort or heal it. At that moment Powder personifies the wounded healer and he empathically feels the helpless agony of the dying animal. While he is in this empathic state, he grabs the arm of the policeman and causes him to feel what the deer is feeling. Powder later explains that he did this because he knew the policeman wasn't conscious of what he was doing and the suffering he was creating. The telepathic merger that Powder creates has elements of Logos Beheld communication and awareness. Powder says: "I opened him up and I let him see. He just couldn't see what he was doing and I let him see."

Powder basically forces a vicarious NDE on the policeman, and like someone who has had an NDE, the policeman exhibits a complete spiritual change. He gets rid of his entire gun collection, and ceases to be an aggressor. If we accept the policeman/hunter as the personification of the world of the ego — the patriarchal realm of governmental control and dominator mentality — we see that the new form has the ability to transform the ego by forcing empathic awareness into it.

Powder is also called by a more conscious and sympathetic policeman to do hospice-like deathbed service for his wife. Powder forms a telepathic bond with the dying woman allowing her to express her wish that the policeman reconcile with his estranged son. With her last wish expressed, the wife can be released into death and Powder reports to the policeman, "She didn't go some place... your wife. I felt her go. Not away, just out... everywhere."

Powder's statement exemplifies his pantheistic unity consciousness, the opposite of egoistic consciousness. He articulates his unity vision in an exchange with Lindsey:

Powder: "It's because you have this spot that you can't see past. My grams and gramps had it, the spot where they were taught they were disconnected from everything."

Lindsey: "So that's what they'd see if they could? That they're connected?"

Powder: "And how beautiful they really are. And that there's no need to hide, or lie. And that it's possible to talk to someone without any lies, with no sarcasms, no deceptions, no exaggerations or any of the things that people use to confuse the truth."

Lindsey: "I don't know a single person who does that."

Lindsey: "What are people like, on the inside?"

Powder: "Inside most people there's a feeling of being separate, separated from everything."

Lindsey: "And?"

Powder: "And they're not. They're part of absolutely everyone, and everything."

Dream of a Transforming but still Dangerous Ego

In 1996, while I was writing a study about the relationship of the ego and the Singularity Archetype, I had a powerful dream the night before I was ready to complete the study. Although the dream could be read as an unflattering depiction of the state of my own power complex, the timing of the dream, occurring just before I was to wake up and write about the role of the ego in evolution, inclined me to believe that the dream has a collective significance. The morning after the dream I found myself personifying the ego, mythologically amplifying its personification in the dream. What follows is the study of the dream I wrote in 1996.

In the dream I am present only as a witness or disembodied point of view. A group of people is standing before an enormously complex, futuristic control panel that has the curved amphitheater shape of the keyboard of a great pipe organ. Information in the form of rapidly moving green LED numbers is pouring out of the control panel. The control panel has been made to be aesthetically pleasing and to have a "natural" look of polished wood and green transparent panels. But part of the numerical display on the right-hand side is erratic and there is obviously a malfunction. The control panel is apparently a new prototype. A man in military garb who is sitting at the control panel is in a state of acute panic. He is afraid because at the center of the small group of white-coated scientists viewing the malfunction of the control panel is Darth Vader. But Darth Vader does not look like he does in the *Star Wars* films. To my surprise, I see that Vader's appearance is altered. He is wearing an abbreviated version of his famous black outfit and no breath mask or helmet. His head is exposed and he has the mustachioed, elegant, intelligent face of an elderly Vincent Price. To be more exact, this is the face of Vincent Price shortly before his death when he appeared in Tim Burton's film *Edward Scissorhands*. In the dream, Darth Vader seems uncannily intelligent and patient. He has a visible aura of power that shrouds his head like a hood, but he also seems frail and elderly.

The scene shifts and we see Darth Vader walking on a dirt road below a wall of natural rock, a side of a small canyon or cliff. He is now elegantly, aristocratically dressed in an immaculate white suit. He seems extremely intelligent, dignified and in control, but as before there is the undisguised frailty of age. A bodyguard, a brutal young man wearing a light-colored suit, stands with his hand on his gun. The gun, in a very phallic manner, is bulging from his trouser pocket and he stands ready, even anxious to use it at the first sign of trouble. Vader strolls with perfect composure paying no attention to the bodyguard who, to him, is merely a background detail. Vader is staring curiously at the wall of rock. There are Egyptian hieroglyphs drawn on the wall in colored chalk. I intuit that the designs were drawn very recently by adolescents. The dream ends with him looking curiously at the hieroglyphs.

Darth Vader, as the *Star Wars* character, is an almost archetypal personification of the demoniac aspect of the ego and the highly related concept of the patriarchy. When we experience him in the first (first to be released) film of the series, *Star Wars: A New Hope*, he appears to be completely motivated by the will to power. He hides his humanity behind a mask, his costume shields him in technology, and the shape of his helmet has an obvious Nazi aesthetic. He is man trying to become machine. But Vader is also the most complex of the *Star Wars* characters, and he undergoes the greatest transformation though the course of the series.

In *The Empire Strikes Back* we see a fascinating glimpse of Vader's humanity. He is apparently in his private apartment, which is a very small bombproof cubicle with an utterly functional interior of control panels and metal surfaces. This interior is Vader's cocoon, a small lightproof, airtight container, a little high-tech thermos insulating him from anything alive. Then, for a moment, we are shown a single glimpse of the back of his unhelmeted head, which reveals that there is vulnerable, scarred human tissue under the costume. He is a human being, and not merely an archetype of evil.

As the original trilogy of films continues, especially as we near the end of *The Return of the Jedi,* it becomes apparent that Vader, whose psyche at first seemed to be electrified by a pure will to power, is now torn between power and love for his son, Luke Skywalker. In the dramatic duel scene in *The Empire Strikes Back*, Vader, in an effort to seduce Luke into an alliance, makes the statement, "Join me, and together we can end this destructive conflict and bring order to the galaxy." The patriarchal will to power, with its pretense of rationalism, is obvious in the phrase, "bring order to the galaxy." But there is also for the first time a suggestion that Vader might be weary of war and does not favor destruction as an end in itself. He is intelligent enough to want to "end this destructive conflict..." Vader, like the ego, may be aware that he is in a conflict with another powerful principle that he cannot fully dominate, and he may be growing weary of the struggle. And then there is the opposing love principle in his statement, the emphasis on "joining" and being "together."

By the end of *The Return of the Jedi,* Vader's transformation is complete and he has sided decisively with love and surrendered power. He accepts his mortality and in his death scene asks his son to remove his breath mask so that they can have a moment of human contact. Vader/ego gives up the power principle, acknowledges love and immediately thereafter perishes.

Darth Vader's transformation in the *Star Wars* films represents one possible developmental track for the ego. From a place of utterly unfeeling will to power he grows weary, discovers love, surrenders and dies. There are numerous actual cases in which particular human egos have traveled this exact developmental path. Let's consider a hypothetical case history of a man in his fifties who is a ruthless, hard-driving workaholic businessman. Ambition was more important to this businessman than his family, and his marriage ended in divorce and estrangement from his children. But now he is in the hospital dying of cancer. His only son comes to visit him, and seeing his dying father hooked up to tubes and machines, he feels a sudden empathy for this brutal man that he never experienced before. The father, in return, feels an overwhelming love for his son who will live after he is gone. He surrenders his ego, accepts mortality, and dies.

The ego, in some collective sense, may also be aware that it is aging and has cancer, just as Vincent Price obviously was during the filming of *Edward Scissorhands*. As an association occurring in my dream, I remember finding Vincent Price's poignant role in the film made more poignant by

Vincent Price, in *Edward Scissorhands*

my having read that he was ailing with cancer when he played the role, and that it was his last film. His character in the film also dies in a poignant way, and Tim Burton, who had a great personal affection for Vincent Price, cast him aware that he was dying.

The imagery of the dream suggests that the ego is interested in rehabilitating its image. But one gets the feeling that these public-relations efforts to reveal a kinder, gentler ego should be viewed with a certain suspicion and wariness. For example, the "natural" green and wood-toned control panel may be viewed as an attempt at subterfuge or misdirection. It is shaped like the keyboard of a giant "pipe organ," so perhaps it represents a phallic will to control. It is a cosmetic softening of what is either the control panel of a Death Star or some Luciferian control panel for the earth. The ego is closely allied with what Jung called the "persona" — the outward, socialized mask we present to the world. The ego wears an immaculate white suit in the second part of the dream, as might befit the British Viceroy of India at the height of Imperialism. The suit, with its aristocratic all-whiteness, carries an association of racial superiority. The immaculate whiteness is also a striking contrast to the natural setting of the dirt road and canyon or cliff wall of raw rock. The ego obviously still feels superior and apart from messy nature, which must be put under control. And for all the ego's veneer of civilization, and dignified bearing, nearby is the brutal, phallic bodyguard, his hand hoping to draw the gun. The panic of the soldier at the control panel was no doubt an appropriate response to a Vader who still holds an iron fist beneath his white linen gloves.

From one point of view, we could say that the devil hath the power to assume a somewhat more pleasing shape. The ego, no doubt, has cards up its sleeve. Perhaps it is allowing itself to appear mortal and vulnerable so that we let down our guard. Possibly there is a laboratory on the Death Star where scientists work round the clock building a cyborg body for the ego. It plans to transform itself into a cyborg and achieve technological immortality and everlasting freedom from the living, dying organic world. The ego is a resilient structure and it has a genius for creating illusion and deception. One would have to be a really gifted paranoiac to invent motives and subterfuges darker and more devious then those of the power-oriented ego.

Although these suspicions are more than warranted, my inclination is to view the dream as a message about the ego's transforming duality. Its Luciferian aspect is still clearly present. Call me paranoid, but there's something about a guy named Darth Vader standing before a world control panel that I can't fully trust. On the other hand, the ego is not in control of the dream, and there is a feeling that the elderly Vincent Price aspect of him is also real. I think presently we find that the ego is in an increasingly schizoid state, and is not sure where he stands. The efforts at power, control and deception are still there, but he is also aware that the control panel is malfunctioning, that its body is aged and there is strange adolescent handwriting on the walls. But before we consider the ego's possibly transformed awareness of mortality, let's consider the relationship of its Luciferian aspect to nature.

The Ego and Nature

Just as Lucifer, according to the Bible, was once the brightest angel before the fall, the ego was once nature's brightest, most favored prodigy. Lucifer, according to the Bible, was created by God, even though he sets himself apart from God and plays an adversarial role. Similarly, the ego was created by nature, even though it sets itself apart from nature and plays an adversarial role. Is God really separate from Lucifer, his own creation? Is nature really separate from the human ego, its creation?

Nature created an interventional, adversarial species that extrudes technology and environmental toxins. If the human species and its ego are mistakes, then we might as well blame nature. The ego is a child of nature as much as a daisy or a virus. To understand the ego, we must discredit the view that it is unnatural. It is actually the ego itself that wants to view itself as unnatural. Like Lucifer, it's trying hard to forget where it came from and where it's going back to.

CROSSING THE EVENT HORIZON 137

Many people coming from the ego, use the term *"natural"* in a way that is filled with deception. I'm not sure that anything is outside of nature. Is the Empire State Building less natural than a beehive, or are they both structures created by earth organisms out of patterned energy? Most people call *"natural"* that which they prefer. For example, homosexuality, even though it occurs in hundreds of species and all human societies will be judged by some people as *"unnatural."* Those same people will view manmade social institutions, like the particular form of marriage approved of by their culture, as "natural." And, of course, it is claimed that God endorses these ego preferences. The God such people worship is really a man in a white suit who has their identical prejudices.

"Natural" carries an unconscious association with a Rousseau-like, sentimentalized view of kindly, gentle mother nature. For example, many food products boast that they have "all natural ingredients." But a soup made of cobra venom, scorpion tails and bubonic plague could make the identical claim. Polio virus is natural, the vaccine is manmade. The ego is natural, if anything is, and the tendency to view the ego as bad because it is distinctively human is in itself an ego-based illusion.

The ego, in its Darth Vader personification in the dream, may be slightly reforming its relationship to nature. Although it stands before the control panel with white-coated scientists and later strolls in a suit of sterile whiteness, it has made, at least, some aesthetic concessions to nature. The "natural" look of the control panel is in striking contrast to the synthetic high-tech look of Vader's world in the films. Perhaps the natural-looking control panel, which may be a world control panel, reflects a dawning concern the ego has for controlling the environment in a way that doesn't destroy it. Similarly, many of the corporate, ego and power based entities that contributed to the toxification of the environment are beginning to realize that destruction of the biosphere will eventually be bad for business and the bottom line.

A much more significant concession to nature is Vader's willingness to expose his frail, aging face. In the dream, this felt like a profound concession to mortality. Vader also shows some interest in stepping out of his cocoon and into the outside world of nature. He walks on a dirt road and looks at a natural rock face. He is seen struggling to understand evolving human nature as expressed by the colored hieroglyphic chalk drawings of the adolescents.

The ego's personification is dual. He is both Darth Vader, who is in himself dual, and Vincent Price. From the deception point of view we could suspect the ego of wanting to gain sympathy. Vincent Price was always the camp icon of horror films. His flamboyant portrayal of characters who were supposed to be sinister and ominous always seemed arch and humorously entertaining. Almost no one takes Vincent Price seriously as a personification of evil in the way people do take seriously Anthony Hopkin's Hannibal Lechter, for example. We might, therefore, suspect the ego of wanting to make light of any fears of it as boogey man.

But I am more inclined to view this Vincent Price aspect of the ego as revelatory, rather than deceptive. Although the ego borrows the physiognomy of Price's face, he doesn't show a trace of his humor, and there's nothing campy about his appearance or manner. The face seems more a revelation of true form rather than a borrowed disguise.

Let's also consider the role that Vincent Price played in *Edward Scissorhands,* which I believe to be a central and intended association of the dream. In the film he is some sort of eccentric genius, a fairy tale mad scientist who seems as much an alchemist as a technological inventor. Like the actor portraying him, he is at the end of his career and near death. And his final invention is also his only son.

Again, we have a strange duality. From one point of view, Price would seem to be a reincarnation of Dr. Frankenstein, the ego as technological Prometheus seeking to rival and surpass nature's progenerative power. Like Dr. Frankenstein, he is creating birth completely without the feminine, as he is the father of a son with no mother. But unlike Dr. Frankenstein, Price seems very loving and kindly. Perhaps he has created Edward aware that his own demise is approaching and loves Edward as much as any father loves his only son. Edward, like Frankenstein (remember his gentle affection for the little girl), is an unexpectedly feminine creature despite this all-masculine birth. He is portrayed by Johnny Depp as androgynous, sensitive, gentle and caring. Price's meddling with nature has brought something of great value into the world. One is reminded of the belief of the great alchemist, Paracelsus, that man is here to finish God's work, to finish nature.

The first words we hear Edward speak, however, are, *"I'm not finished."* He is referring to his mutant, metallic hands that would apparently have been replaced by normal-looking hands but for the untimely demise of Price before his creation could be finished. These technological hands, which look frightening, are capable of astonishing utility and creativity. But they also make it hard for Edward to do some of the ordinary tasks of daily life like dressing and eating, and he frequently inadvertently, wounds himself.

If the ego is, in a sense, the father, Edward himself is a hybrid. His *"unfinished"* technological hands give him creative power over nature as when he sculpts hedges into amazing creatures. The creative gardener is an almost archetypal personification of man augmenting nature. But Edward, unlike the ego, seeks love, not power, and his too powerful, technological hands make this hard for him. Edward, like Powder, is a post-Singularity adolescent mutant unsure of his identity. Like Powder, he has an unnatural pallor as if he were also partly a corpse. In some other ways, however, he is like a shy, alienated teenager. The technological proficiency that is an ingrained part of his being is much like that of a modern adolescent who has grown up in a world of smart phones, cars and computers; he is innately adept at using these tools and would feel like an amputee without them. But at the same time there is an awareness that these powerful gifts can be harmful, that they can cause self-inflicted wounds and make love difficult. The ego, in his Vincent Price aspect, is reminding us that he is the father of the mutant, and that he cannot be separated from the fate of the next evolutionary step.

Here again we have a strange paradoxical duality. It is true that new life builds on prior forms and the present ego-based psyche will have strong familial connections with whatever succeeds it. The patriarchal ego may have a certain paternal claim. But we also have the ego usurping the power of nature, and claiming the feminine role in creation. The ego, as the story of Frankenstein reminds us, is not to be trusted in the role of creator. The feminine cannot be left out of creation, but the ego prefers an exclusively masculine world. Dr. Frankenstein and Frankenstein, Price and Edward, Darth Vader and Luke Skywalker — each is a father with his only son, and mothers are conspicuously absent. Powder's mother dies in the cosmic event that creates his transformation. It is revealed in the second *Star Wars* trilogy that Vader had a female consort, but, in the first cycle of films, we never hear of her and her children don't know her either. Vader has a daughter, Princess Leia, but he shows little interest in joining with her.

The ego in the dream is surrounded by male scientists, soldiers and bodyguards. His demeanor and presence personifies what Jung referred to as the solar phallic or higher masculine power identified with mind and will. But nearby is the chthonic or lower phallic power of the bodyguard with his relation to power-oriented sex on the level of the genitalia, brutal violence and domination. We see higher and lower phallic principles combined in a typical dream image/word pun in the control panel, which is shaped like a great organ. The ego is as male as ever and it wants to usurp the feminine role in creation. Perhaps that's another meaning of the green and wood-toned control panel.

In the waking life we certainly see the ego standing before control panels altering nature. White-coated or suited ego personifications introduce genetically altered microorganisms, plants and animals into our world. Once we foraged in the forest, then we learned to use our hands to make gardens and farms, but now ego-driven multinational corporations mediate with nature for us and grow genetically altered crops in chemical fertilizers, which are sprayed with pesticides, irradiated, and sold in microwaveable plastic at the supermarket. We've allowed the ego to be in charge of nature and progeneration and can't be sure where that process will end. Given the opportunity to fulfill its ambitions, perhaps the ego will create artificial intelligence that will propagate itself in a virtual world that really will be childhood's end. Is it possible for the ego to create an alternative or parallel evolutionary track to that of the human species? Consider how much computers have evolved in the last fifty years compared to fifty years of human evolution. The ego might seek to avoid mortality by using artificial life to replace or mutate organic evolution. For your next lifetime, why be reborn by messy, inefficient mother nature when you can be rebooted by Turbo-Genesis Incarnater version 7.1? For neurological materialists, at least, consciousness is reducible to wetware, and therefore a digital rebirth seems plausible.

Perhaps the ego has a cybernetic card up its sleeve. In the dream, however, the Vader/Price character seems to be feeling his age and acknowledging his mortality. Similarly, heads of multinational corporations and governments read the statistical projections and know they must content themselves with managing the end of the world. In the dream the ego sees that there is handwriting on the wall. The hieroglyphic handwriting is colorful and adolescent. Since the markings are made with chalk, they are recent and temporally fragile, but they also resonate with the ancient world and appear Egyptian. Its hieroglyphic expression suggests the archetypes and the collective unconscious. In Jungian literature, there is a famous example of the timeless memory of the collective unconscious in the dream of a modern girl that manifests motifs of ancient Egyptian mythology unknown to her waking self. In Terence McKenna's most seminal book, *The Archaic Revival*, he discusses the revival, especially popular with adolescents, of the archaic practices of body piercing, drum circles, paganism, magic, herbal healing and the use of natural hallucinogens. Aspects of the ancient world are returning through the young and the ego isn't sure what to make of them, but it may be intelligent enough to sense that they are harbingers of change beyond its control. The spatial occurrence of the hieroglyphs in the dream is also significant. They are far over the head of the ego and several body lengths out of reach.

The dream tells us that the ego is still powerful, still dangerous, yet also a paradoxical, complex entity with conflicting motives and self-ambivalence. It may be nearing the end of its life, but it will not be without a role in the creation of what's to come.

VIII. My Encounter with the Singularity Archetype

Detail of my first collage entitled "Parallel Journeys" made in 1996. The two b&w images are photos my father took of me at age 8 and as an infant.

NOW that I've introduced the Singularity Archetype, I'll relate the story of how I first encountered it in the external world. I provide the account not as an autobiographical tangent so much as a case history of what an encounter and ongoing relationship with this archetype looks like.

It was a summer afternoon in 1969 or 1970 and I was about twelve or thirteen years old. I was sitting in the tiny breakfast room, an annex to the kitchen of my family home in the Bronx, watching our black-and-white television. A sci-fi film was coming on, a 1960 British movie with an arresting title: *Village of the Damned*. I'm pretty sure my dad was sitting behind me and that he watched the film as well. Nothing I had ever seen on television was so mesmerizing — the story and the serious and intelligent tone of the film were magnetic for me.

Although I didn't share this with my dad, or with anyone, the film left me stunned and shaken. It was a life-changing encounter and the experience had a religious intensity. I felt as though the film came from inside of me. The core of my being began to vibrate and I knew that something of the greatest significance had occurred. Nothing that I had ever seen or heard before in the outer world struck certain of the deepest and most hidden parts of my being as this film had. I felt the stir of destiny like a field of crackling electricity all around me. How did they know? Where had this film come from?

Village of the Damned was my first encounter with a full-blown expression of the Singularity Archetype in the outer world as an artifact of contemporary culture. It was also expressed in one of the most potent carriers of mythology ever created — the movie. A few months ago (writing in the summer of 2010), all across the globe there were many other twelve-year-olds having a similar experience of religious intensity watching the movie *Avatar*.

The same year that I had this experience with *The Village of the Damned,* I came to a life-changing revelation about a nearly fatal paranormal experience which had occurred when I was ten. The revelation had spiritual dimensions and filled me with a sense of the profound meaningfulness and high stakes of life.[44] When I was fourteen, I had a second encounter with the Singularity Archetype, expressed in another potent mythological form. This time the medium was a science fiction novel, Arthur C. Clarke's masterpiece, *Childhood's End.* I carried my battered paperback copy of *Childhood's End* through the halls of the Bronx High School of Science, and it became a ball of light glowing in my hands. Besides the content, what was most disturbing was that somehow what I thought were my most creative and original science fiction ideas, ideas that I expected to write about one day, had somehow shown up in this tattered paperback. I flipped back to the copyright page — 1953, this book was written four years before I was born! How could such a thing be possible? This was probably also the year I encountered Clarke's other masterpiece, *2001,* his visionary collaboration with Stanley Kubrick that brought the Singularity Archetype to the big screen with cutting edge Industrial Light and Magic special effects. Although the film was released in 1968, I probably first saw it as a revival in 1971.

Dostoevsky and the Voice from the Clock-Radio

Another key anomaly occurred during my fourteenth year, though it will not be clear until later how it is directly related to the Singularity Archetype.

I felt something prod me out of the deep sleep of a healthy fourteen year old at two or three o'clock in the morning. Some irresistible inner prompting had me reaching toward my futuristic-looking Panasonic clock radio to switch on the sound. When I did so, I heard a voice coming out of the radio that sounded exactly like my own mind speaking in my head. I was stunned, and wondered if I was still dreaming, but

---

[44] See "A Mutant Convergence — How John Major Jenkins, Jonathan Zap and Terence Mckenna Met During a Weekend of High Strangeness in 1996" ZapOracle.com

everything in the room felt so physical and real. The voice seemed to express my inner most thoughts, the thoughts I had not shared with anyone, and the thoughts and feelings expressed by the voice had what I thought were the unique perspective of my own mind and personality. Suddenly there was a station identification break and I found out what was going on. It was WBAI, FM, the station I tuned into far more than any other.

The WBAI of the Sixties and Seventies was unlike any radio station that has ever existed before or since. "Referred to in a *New York Times Magazine* piece as 'an anarchist's circus,' one station manager was jailed in protest, and the staff, in protest at sweeping proposed changes of another station manager, seized the studio facilities, then located in a deconsecrated church, as well as the transmitter, located atop the Empire State Building."[45] Tuning into WBAI at random, I could find almost anything going on and some of it was mind-blowing. For example, there was a popular show run by hilariously militant lesbians. Males were not even permitted to call the show, but they did anyway, and always to tell the militants how much they loved and supported them. In return the lesbians showered them with verbal abuse — "Well, don't you worry your pretty little head about it!" they would say as they hung up on the male callers.

As we'll see with this and many other examples, a source of cultural novelty is also likely to be a source for strange, sometimes synchronistic encounters with the Singularity Archetype. Some of the stranger radio shows of that era of New York City played an almost internet-like role in informing me about esoteric subjects. The most significant of these was the the famous Long John Nebel all-night radio show, a magnet for all subjects paranormal and the forerunner of Art Bell and the Coast-to-Coast AM franchise. I pulled many all-nighters during my high school years experimenting with photography in our basement darkroom while listening to reports of the bizarre and anomalous on the radio.

After the WBAI station identification break I found out that what seemed like telepathic radio was actually an all-night live reading from Doestoevsky's haunting novella, *Notes from Underground.*

When I was nineteen, and a junior in college, I had the first chance of my academic career to do some independent research. I had always meant to find out who this Dostoevsky was and how he seemed to able to write in a way that uncannily evoked the inner contents of my mind. As with the other encounters, Dostoevsky novels were cases of the supposed firewall that exists between inner and outer blurring out into a wide open portal. Thinking about the psychology of Dostoevsky characters while

---

[45] http://en.wikipedia.org/wiki/Wbai

sitting on a bench at night in a quiet part of the college campus, I crossed a developmental event horizon and experienced the beginning of my adult consciousness. It was such a decisive change that memories before and after that moment have a decidedly different quality, as my fundamental level of self-awareness transformed. The threshold occurred as a cascade of insights that revealed a psychological model and type that characterized myself and many of Dostoevsky's key characters. I called this type "the profound egocentric," but had no idea how it connected to my other obsessions related to the Singularity Archetype.[46]

Having successfully, I thought, penetrated the Dostoevsky anomaly the year before, in the last semester of my senior year at college, I set out to understand the strange uncanny significance I sensed in *Village of the Damned* and *Childhood's End*.

Encounter with Jung

Unlikely help offered itself to me during the course of my studies. The Chairman of the Philosophy Department, though I was an English major, had become my benefactor and opened doors for me in a highly conservative academic environment, allowing me to pursue interdisciplinary research projects into obscure, shadowy areas. But it was actually my mom, a psychologist whose career spanned forty-four years, who provided the crucial suggestion that I read what a Swiss psychiatrist named Carl Jung had to say about the "archetypes and the collective unconscious." I looked him up in the encyclopedia and wondered what this dead Swiss guy, who was born in the Nineteenth Century and was the son of a minister, could possibly tell me, a Jewish kid from the Bronx, about my obsession with certain works of science fiction?

---

[46] The resulting paper, "Dostoevsky and the Profound Egocentric," can be found at ZapOracle.com.

And so I came to stand before the many elegant black volumes of the Princeton Bollingen edition of Jung's collected works. I scanned the index volume for a few minutes and came across a late work, *Flying Saucers, A Modern Myth of things Seen in the Sky,* published when I was a few months old. That was a bit of a shock, as UFOs were a major part of the science fiction that obsessed me and informed my esoteric research. Jung's flying saucer book was included in volume ten of the collected works, *Civilization in Transition,*

Carl Jung in his study, photographer unknown

a title that has always struck me as both ominous and an almost comic example of Swiss understatement. The UFO subject seemed to haunt Jung near the end of his life. At the end of the book it seemed like he couldn't let go of the subject — there was an afterward, followed by an epilogue, followed by a supplement.

As I glanced through the supplement, I felt the air crackling with electricity again and my eyes dilated in amazement. Jung had devoted this final supplement to analyzing mythological layers of meaning in the British science fiction novel, *The Midwich Cuckoos,* by John Wyndham. This was the novel that *Village of the Damned* was based on! It was like the dead Swiss guy had stepped out of the bookcase, like a holographic projection of a wizard bearing a torch, and he was looking over my shoulder and saying, "Yes, I was fascinated by that one too, and here's what I thought." From that moment forward Jung became my mentor in unraveling the mystery of the Singularity Archetype.

Even then however, I could see that Jung's supplement on *The Midwich Cuckoos,* with its strange placement after an afterward and an epilogue, seemed to have been the hastily thrown together afterthoughts of a restless mind obsessed with a subject on which there could be no closure. Jung was writing near the end of his life, and the flying saucer mythology he was studying was only in its infancy. Jung did not, by the way, assume that UFOs were merely hallucinations. He noted that they often reflected radar and wondered aloud if they might not be physical exteriorizations of the collective unconscious. Jung's supplement spent two paragraphs summarizing the novel and then just two paragraphs speculating about some of its implications and mythological motifs.

Some of Jung's observations paralleled my own. I sensed, as Jung did, that unlike Arthur C. Clarke, Wyndham was viewing the singularity from the fearful vantage of the old form. Jung's brief study ends with a sentence, also the last sentence of the entire book, that seems to reflect the state of extreme unfinished ambiguity that Jung was feeling about the whole subject: "Thus the negative end of the story remains a matter for doubt." What a strange sentence to end a book with! At the same moment that I recognized Jung as my mentor, and would soon discover that I needed to stand on his shoulders to get a clearer view of the mystery, I also sensed the unfinished place where he had left things. Amazingly, he had left off at exactly the place where I had begun.

The Singularity Archetype and the Profound Egocentric

Jung also provided me a hint that revealed an unexpected connection between the paper I had written on Dostoevsky while in college and my next project on the Singularity Archetype. When I wrote the paper I recognized that certain other writers, especially Kafka and Nietzsche, were also profound egocentrics. I also noticed that many of the mutants depicted in novels and movies inspired by the Singularity Archetype were profound egocentrics as well. The connection, however was not clear to me until I stumbled across an observation that Jung made about Nietzsche. In his collected works, Jung speculates that Nietzsche's inner torment was caused by the sensory basis of language being insufficient for him to express himself. This hint sparked a key speculative realization — the profound egocentric personality type was primarily the outcome of psyches who probably had the latent capacity for a new means of communication, and for whom ordinary language was not sufficient, but who were living in a social matrix where no such new means of communication was supported.

In 1978 I described the realization this way:

> "The profound egocentric's intense isolation seems to begin with earliest childhood. If we postulate that the profound egocentric is capable, or partially capable, of a new means of communication while humanity as a whole is not, we could establish an excellent cause-and-effect relationship with the whole phenomenon.

> "In his *Symbols of Transformation*, Jung discusses the sensual base of all language and the resultant limitations imposed on

abstract thought. Jung suggests that the bitterness, loneliness and eventual despair of Nietzche was the result of the inadequacy (for him) of language. If there are individuals whose mental processes have developed enough to make our present form of communication inadequate, then perhaps a new one will evolve to parallel that development."

The finished product of my initial investigation was a philosophy honors paper entitled "Archetypes of a New Evolution," which I finished in the late Spring of 1978.[47] This paper, written when I was twenty, was the first step in a new life phase for me that has continued into the present, of a conscious awareness of the Singularity Archetype. I have been actively writing and speaking on the subject ever since. During the summer of 2010, thirty-two years after my initial paper in college, the time arrived to crystalize my findings and begin the book you are currently reading.

---

[47] http://www.zaporacle.com/archetypes-of-a-new-evolution/

IX. Some Dynamic Paradoxes to Consider When Viewing the Singularity Archetype in an Evolutionary Context

Dynamic Paradoxes Collage by the author

(The following is a brief excerpt from the beginning of my essay "Dynamic Paradoxicalism — the Anti-ism ism.") [48]

"Words that are strictly true seem to be paradoxical." — Lao-tse

"There is nothing absolute and final. If everything were ironclad, all the rules absolute and everything structured so no paradox or irony existed, you couldn't move. One could say that man sneaks through the crack where paradox exists."   — Itzhak Bentov

"Dynamic paradoxicalism is my attempt to create a meta-philosophy that is a counter to fundamentalist and absolutist thought, which is nearly as common amongst New Agers and the Left as it is amongst religious fundamentalists and the Right. The greatest of life skills is the ability to live with ambiguity, ambivalence, and paradox, without trying to regularize these uncertainties into finished, absolute truths. Dynamic paradoxicalism recognizes that most important areas of truth exist as a paradox, where seemingly contradictory elements have a dynamic level of validity based on context specific circumstances. Although a greater conception that synthesizes the disparate elements of a paradox into a grand unit is an awesome addition to the conceptual toolbox, it is not always the most useful tool in the box. Dynamic paradoxicalism

---

[48] http://www.zaporacle.com/dynamic-paradoxicalism-the-anti-ism-ism/

recommends an ability to slide between the poles of a paradox, in some circumstances favoring the point of view of one side of the paradox, in other cases the other pole, and in still other cases favoring the unified view.

"Dynamic paradoxicalism is based on the the principle that the opposite of a profound truth is often another profound truth."

I believe that the perspective of dynamic paradoxicalism is necessary to comprehend the Singularity Archetype. Non-paradoxical views of the Singularity Archetype flatten and distort it. We've already discussed one of the essential paradoxes: From one point of view the Singularity Archetype is about the collective approaching the event horizon of an evolutionary singularity. From another point of view, the Singularity Archetype is about the individual approaching the event horizon of death.

Another key paradox has to do with linear and circular time. From the perspective of circular time, the Singularity Archetype is an eternal archetype of death and rebirth that cannot be located in linear time. The Singularity Archetype lives in a nowever state, and people from whatever place and period encounter it.[49]

From the perspective of linear time, historical time, the Singularity Archetype is the end of the human narrative. There are overshadows of the Singularity Archetype from the very beginning of the story, but in the later chapters the focus on the central organizing idea of the story intensifies, building toward a denouement. From the perspective of dynamic paradoxicalism, both the circular and linear perspectives of the Singularity are true, but incomplete in isolation.

The unified view of this paradox would be the elongated spiral. The spiral circles around but also has a linear direction. For example, for the last thousand years the seasons have continued to circle from winter, to spring, to summer, to fall. All the days have circled from sunrise to sunset, and so on. But while all that circling has been happening, there has also been astounding linear change, such as the development of technology. Birth, death and rebirth may revolve in a circle, but during the span of a single human incarnation there is a very linear process called aging. The narrative of an individual life keeps unfolding, page-by-page, day-by-day in a linear process that includes a beginning and an end.

Parallel paradoxes appear when the Singularity Archetype is viewed from the perspective of evolution. For example, from the perspective of the ego, the Singularity Archetype is like the wing of the devil, it

---

[49] See The Myth of the Great Ending: Why We've Been Longing for the End of Days Since the Beginning of Time by Joseph M. Fesler

manifests as the worst thing possible — the end of all things, death and/or extinction as oblivion. From the perspective of the Self, however, the Singularity Archetype is about death and rebirth. The caterpillar must die to become a butterfly. It's said that sixty-five million years ago, life on this planet crossed an event horizon when the earth collided with a giant asteroid. From the perspective of the dinosaurs this was the worst thing possible, the end of days, a steep descent into extinction and oblivion. From the perspective of the mammals, this looked like the worst thing possible when it happened. But the mammalian perspective changed much later when the mammals emerged from the ashes of aesteroidal apocalypse to find that they were in a new world that was amazingly fertile for their further evolution.

From the Western perspective of progress there is a positive linear development of life and human culture and technology. In the postmodernist world, progress is often seen as a naive perspective, especially since it's become apparent that the progress of technology threatens the life of the planet. In parallel, sci-fi fantasies have gone from being largely utopian to almost exclusively dystopian. But this perspective, which has some true aspects, is in a highly charged paradox with other principles such as the Hindu devolutionary perspective, as well as the perspective of some, but not all, of the models generated by evolutionary biology.

Evolution or Devolution?

Michael Cremo, especially in his books *Forbidden Archeology* and *Human Devolution: A Vedic Alternative to Darwin's Theory,* points out substantial, well-documented evidence that there are dramatic flaws in accepted timelines of human evolution and with many aspects of Darwinian evolutionary models. For example, in an introduction to *Human Devolution,* Cremo writes:

> "The Darwinian theory of evolution is in trouble right from the start. Although the origin of life from chemicals is technically not part of the evolution theory, it has in practice become inseparably connected with it. Darwinists routinely assert that life arose from chemicals. But after decades of theorizing and experimenting, they are unable to say exactly which chemicals combined in exactly which way to form exactly which first living thing. As far as evolution itself is concerned, it has not been demonstrated in any truly scientific way. It remains an article of faith. The modern evolutionary synthesis is based on genetics. Evolutionists posit a relationship between the genotype (genetic structure) of an organism and its phenotype (physical structure). They say that changes in the genotype result in

changes in the phenotype, and by natural selection the changes in phenotype conferring better fitness in a particular environment accumulate in organisms. Evolutionists claim that this process can account for the appearance of new structural features in organisms. But on the level of microbiology, these structures appear to be irreducibly complex. Scientists have not been able to specify exactly how they have come about in step by step fashion. They have not been able to tell us exactly what genetic changes resulted in what phenotypic changes to produce particular complex features of organisms. This would require the specification of intermediate stages leading up to the complex structures we observe today. In his book *Darwin's Black Box* (1996, p. 183), biochemist Michael Behe says, 'In the past ten years, *Journal of Molecular Evolution* has published more than a thousand papers... There were zero papers discussing detailed models for intermediates in the development of complex biomolecular structures. This is not a peculiarity of JME. No papers are to be found that discuss detailed models for intermediates in the development of complex biomolecular structures, whether in the *Proceedings of the National Academy of Science, Nature, Science, the Journal of Molecular Biology* or, to my knowledge, any science journal.'"

Of course, to become familiar with all the models, controversies and new findings of evolutionary biology is a lifetime's endeavor, so I am in no way presenting myself as competent to arbitrate the relative validity of different models. I will, however, make some general points relevant to my view of the Singularity Archeytpe and evolution as dynamic paradoxes. Many of the findings of NDE research, explored in Chapter III of this text, could be used, and Cremo does use them, to support a Vedic devolutionary model. This model stipulates that we are originally spiritual beings that descended into flesh and the relative darkness of the material world. When people experience states of incredibly enhanced awareness, and planes of existence that seem more evolved than the mortal coil, their experience is usually that they are "coming home," that they are experiencing a state that they came from, but lost touch with, while human incarnation and corporeal existence eclipsed their awareness. The other side of the devolutionary paradox would be a progressive orthogenetic evolutionary model such as Pierre Teillhard de Chardin presents in *The Phenomenon of Man*. In this model, life is progressively developing toward more self-awareness. When I say that a progressive orthogenetic model is on the "other side" of the paradox, I am not implying that there are only two sides. Many other evolutionary models have considerable evidence supporting their points of view. For example, natural selection has been very elegantly demonstrated in the recent evolution of the peppered moth in England.[50]

My own informal model assumes that many different evolutionary mechanisms are at work, and some of them relate as dynamic paradoxes. For example, if the Vedic model is true, and we "devolved" from a more spiritual dimension into the dark and dense material world, there could still be considerable evolution involved in making such a descent. According to The Taoist I Ching, evolution occurs by "returning to the Tao." From the perspective of this model, we are born, like most organisms, completely in tune with the Tao, but then acquired conditioning causes us to lose touch with our essence. If, however, we are strong and aware enough to follow the path of "reverse alchemy," and return to our essence, we will have evolved considerably. Simpler organisms — daisies, spiders, etc. are born in tune with the Tao, never deviate from it, but also don't evolve as much as a person on the path of reverse alchemy. The process of becoming displaced from essence, and then working your way back to it, is quite developmental and promotes self-awareness.

Although the material world, according to the Vedic model, has a devolutionary relationship to the spiritual world, progressive evolution may still occur within certain linear time frames of the material world. The Spiral Dynamics model of evolution presents evidence of an elongated spiral in the evolution of human consciousness. As we travel through linear time, more advanced human types gradually tend to preponderate according to this model. Still another model, what Aldous Huxley called "the Perennial Philosophy," includes and coincides with the Vedic view, and finds that human evolution in the material world cycles in a circular pattern — evolving, devolving, then evolving again, etc. From the position of dynamic paradoxicalism, all of these models have validity when seen from certain perspectives and time frames.

Teleology and the Singularity Archetype

From the perspective of circular time, the Singularity Archetype is always present and doesn't "finalize" at some particular date. The event horizon is, like the everyday horizon, ever receding so that you keep approaching it indefinitely. Certainly the Singularity Archetype is already present and not to be located exclusively in the future. People have been encountering the Singularity Archetype for thousands of years during visionary states, near-death, etc. The circular time perspective of the Singularity Archetype, however, is incomplete.

---

[50] http://en.wikipedia.org/wiki/Peppered_moth_evolution

A full perspective of the Singularity Archetype also requires the perspective of linear time. The evolutionary aspects of the Singularity Archetype are not merely illusions generated by linearity, but are core aspects of the collective face of the archetype. The linear evolutionary model does imply teleological evolution, evolution with a goal, which presently has a disreputable status amongst most evolutionary biologists.

A detailed case for teleological evolution is beyond the scope of this book, but some general points about teleology will be necessary to understand the paradoxical relationship the Singularity Archetype has with evolution.

"Orthogenesis" (also sometimes referred to as "orthogenetic evolution," "progressive evolution" or "autogenesis") is the hypothesis that there is in an innate tendency, due to internal or external forces, for life to develop in a linear direction. Orthogenesis, however, does not posit a goal for this linear movement. While some well-known, early models conflated the linear drive of orthogenesis with goal-orientation, the later form of evolution is more properly called "teleology."

Teleology's disreputable status in evolutionary biology has a very long history. More than a 100 years ago, biologist Ernest William von Brück put it this way: "Teleology is a lady without whom no biologist can live. Yet he is ashamed to show himself with her in public."[51] This shamefulness originally derived from assumptions that teleology implied a divine force or that it supported discredited notions of progress. But teleology does not require a divine force, and recently it has been making a comeback in evolutionary biology, though not without continued controversy. Darwin was a supporter of teleology, which he saw as a natural process and not a result of anything supernatural or divine. For example, in 1863 when biologist Asa Grey wrote a letter congratulating Darwin for some findings that supported teleology, Darwin wrote back: "What you say about teleology pleases me especially and I do not think anyone else has noticed the point."

Although many in the scientific community still abhor teleology, it certainly has supporters. For example, British physicist Paul Davies wrote in *The Fifth Miracle*: "The laws of nature are rigged not only in favor of life, but also in favor of mind. Mind is written into the laws of nature in a fundamental way." If Davies is correct, then Homo sapiens is the spearhead of a teleological evolution unfolding on this planet.

The speculative teleological models of evolution presented by Terence McKenna and Pierre Teilhard de Chardin work extremely well with many of the implications of the Singularity Archetype. I regard de

---

[51] From Dr. Kenneth Ring's Lessons from the Light: What We can Learn from Near-death Experience, page xvi

Chardin's *The Phenomenon of Man* to be an essential text related to the Singularity Archetype. His work is so well known, however, I won't attempt to summarize it here, but I encourage everyone interested in the Singularity Archetype to read *The Phenomenon of Man*. Here's a brief quote from this seminal work:

> "Thus we see not only thought as participating in evolution as an anomaly or as an epiphenomenon; but evolution as so reducible to and identifiable with a progress toward thought that the movement of our souls expresses and measures the very stages of progress of evolution itself. Man discovers that *he is nothing else than evolution become conscious of itself,* to borrow Julian Huxley's striking expression" (221).

So far in this section I have lightly surveyed aspects of evolution that would more properly be introduced by a shelf load of heavy volumes. The purpose here is not to break new ground in evolutionary biology, but to outline my view of the Singularity Archetype as having a dynamic, paradoxical relationship to evolution.

Further Speculations on Human Evolution

Our need to evolve may express itself in ways that seem paradoxical and disturbing. For example, there is much reason to believe that this evolutionary rebirth may become possible only as we push the species toward the brink of extinction. If you'll continue to indulge me, I'd like to offer some further speculations about human evolution.[52]

The Last Great Evolutionary Jump

The last great quantum jump in evolution on this planet was the development of the human capacity to think and express itself in words. Stanford anthropologist Richard Klein called the human development of language "the brain's big bang." Noam Chomsky and others have pointed out that all human languages are essentially the same on the level of deep syntax.

The exact origins of human language are, of course, unknown. There is debate about whether it developed gradually or suddenly. Linguistic monogenesis is the hypothesis that there was a single proto-language,

---

[52] I want to emphasize that word again: *speculation*. Indeed, some of what follows might even be reasonably called under-informed speculation. A vast amount of unfinished theoretical work exists on the origins of human language. Most of this work is being done by evolutionary biologists, linguists and neuroscientists like Terence Deacon, author of *The Symbolic Species: The Coevolution of Language and the Brain*. By contrast, I took one linguistics course in grad school and don't have even an introductory grasp of the many competing models for the origins of language. What follows is not a theory, but a very general speculation.

sometimes called Proto-Human, from which all other vocal languages spoken by humans descend. There is no single, unprecedented brain structure associated with language. Language processing occurs in many different brain structures all of which existed before language is believed to have originated.

One way of imagining an evolutionary jump is to consider the possibility of an individual mutation that is capable of superior functioning. Most mutations, of course, are disadvantageous and bred out, but occasionally even random mutagenic forces can generate something superior. This model wouldn't work very well for the evolution of language, however, which is a collective phenomenon. A single mutation capable of language wouldn't have anyone to develop language with. Therefore, one can speculate that the structures in the brain that allowed the capacity for language developed gradually, and that for a long period of time some latent capacity for language existed in a great many individuals without it being manifest.

One possibility would be some sort of punctuated equilibrium. Some subset of early humans was experiencing acute stress that would not allow the old equilibrium of survival to continue. With this ultimate pressure acting as a catalyst, the long-latent capacity for language becomes manifest as a new survival adaptation. The superior consciousness and communication made possible by this adaptation allows the early human subset to survive. Perhaps the advantages incurred by this adaptation allowed early humans to overtake competing hominid species. Some aspects of this speculative scenario may have an analogous relationship to the present situation of modern humans.

Organisms and Change

Putting aside our species in particular for a moment, let's consider in general the nature of organisms and change. Organisms are extremely complex structures, living processes rather than fixed objects. The coherence of these extremely complex processes is constantly being threatened by various insults — attacks by other species, weather and climate change, cosmic rays, environmental toxins, etc. — that can degrade the coherence of the entire pattern/organism. Enough degradation of this coherence and the process may completely destabilize as in disease and especially in death, where there is the most radical apparent loss of coherence and complexity. Organisms, therefore, are conservative in nature, striving to maintain their inner coherence. Biologists refer to this drive toward maintaining inner coherence as "homeostasis." Similarly, a species seeks to ensure the survival and reproduction of its genome — a coherent genetic pattern changing relatively little between generations.

Human individuals are obviously also organisms. If we change our frame and look at the human species, or at the human psyche, we are still viewing an organismic phenomenon, an extremely complex living process. Both Freud and Jung agreed that the human psyche is essentially conservative. The psyche has its own homeostasis, a powerful drive to maintain its coherence and particular identity. Generally, it strives mightily to maintain that coherence and resist change. An organism will defend homeostasis even if that homeostasis is unsuccessful in some ways. A neurotic psyche, for example, will maintain its coherence, including pathological aspects that produce much suffering and that could be changed; proverbially, better the devil I know than the devil I don't know. Addicts remain in their addictions. People stay in their comfort zones even if they are suffocating in them. The human psyche is a complex and vulnerable structure living in an acutely stressful environment. Most people maintain their feelings of sanity and manufacture a socially acceptable identity by strained, tenuous repression of the irrational. All sorts of powerful, unconscious forces that don't fit into the model of themselves that society has trained them to create must be repressed. They may feel about change what a sentient house of cards might feel about gusts of wind.

The collective psyche of a society or culture can be even more resistant to change. And when such conservative psyches, individually or collectively, sense the approach of a singularity that will thoroughly punctuate their equilibrium, they perceive it as apocalyptic. And their perception may not be far off, as powerful change may require apocalyptic shocks. An analogy to such a threatening level of change can be drawn to tribal rites of initiation. Many tribal cultures take an adolescent and put him or her through life-threatening experiences. For example, the Amazonian Xircrin people put adolescents through an ordeal that involves venomous wasp stings. The wasp attack they must endure frequently results in blindness or death.[53] Perhaps the human species, sensing its adolescent crisis and need of initiation, is creating its own perilous rite by toxification of the environment.

Terence McKenna and the Attractor Point

Terence McKenna has written a number of fascinating books that make similar speculations about evolution. The parallels to the ideas I've reached through different means are so numerous that I can only conclude that we are either experiencing exactly the same form of mental illness or are perceiving the same truths. McKenna, for example, refers to what I call the Singularity as either "the end of history" or as "the strange attractor." McKenna adopted the term "strange attractor" from chaos

---

[53] http://findarticles.com/p/articles/mi_hb3120/is_4_76_n29082049/.

mathematics. A strange attractor, as McKenna uses the term, is an event in the future that is able to bend and warp causality toward it. Although from the point of view of linear time it is an event that has not yet occurred, its influence is pervasive.

I can't pretend to have much understanding of chaos mathematics, but an analogy occurs to me that what the strange attractor is for the life of the species, death is for the individual. Death is a strange attractor in the life of every individual. While we live, death is obviously a future event that has not occurred but which is inevitable. Our mortality, the fact that we move inexorably toward that attractor, shapes and influences every aspect of our lives. Also, although it is definite that we must pass into that attractor, the moment it will occur and the manner of our passing are not necessarily determined. The inevitability of the attractor is beyond our free will and individuality, but the time and manner of it are often influenced by our choices and personality. I can't choose whether or not I will die, but the way I care for my body, the life choices I make, the risks I choose, the option of suicide, all demonstrate that the attractor may not be fully determined outside of my will. Like entering a singularity in space, we also don't know for sure what will happen when we pass the event horizon of death. Spiritual teachings from many cultures and periods, NDEs, etc. suggest that death is a doorway. Conversely, neurological materialists view death as a dead end. As one put it to me, "It's just lights out and that's it." From the untranscendent vantage of the ego, the strange attractor of death is viewed as an apocalyptic extinction. Similarly, our species is heading toward a strange attractor. Many view it as extinction — unredeemed apocalypse. But others view it as a doorway. Where we go when we pass through that doorway may be greatly influenced by the choices that we make in life.

Approaching the Singularity

To engage another speculative area, let's consider what may happen as our species approaches the evolutionary event horizon. Our present world may be viewed as being in a rather tense position between realms of matter and spirit. Much in our world can be explained by Newtonian physics and a very mundane, mechanical model of reality. But those of us not actively trying to repress the atypical recognize that there are many white crows in our world. Anomalous events occur that can't quite be explained by coincidence or cause and effect. Numerous well-designed and controlled scientific experiments have demonstrated the reality of a number of parapsychological abilities and effects. I'm not going to try to recapitulate that evidence here, but instead will refer interested readers to the work of Dr. Dean Radin, especially his book *Entangled Minds*. Yes, as in any field, we can also find examples of purported effects that were the result of fraud and/or poor methodology, but if we have even a single authentic instance of one individual exhibiting telekinesis, communicating telepathically, reaching another person through their dreams, etc. — just one example in all of human history — then the door to extraordinary functioning and consciousness is thrown wide open for the whole species. And many of us can point toward a number of such events in our lives. A miraculous evolutionary capacity in human beings, that is mostly latent now, has been manifesting episodically for a long, long time. Certainly, as we've discussed at length in the section on NDEs, we have abundant evidence of paranormal function as people approach the individual event horizon of death.

X. Apocalypticism, Prophecy, Dreaming of the End of the World and the Singularity Archetype

My friend, the late Keith Haring, first gained popular attention with a form of guerrilla art he invented in the early Eighties in NYC. To prevent image bleed through, before new ad posters were put up in subways, the old ads would first have black paper pasted over them. These black surfaces became canvasses that Keith would draw on at high speed with white chalk.

> "Historically, it is chiefly in times of physical, political, economic and spiritual distress that men's eyes turn with anxious hope to the future, and when anticipations, utopias and apocalyptic visions multiply." — C.G. Jung (MGE 13)

> "There is no such thing in nature as an H-Bomb, that is all man's doing. We are the great danger. The psyche is the great danger." — C.G. Jung[54]

AS I discussed in the introduction, prophecy is the most unreliable of human enterprises. Dieting, falling in love, betting on the stock market or horses, all have far higher success rates than prophecy. Lottery tickets pay off at least as frequently as prophecies do. But of all types of prophecy there is one that from the perspective of linear time has been wrong 100% of the time. It is also the most popular type of prophecy —

---

[54] From Jung on Elementary Psychology (1979)

apocalypticism. Apocalypticism is a nearly universal, addictive habit of the human psyche.

Narratives about the end of the world have existed since the beginning of recorded history. The tale of Noah and the Flood, the Norse myth of Raganrok... the Hindu myths of recurring worldly annihilation and regeneration, and selected Zoroastrian, Babylonian, Sumerian, Buddhist, Islamic, Greek, Roman, African, Mayan, and Native American myths describe the destruction and transformation of the world, the struggle between the powers of good and evil, and the divinely determined destiny of humanity and the cosmos. As historian of religion Mircea Eliade notes, "The myth of the end of the world is of universal occurrence; it is already to be found among primitive peoples still at a paleolithic stage of culture... and it recurs in the great historic civilizations, Babyloninan Indian, Mexican and Greco-Roman" (*EOW* 5).

My friend, Rob Brezsny, in his revitalizing and wildly creative book, *Pronoia is the Anecdote to Paranoia: How the Whole Universe is Conspiring to Shower you with Blessings,*[55] provides a great summary of the millennia long popularity of apocalypticism:

LET'S EXPOSE THE OBVIOUS MIRACLES, Part 6

Many people alive today are convinced that our civilization is in a dark age, cut off from divine favor, and on the verge of collapse. But it's healthy to note that similar beliefs have been common throughout history.

As far back as 2800 BC, an unknown prophet wrote on an Assyrian clay tablet, "Our earth is degenerate in these latter days. There are signs that the world is speedily coming to an end." In the seventh century BC, many Romans believed Rome would suffer a cataclysm in 634 BC.

Around 300 BC, Hindus were convinced they lived in an "unfortunate time" known as the Kali Yuga — the lowest point in the great cosmic cycle. In 426 AD, the Christian writer Augustine mourned that this evil world was in its last days. According to the Lotharingian panic-mongers who lived more than a 1,000 years ago, human life on earth would end on March 25, 970.

Astrologers in 16th-century London calculated that the city would be destroyed by a great flood on February 1, 1524. American minister William Miller proclaimed the planet's "purification by fire" would occur in 1844. Anglican minister

---

[55] Rob's book is available for purchase at Amazon: http://bit.ly/Pronoia or Powells: http://bit.ly/PronoiaPowells.

Michael Baxter assured his followers that the Battle of Armageddon would take place in 1868. The Jehovah's Witnesses anticipated the End of Days in 1910, then 1914, then 1918, then 1925.

Oddly, no major prophets forecast cataclysm for the years between 1930 and 1945. Is there any time in history that was more deserving of being called the "Apocalypse" than that period? The Great Depression was the most widespread, long-lasting economic disaster ever. During World War II, 50 million civilians and 25 million soldiers were killed.

John Ballou Newbrough ("America's Greatest Prophet") wasn't impressed with the tragedy of that era. After the war, he promised mass annihilation and global anarchy for 1947.

The website "A Brief History of the Apocalypse" at tinyurl.com/yqb83n lists over 200 visions of doom that have spilled from the hysterical imaginations of various prophets in the last two millennia.

Our age may have more of these doomsayers per capita than previous eras, although the proportion of religious extremists among them has declined as more scientists, journalists, and storytellers have taken up the singing of humanity's predicted swan song.

In her book, <u>For the Time Being</u>, Annie Dillard concludes, "It is a weakening and discoloring idea that rustic people knew God personally once upon a time but that it is too late for us. There never was a more holy age than ours, and never a less. There is no whit less enlightenment under the tree by your street than there was under the Buddha's Bo tree."

I invite you to go sit under that tree by your street.

One of the reasons that prophecy has been so unreliable relates to the perpetual confusion in the human psyche between the inner world and the outer world. The confusion is only to be expected given that there is often a blurred boundary between inner and outer. Inner and outer converge through synchronicity and through many causative mechanisms such as self-fulfilling prophecies. The most classic confusion of inner and outer is interpersonal projection. We project some disowned part of ourselves on to another or others. For example, a man may project the disowned feminine aspect of his soul onto a beautiful woman he sees walking down the street. He looks at her and feels this sense of eternal recurrence — *she was meant for me! I've known her from other lifetimes!* In a sense, the perception is correct, this aspect of his soul is meant for him, and it has been with him from time immemorial. The incorrect part, and it can be disastrously incorrect, is the confusion of inner and outer, the acting out interpersonally of what is intrapsychic. Most interpersonal violence, as well as genocide and other forms of collective violence, occur in a state of shadow projection, where disowned and dreaded parts of oneself, or of the collective, are projected onto a despised other or another race, etc.

Anything with a strong emotional charge in the psyche, and especially if the charge is uncomfortable, will be projected outside. One of the strongest charges in most psyches is anxiety about death. A classic projection is for a person to feel his own mortal vulnerability, the imminence of his own death that may come at any time, and to attribute that feeling to the world: *I can feel it, this is all temporary, this world is going to end; I am living in the end times!* Again, the perception is correct except for the confusion of inner and outer. Every mortal is always living in end times, death is always imminent and even if any of the many possible causes of premature death are avoided, the years left are still only a one or two digit figure. The uncomfortable feeling of perilous temporal fragility must go somewhere and an end of world prophecy is like a lightning rod for this intensely uncomfortable inner charge.

Like a fractal or a hologram, the life cycle of the individual to some extent recapitulates the life cycle of the species. An individual has a certain limited life span before they cross the event horizon of death, and a species also has a limited life span before it becomes extinct. The average life span of a mammalian species is a million years. Because of the parallelism, it is easy for someone to confuse the imminence of personal death with collective eschaton. This confusion is also well motivated as it seems to displace much of the individual anxiety about death, which is usually faced alone, onto a "we're all in it together" general event that has strong elements of high drama and excitement associated with it. Instead of a feeling of powerlessness about the inevitability of one's own death, the prophet feels empowered by his sense that he has been privileged with secret knowledge withheld from the common person. Also, the ego is very concerned about its place in the social hierarchy and is appalled by the idea that it could cease to exist while others continue to live. If everyone checks out at once, however, then death involves no such social humiliation. Even better, if there is some sort of Rapture, where the ego is part of an elect that becomes immortal while others of the sort the ego doesn't like are annihilated or left behind to deal with the Antichrist and Armageddon, then personal anxiety about death gets channeled into an all-satisfying scenario. As Joseph M. Fesler writes, "Even Saint Thomas Aquinas — perhaps the greatest philosopher of the Middle Ages — suggested that part of the joy of being in Heaven was gazing down into the dark abyss of Hell and enjoying the eternal torment of the damned" (*MGE* 61).

For these powerful psychological reasons, prophecies of the end of the world usually seem to be conveniently scheduled to occur before the end of the prophet's expected lifespan, allowing the eschaton to upstage anxiety about personal death.

Many years after I formed this hypothesis, I heard of an episode that gave it anecdotal support. Elizabeth Steen, a woman some considered clairvoyant, predicted a massive earthquake would happen in the Bay Area on Aug 14, 1969. In copycat fashion other psychics began to predict a quake on the same day. Elizabeth was sincere in her prediction, and at great expense she relocated her family from the Bay Area to Spokane, Washington. On the predicted date there was no earthquake, but Elizabeth was not there to see the failed prophecy. According to the her obituary dated March 29, 1969 in the Spokesman Review, she died the day before at the age of 29 from a usually non fatal form of lupus.

It should not be surprising that personal death and eschaton should get conflated, displaced and otherwise mixed up with each other since both are faces of the Singularity Archetype. Depending on how the conflation works itself out, apocalypticism is the most significant way that the Singularity Archetype can pathologize in the individual and collective psyche. But sometimes, even in the darkness of apocalypticism, like the white yang dot in the black yin portion of the familiar yin-yang symbol, transcendent aspects of the Singularity Archetype shine through. This is particularly true when apocalyptic visions occur spontaneously rather than through cultural indoctrination. This light, hidden within visions of apocalypse seems to be part of the etymology of the word, "apocalypse." Its origin is from Old English which inherited it from Old French and ecclesiastical Latin which derived it from the Greek *apokalupsis*, from *apokaluptein 'uncover, reveal,'* from *apo- 'un-'* and *kaluptein 'to cover.'*

The Most Successful Prophets

Apocalyptic prophecy has the highest failure rate of what is already the most unreliable of human enterprises. Especially bad at prophecy are those who call themselves prophets and who are associated with fundamentalist religion. New Age prophets, psychics and seers are just as bad. There is one group, however, that has had some spectacular successes — fiction writers. It is probably no coincidence that science fiction writers have also given us our most penetrating visions of the Singularity Archetype. Fiction writers have enormous advantages over fundamentalists and professional seers. Their art gives them access to the collective unconscious, but they are not obliged to perceive visions through the rigidities of established traditions. Also, since they aren't invested in ego-identities like "psychic," "seer," and "prophet," they are less likely to take themselves too seriously and to feel obliged to pump out supposedly visionary product when they are uninspired. The fact that they usually don't know that they are doing prophecy can make them clearer channels by reducing ego involvement. For all these reasons, science fiction writers are great prophets of the Singularity Archetype.

In his extraordinarily perceptive essay, "An Arrow Through Time,"[56] cognitive scientist, philosopher and journalist Stephan A. Schwartz discusses the reliability of various forms of future-gazing. He singles out fiction writers for achieving the most remarkable success. For example, he points out Edgar Allan Poe's 1838 novel, *The Narrative of Arthur Gordon Pym [pseud.] of Nantucket.* In the novel, Poe "describes the shipwreck of the brig Grampus, including an account of three sailors and a cabin boy lost at sea in a small boat. The desperate sailors kill and eat the cabin boy, whose name is Richard Parker. In 1978 *The Times* in London ran a contest on coincidence, that was judged by Arthur Koestler. The winning entry was a true story of a uncannily similar shipwreck — three sailors and a cabin boy escape in a small boat, and the boy is killed and eaten. The boy's name: Richard Parker. When the real sailors who had been caught were tried for their crime Poe's book was discussed at their trial."

Schwartz also provides an interesting history and summary of a rejected manuscript Jules Verne wrote in 1863, entitled *Paris in the Twentieth Century.* Verne's publisher, in correspondence discovered with the manuscript, felt it was too unbelievable and would be a commercial disaster. The neglected manuscript became a kind of time capsule sealed in a forgotten safe. According to Schwartz,

> "Verne put it in a safe where it remained forgotten for more than a century. It was re-discovered in the 1990s by an heir who found the safe in a barn on a Verne family country estate that had come down to him. When the safe was opened by a locksmith, the manuscript and the correspondence were found. *Paris in the Twentieth Century* was finally published in France in 1994."

The protagonist of the novel is a sixteen-year-old boy who has graduated with a major in literature and the classics, but finds that this course of study is useless in the futuristic world of 1960, where only business and technology are valued. Among the more specific predictions, Verne describes a geometric, modern centerpiece built for the Louvre in Paris. In 1989 a modern, geometric, glass-and-steel pyramid structure designed

---

by architect I.M. Pei was unveiled in the courtyard plaza of the Louvre. It is now a Parisian landmark.[57]

Schwartz summarizes some of the other extraordinarily accurate predictions Verne makes in this novel:

"Verne describes 20th Century Paris as having a skyline dominated by a large metalwork tower. The streets are paved. Technology and business dominate Parisian life, and women are 'Americanized' as is the French language, which is filled with adapted American words. The horses that jammed and polluted Parisian streets in 1863, are gone, replaced by vehicles of metal. Average people work for big corporations (uninvented in their modern sense at the time he was writing). They sit in offices and work at computers, and send paperwork to one another by facsimile machines. Yes, he even uses the word."

The most famous case of literary prediction is *Futility*, an 1898 novella by Morgan Robertson, published fourteen years before the sinking of the Titanic in April of 1912. *Futility* features an ocean liner named "Titan," which sinks in the North Atlantic after striking an iceberg. The Titan was the largest craft afloat, seen as the greatest work of men and considered unsinkable. Due to the hubris of its designers, it carries an extremely deficient number of lifeboats resulting in a tragic loss of life when it sinks on an April night.[58]

Schwartz provides a table listing some of the main similarities between the novel and the actual incident:

	TITAN	TITANIC
Fatal Sailing Date:	April	April
Flag:	English	English
Length (in Feet):	800	882
Number of Propellers:	3	3
Top Speed (in knots):	25	24
Water-tight Bulkheads:	19	15
Passenger Capacity:	3,000	3,000
Passengers Aboard:	2,000	2,200
Number of Lifeboats:	20	24
Cause of Sinking:	Struck Iceberg	Struck Iceberg
Side of Vessel Breached:	Starboard	Starboard

---

[57] http://en.wikipedia.org/wiki/Paris_in_the_Twentieth_Century
[58] http://en.wikipedia.org/wiki/Futility,_or_the_Wreck_of_the_Titan.

The Nineteenth Century's other most famous science fiction writer, H.G. Wells, had, like his French colleague, Jules Vernes, some amazing predictive successes. As Schwartz notes,

"In his various novels Wells predicted gas warfare and tanks, aerial bombardment and nuclear war, as well as industrial robots. But if you ask scientists what impresses them most about Wells' predictions they say it is the infrared lasers in *War of the Worlds*. First published in 1898, the same year as *Futility*, the story centers on the invasion of earth by aliens and contains this description of the aliens' principal weapons system: '...this intense heat they project in a parallel beam against any object they choose, by means of a polished parabolic mirror of unknown composition, much as the parabolic mirror of a lighthouse projects a beam of light... However it is done, it is certain that a beam of heat is the essence of the matter. Heat, and invisible, instead of visible, light. Whatever is combustible flashes into flame at its touch, lead runs like water, it softens iron, cracks and melts glass, and when it falls upon water, incontinently that explodes into steam.'"

Schwartz continues:

"Writing as Harrison James, Rusk tells the story of the kidnap of a young college student named Patricia, daughter of a wealthy and prominent right wing figure, by an angry black man leading a terrorist gang. So close were the similarities that when Patricia Hearst was kidnapped in 1974, Rusk received a visit from the FBI, and the book – as with Poe's *Pym* – came up in the trial. *Grove Press* later reissued the book with transcriptions of Patricia Hearst's testimony and explicitly focused on the similarities between what it called 'Fiction before Fact.'"

Schwartz concludes his essay with an instance of fiction writers and movie directors being employed to predict the future by the U.S. military:

"After 9/11 occurred, *Variety* reported that US military intelligence experts invited a group of screen writers and directors who specialized in thrillers to, as one source told the magazine, focus 'on the short-term threats.' Included in the group were Steven De Souza (*Die Hard*) and David Engelbach (*McGyver*), and directors Joseph Zito (*Delta Force One, Missing in Action*, and, *The Abduction*) and Spike Jonze. The virtual meeting took place by cyberlink at the University of Southern California's Institute for Creative Technologies, formed in 1999 at the US military's initiative, to develop virtual training programs for servicemen. The group talked about "possible terrorist targets in the United States and how best to confront terrorist threats, in the wake of the September 11 terror attacks against the World Trade Center and the Pentagon."

Someone who probably should have been part of the panel, but is not mentioned in Schwartz's essay, is thriller-writer Catherine Coulter. The *CLG Newsletter* reports:

"An FBI thriller, *The Edge*, by Catherine Coulter, was published in 1999. The book is part of Coulter's ongoing 'The FBI Thriller Series.' *The Edge* reached number six on *The New York Times* Best-Seller List[59] for fiction on the 5th of September 1999.

"Given the contents of the book, one wonders whether or not the FBI deserves credit for collaborating on the plot. A scan of Coulter's thriller includes the following sentence on page 19: *'Maybe I had a chance not to be, in the Counter-Terrorism section; particularly after 9/11 when the world had changed.'*

"*The Edge* was copyrighted by Catherine Coulter in 1999. The paperback version was released in 2000."[60]

Positive Encounters with the Singularity Archetype

Something I've noticed is that positive encounters with the Singularity Archetype tend to occur for people who are dealing with apocalyptic circumstances in their waking lives. These encounters will often occur during the dreamtime. For example, on August 24th, 1945, three weeks after surviving the bombing of Hiroshima, a Japanese man had the following dream:

"I was in Tokyo after the great earthquake and around me were decomposing bodies heaped in piles, all of whom were looking right at me. I saw an eye sitting in the palm of a girl's hand. Suddenly it turned and leaped into the sky and then came flying back toward me, so that looking up I could see a great bare eyeball, bigger than life hovering over my head, staring point-blank at me. I was powerless to move. I awakened short of breath and my heart pounding."[61]

Jung believed that dreams were mostly compensatory, making up for defects and one-sidedness in the waking attitude and life. After witnessing an actual apocalypse, the feminine appears as a girl holding an eye in the palm of her hand. What is especially fascinating is that it is

[59] http://www.hawes.com/1999/1999-09-05.pdf
[60] http://www.legitgov.org/FBI-Thriller-Published-1999-References-911.
[61] Hill, Michael Ortiz. *Dreaming the End of the World — Apocalypse as a Rite of Passage.* 2nd Ed. Putnam, CT: Spring Publications, INC, 2004. 49.

the eye, the embodiment of the Logos Beheld aspect of the Singularity Archetype, that becomes a spontaneously occurring symbol of the godhead and of collective consciousness.

Michael Ortiz Hill, who recorded the above dream in his book, *Dreaming of the End of the World: Apocalypse as a Rite of Passage,* pointed out some other dreams and statements that reveal the convergence of apocalypse and singularity as life-affirming metamorphosis.

For example, William Laurence called the rumblings of the Trinity explosion the "first cry of a newborn world" (19).

In his memoirs, Curtis LeMay, who coordinated the World War II air combat over Japan, the bombing of Hiroshima and Nagasaki, wrote of "the nuclear baby clinging as a fierce child against its mother's belly" (19). LeMay was also the strongest advocate for all out nuclear war with Russian during the Cuban Missile Crisis.

Even more extraordinary is the following dream:

> "There is a distinct crater left by the Bomb, and it is filled with water. We walk around the crater with a kind of awe — there is an odd sort of beauty attached to it. A mother is baptizing or drowning her baby in the water of the crater. I am aware of the intense radioactivity that must be in the area and can't resolve whether she is baptizing the infant or killing it. There is a deep sense of mystery to this...

> "Then, in the dream, a voice ordered, 'Make a child.' I refused and yelled back, 'I can't. I'm forty-six; there are no facilities left to test for birth defects; I've had cancer; I've had two children; the world is destroyed. I cannot, will not make a child!' The voice remained kind but adamant: 'New life,' it demanded; 'New life!'" (57-58).

White Raven Rising — Dream of Apocalypse and Transcendence

One morning in the summer of 2004, I was talking to a small group of people about their dreams. We were at a wilderness gathering in the Modoc National Forest in Northeastern California. It was a high desert, perhaps nine thousand feet of elevation and uncommonly beautiful. It was my first morning at this gathering, and I remember the air was scented by high desert plants, especially sage. As the conversation was breaking up, a man in his early forties (we'll call him Kyle), who had been listening attentively, asked if he could speak to me in private about a dream that would not be appropriate to share with the group. I assumed the dream had some sexual content that Kyle felt embarrassed about sharing with the others. I followed him to a secluded spot where we sat surrounded by sage brush.

Kyle told me that he had been in a branch of the U.S. armed services and was employed as a mine sweeper in Nicaragua in the 1980s. After coming out of the service his life was in a terrible state and he was suicidal. He had experienced some horrible things during his time in Nicaragua and was suffering from post traumatic stress disorder. One experience in particular haunted both his waking life and his dreams.

A guerrilla group had apparently planted mines in a school yard. A couple of small boys had wandered into the yard during the weekend when school was not in session and were killed by a mine. Kyle was called in to deal with the situation. The boys had been dead for two days in the tropics and the bodies were in about as horrifying a condition as they could be. Kyle removed the mines and felt obliged to rescue the bodies so that the family of the boys could bury them. He vomited several times before he could summon his will to go out there and wrap what was left of the boys in a couple of blankets.

During the depth of his suicidal phase after returning from Nicaragua, Kyle had a series of six nearly identical nightmares. In the nightmares he would be at the school yard and he would hear one of the boys calling to him for help. In each case he would get to the boy and find him in a terrible state, a state where no one could possibly be calling for help, and he would hear the death rattle, the characteristic sound of a body's final exhalation, something he had also witnessed during his time in Nicaragua.

Each time Kyle would awaken from the nightmare in a cold sweat and he felt like the nightmares were trying to drive him to suicide. The seventh dream begins exactly like the other six, he gets to the dismembered boy and hears the death rattle, but this time a white raven is spiraling down from the sky. The raven lands on the boy's head and the boy, suddenly intact, gets up and begins dancing. The white raven also does a strange dance. Kyle showed me with his arms how the raven held its wings out and did a kind of dance like a shaman would do. After the dance, the white raven looks at Kyle and says, "I think you ought to see this."

The white raven flies up in a spiraling manner and as it spirals above him, Kyle feels himself being pulled up, as if the spiraling were a tornado. Kyle finds himself elevated above the earth, and he has an experience of indescribable mystical transcendence. He is no longer bound in time and finds himself experiencing eternity, as well as a direct and ineffable sense of a harmonious meaning and reason for everything. The state he describes seems to be a spontaneous experience of what

Hindus and Buddhists called "Samadhi." The experience leaves him permanently transformed; the suicidal despair is gone and he is able to set his life on a positive course.

Kyle had one of the most direct encounters possible with the Singularity Archetype. In the depths of the dark night of the soul he experienced a true apocalypse (an unveiling) at the end of time. The end of time does not have to mean the end of the world, history or the species. In this case it means the end of linear time, which on the scale of an individual life could be a transcendent samadhi-type experience, a shattering dark night of the soul or the event horizon of death. The singularity archetype pulls Kyle into its transcendent spiral at the "end of time" where linear time gives way to eternity. He emerges on the other side of the event horizon permanently transformed.

Dreams about apocalypse that contain the transcendent qualities of the Singularity Archetype do not, of course, require apocalyptic waking circumstances. In the introductory chapter, I gave the example of a young man who dreamt of what seemed the end of the world:

> The sky is turning very dark. Underground tremors occur and escalate to where the earth seems to be shaking itself to pieces. There is fire and lightening and it seems to be the end of the world. Then everything calms down. Sunlight breaks through the dark clouds and illuminates a large white eagle, which comes spiraling down from above. In its talons it holds a golden egg with a glowing aura. Carefully, it deposits this egg in a nest at the top of a great tree.

I met the artist Brenda Ferrimani at a Jeremy Taylor dream seminar in 2007 where we discussed the dream that inspired this extraordinary painting. Here is Brenda's description of the her dream:

"The painting retells the dream I had the night after 9/11, and is the reason why I have chosen the Trade Towers burning as the backdrop to this work.

"I am in my bed at night. I hear coyotes in the distance. There's a window at the foot of the bed and a light in the sky, shinning in. I sense there's something out there. I move toward the window and as I do I am sucked out the window, and I begin falling into endless darkness! I am falling

Fall into Fear
Original Painting 6' x 4 acrylic medium Prints available upon request to the artist
http://brendaferrimanidreamart.com/Artwork/FallFear.html

down, down into the deep darkness. I feel like screaming, but then I remind myself I am dreaming. At this point I become lucid. I can see and feel everything slow, and I stop falling. I ask, 'What's out there for me?' I demand, 'Show me! Show Me!' Then, I begin to move upward. I see the stars as i am traveling up to the heavens. Then huge metal discs with alien writing start moving up around me. I yell once more, 'Show Me!' — I even say this out loud in waking reality and I wake myself up..."

The descent into apocalyptic darkness causes the artist, a seeker of visions, to demand that it be a true apocalypse — an unveiling. Her demand "Show me!" is rewarded with a Logos Beheld revelation. The metal discs could have many levels of meaning, but the alien writing suggests that they are linguistics intentions made visible and concrete.

The next section will give a couple of other very interesting examples of this type of dream where dark and light, apocalypse and evolutionary singularity arrive together in the dreamtime.

Genevieve's Dreams about the Singularity Archetype

In 2009, an hour or so after I finished an extensive revision of an earlier work on the Singularity Archetype, I received two dreams sent to me via email from a friend, Genevieve, a successful software engineer in her mid-twenties. These dreams seem to me like an epilogue sent by the collective conscious, and an update on the Singularity Archetype.

Genevieve has had a long-term interest in the paranormal, exposure to writings about Mayan prophecy, and has also read a number of my writings. From one point of view, she could be viewed as a hopelessly contaminated dreamer of the Singularity Archetype because she has so much waking-life influence from related material. There are a few reasons why I don't think this disqualifies Genevieve dreams. One is that if we disqualify her, then we would also be disqualifying ourselves. Any reader who has read this far has heard about the Singularity Archetype and would similarly have to disqualify any related dreams that they might have. Also, from the contamination point of view, every dreamer is disqualified because everyone has been exposed to and influenced by any number of forms of apocalypticism. The dominant forms of apocalyptic influence are: the grim ecological point of view, religious fundamentalism, the dystopian science-fiction view and New Age prophecy. Unless you've grown up off planet, the likelihood is that you have been influenced, in one way or another, by all of the above.

Another reason for including Genevieve's dreams is that waking consciousness is usually not in control of the dreamtime. Dreams often confound waking consciousness.

Another disclaimer before proceeding, since this will be an extended case of me interpreting someone else's dreams it might be worth stating the obvious. Dream interpretation is highly subjective. One human psyche is interpreting the artifact of another human psyche, or of its own psyche, and that's as subjective as it gets. Subjectivity is the baseline for all dream interpretation. I agree with Jeremy Taylor's idea of "projective dream work," which begins with the premise that all dream interpretation is projection. In projective dream work, every interpretation begins with the acknowledgment, "If this were my dream..." The interpreter will often narrate parts of the dream in the first person as a further acknowledgment that what they are interpreting is their own experience of the dream.

Subjective material is too valuable to exclude from consideration. If we acknowledge the subjectivity of our point of view, and attempt to discern things as rigorously as we can, we may gain priceless insights by looking into the subjective. Acknowledging the subjective is not the same as being a relativist; it does not mean that every point view is merely the conditioned product of shifting cultural context. Looking into subjective material means that we could very well be fooled, deceived and deluded, but it does not exclude the possibility that we may also discern crucial truths. And many of those crucial truths are never going to be accessible to the person who thinks they can exclude subjectivity from their worldview. They will also not be available to the person who is not discerning in their relation to subjective material. If you are credulous, literalist, absolutist, or just plain sloppy in your approach to subjective material, it is very likely to swallow you whole. My assumption is that you, the reader, are skeptical, and that you are examining my speculative thoughts, and everyone's speculative thoughts, from your inner truth sense and discerning point of view.

Dream 1: Ray of Light

Genevieve first dream, which she titled "Ray of Light," occurred on January 5, 2009:

> "So first of all, I woke up at 3:23 this morning, no idea what awoke me, but I was having a boring dream about trying to match items from an Avon catalog that I had picked out the night before... I could not fall back asleep for some time... but finally did, then had this crazy dream:

> "I was in my bedroom where I grew up... I think in the dream, my boyfriend was with me... but I looked out the window, it was nighttime, and I saw all this crazy shit going on in the sky. Looked like a meteor shower — orange lights streaking all over the place... I kept watching and then could see what looked like Saturn maybe? All huge...

> "Then I noticed that there were these Asian-looking people sitting outside my window. They didn't seem to notice me, but some of the women were naked and had lots of tattoos covering their bodies. They looked tired. We ducked down, not really wanting them to see us.

> "I remember walking around the house trying to figure out what time it was, but all the clocks said different things. I think my boyfriend said it was 12 — and I thought he meant 12 noon and that I was late for work. Still it was dark out and I couldn't figure out what time it really was.

"Then at some point after that, I looked out the window again, and there was this giant ray of light that shone directly on me. It was an immense amount of energy — and when I tried to talk, I couldn't speak — I just made a sort of gagging sound. All of this dream seemed very real. I just sort of sat there, with my eyes closed, and absorbed the energy from the ray. My whole body felt tingly and energized — it was a really amazing feeling. It was like I knew it was updating my genetics, activating things in me. I just breathed deep and tried to relax — but could not speak.

"After the ray released me, I found myself in a coffee shop with a bunch of people. It still seemed like nighttime. I started talking to the people and they told me about an experience they had just had that was totally like mine! They had also experienced the big ray of light and not being able to speak, etc."

"Ray of Light," Interpreted

So first of all, I woke up at 3:23 this morning, no idea what awoke me, but I was having a boring dream about trying to match items from an Avon catalog that I had picked out the night before...

In her dream narrative, Genevieve gives us the exact hour and minute that she wakes up. Three o'clock in the morning is traditionally considered the "witching hour." The number 23 has many mystical associations.[62] These mystical associations inspired a major Hollywood film, *The Number 23*, starring Jim Carrey, which was released in 2007. At this mystical time in the waking life, Genevieve wakes up from a dream that reflects and amplifies the mundane world where one gets immersed in everything an Avon catalog would represent — materialism, consumerism, the cosmetic approach that emphasizes the persona and the world of surfaces and appearances. It is as if, through the law of opposites, the mundane is needed to potentiate a revelation of the divine.

I could not fall back asleep for some time... but finally did, then had this crazy dream:

I was in my bedroom where I grew up... I think in the dream, my boyfriend was with me... but I looked out the window, it was nighttime, and I saw all this crazy shit going on in the sky. Looked like a meteor shower — orange lights streaking all over the place... I kept watching and then could see what looked like Saturn maybe? All huge...

---

[62] http://en.wikipedia.org/wiki/23_Enigma

Genevieve is in familiar circumstances but then she sees and experiences some anomalous events:

> *Then I noticed that there were these Asian looking people sitting outside my window. They didn't seem to notice me, but some of the women were naked and had lots of tattoos covering their bodies. They looked tired.*

I emailed Genevieve a question about this: "The tribal people are naked and tattooed — did they seem tribal or more like tattooed modern persons who were undressed? Did their tiredness seem to be from exertions, as if they were weary from a long hike, or was the tiredness more from temperament, like they were sluggish, low energy people. What's your sense of the tiredness?"

Genevieve's response: "They were more like tattooed modern persons who were undressed. Their tiredness seemed more from temperament, like they were low energy people, but possibly also from a long life of hard work that had worn them out."

> *We ducked down, not really wanting them to see us.*

Question emailed to Genevieve: "What were you anxious about happening if they saw you? Was it just out of an instinctive urge toward privacy, or did you think they might be dangerous or solicit you as beggars or what?"

Genevieve's response: "I think it was somewhat out of an instinctive urge toward privacy, but also because I thought they might be dangerous — and being directly outside my bedroom window, looking at us, I was sort of freaked out."

> *I remember walking around the house trying to figure out what time it was, but all the clocks said different things... I think my boyfriend said it was 12 — and I thought he meant 12 noon and that I was late for work. Still it was dark out and I couldn't figure out what time it really was.*

Linear time has been irrealized, but there is still the pull of the mundane and anxiety about being late for work. Time depends on perspective and her boyfriend apparently thinks it's midnight, and Genevieve thinks it's noon.

> *Then at some point after that, I looked out the window again, and there was this giant ray of light that shone directly on me. It was an immense amount of energy — and when I tried to talk, I couldn't speak — I just made a sort of gagging sound. All of this dream seemed very real. I just sort of sat there, with my eyes closed, and absorbed the energy from the ray. My whole body felt tingly and energized — it was a really amazing feeling. It*

was like I knew it was updating my genetics, activating things in me. I just breathed deep and tried to relax — but could not speak.

The emphasis on not being able to speak is very interesting. We have already discussed nonverbal communication and a visual telepathy as key aspects of the Singularity Archetype. Although, the new means of communication is not clearly realized here, we do find that the old means of communication is shut down. Genevieve discovers that she is mute while her genetics are being updated by a ray of light. Apparently the evolutionary upgrade makes speech unnecessary.

After the ray released me, I found myself in a coffee shop with a bunch of people. It still seemed like nighttime. I started talking to the people and they told me about an experience they had just had that was totally like mine! They had also experienced the big ray of light and not being able to speak, etc.

That the other people had the parallel experience, even if Genevieve wasn't aware of them while it was happening, suggests a communal telepathy as well as a global evolutionary metamorphosis.

Dream 2: Message from the Stars

Genevieve's second dream, "Message from the Stars," came to her on February 18, 2009:

Had another one of these dreams again last night. They are always very vivid, very intense, very colorful.

I was in what was supposedly my house and several of my friends were there, but in another room. It was nighttime, and dark enough out that I could see the stars well just by looking out my big picture window in the back of the house. I must have been looking at just the right moment, because suddenly, from the middle of the sky, the light started to get brighter, and then like a laser, a beam of light shot out of space and towards my right.

It seemed like it was very close, and that it had hit the ground. The sky was very lit up from this in amazing colors. I ran through the house to the front of the house, yelling to my friends what I had just seen. When I looked outside, it was striking right in front of my house, leaving a huge and deep gash in the front yard.

While the beam was striking right there, in front of my eyes, there were all sorts of visual messages I was receiving.

They depicted what felt like a warning. There were images of a cartoon devilish character, and what felt like destruction, but at the very end an image of a seedling, or of grass regrowing.

I felt like it was telling me that I need to meditate, that my very survival depends on it. I felt as if I didn't take heed of this warning, I would not survive. I vowed to meditate more.

After the blast had concluded, we were looking at some art pieces that were on my wall. Apparently I had photographed them with a camera phone before the blast, and we could now compare them to what they looked like now. They were both reddish (like natural clay red) and made of something like a clay material. The first one had been a depiction of Jesus, or something like that, not the typical Jesus picture though, but more of a tribal depiction. The clay was now blemished as if from extreme heat, and bubbly on the surface.

There was another clay piece which depicted a Mayan god, and had before been in a somewhat peaceful pose. It was now taking a more active stance. A feather in its hand had transformed into a knife, ready to strike.

The atmosphere felt intense, and as I looked out to the sky again there were brilliant nebula clouds of colors forming, flashing and fading. All sorts of activity and it was brilliant. I noticed in the room where I was, were only some of my younger friends. Throughout the house there were two other rooms with older, and yet older groups of people. I tried to urge the younger of the two groups to come and see what was going on in the sky.

After sometime, maybe it was the next day, because it seemed light outside again, I went out to the front to examine the damage that had occurred to the yard. The yard was right up against a street, and the gash was the entire length of my house. It was only in front of my house — as if the message had been directed solely at me, however it was mostly parallel to the street. There was no grass, it was just like hardened dirt and there were all these mysterious shapes carved out of it. Each of the shapes seemed to be one of the parts of the messages I had felt I received.

"Message from the Stars," Interpreted

While the beam was striking right there, in front of my eyes, there were all sorts of visual messages I was receiving.

Now it becomes explicit that the beam of light includes visual telepathy. The beam is literally the "Logos Beheld" and, in particular, the Logos Beheld as a central aspect of the Singularity Archetype.

> *They depicted what felt like a warning. There were images of a cartoon devilish character, and what felt like destruction, but at the very end an image of a seedling, or of grass regrowing.*

Here we have a very concise description of the Singularity Archetype in a single sentence. We see the wing of Satan again, the devil, but it is cartoonish. The message seems to be that the singularity may seem sinister, but only from the childish ego-bound perspective. Still, there are warnings of a great destruction, but with the strong implication that this is necessary for rebirth.

> *I felt like it was telling me that I need to meditate, that my very survival depends on it. I felt as if I didn't take heed of this warning, I would not survive. I vowed to meditate more.*

In many apocalyptic visions and projections there are cataclysmic events in which a great many human souls are unsheathed from their bodies. For example, the extra-Biblical evangelical expectation of the Rapture involves an apocalypse where only the Christian elect are relieved of their imperiled mortal bodies and whisked away to heaven in glorified bodies. A technological materialist like Ray Kurzweil may imagine an ecological apocalypse where only those who have been lucky enough to have their consciousness downloaded into a quantum computer survive. Essentially, the archetypal expectation is that only those able to transcend the corporeal body survive, and they do so because they have perfected their spirit body (or their "information body," if you are a salvation-via-technology singularity theorist). There is a very long tradition, in many spiritual disciplines, that only those who have learned to transcend their egos, especially through the practice of meditation, are sufficiently prepared to cross the event horizon of personal death, and we've already discussed that personal death parallels collective eschaton. Also, meditation is a practice highly related to the Logos Beheld idea that the evolutionary transformation will involve a sudden transition from verbal communication to visual telepathy because meditation is all about quieting the internal chatter, the psyche's tendency to default into word-based thinking.

> *After the blast had concluded, we were looking at some art pieces that were on my wall. Apparently I had photographed them with a camera phone before the blast, and we could now compare them to what they looked like now. They were both reddish (like natural clay red) and made of something like a clay material. The first one had been a depiction of Jesus, or something like that, not the typical Jesus picture though, but*

*more of a tribal depiction. The clay was now blemished as if
from extreme heat, and bubbly on the surface.*

Questions emailed to Genevieve: "Can you say more about the Jesus art
piece? Did it look tribal before or only after? What does it mean that he
looked tribal? Did he look more Semitic than the conventional Nordic
Jesus? How was he dressed and exactly what did he look like? How did
you feel about the changes to the art piece? Did it feel like it was partly
ruined or that it had been altered in an interesting way or what?"

Genevieve's response: "Well, it didn't really look anything like Jesus at
all. I guess I just knew in the dream that that was what it was. It was a
Greyish or reddish clay material, all one color, and it was textured. It
always looked tribal — both before and after — and by tribal I mean that
it looked like an Indian — a guy in a headband with very Mayan-like
features. After the comet/star landed, the heat from it made the clay
bubble, so the texture was no longer as smooth. I didn't feel like it was
ruined; I was just intrigued at what had happened to it, and the
transformation felt somewhat symbolic — because there wasn't any other
heat damage anywhere else in the house that I recall."

This mutated representation of Jesus is emblematic of the strange
intermingling of prophetic traditions happening today. It seems to be a
product of multicultural hybridization and it is messianic, but not
necessarily in the way that any one tradition might anticipate. Also,
unlike a static tradition, the emblem mutates with the cosmic trigger
event. A possible implication is that this is a time where one static
mythology no longer serves, but where there is a spontaneous eruption of
mutating, hybridized mythologies. Genevieve, like so many today, is a
cultural and ethnic hybrid, half Jewish/ half Catholic, and with no
particular commitment to either of these Abrahamic faiths. She seems,
like many open-minded seekers of this era, to be looking for insight from
whatever fields — science, spirituality, paranormal studies — and from
whatever cultures — Abrahamic, tribal, Mayan — that have relevance in
an unprecedented time. These once very disparate elements hybridize,
bubbling together in an alchemical cauldron. The signs of heating,
especially since they are not observed elsewhere, indicate the imperative
need for our prophetic traditions to be reheated and hybridized, to be
returned to the kiln of the unconscious and reformed.

*There was another clay piece which depicted a Mayan god, and
had before been in a somewhat peaceful pose. It was now taking
a more active stance. A feather in its hand had transformed into
a knife, ready to strike.*

Question emailed to Genevieve: "What feeling did you get from the
change in the Mayan clay piece? Did it seem threatening and ominous or
just different?"

Genevieve's response: "It didn't seem threatening, just different, perhaps a bit ominous."

Mayan prophecy in particular seems activated and ready to be fulfilled. The sense of Mayan prophecy as about to strike in some aggressive way would seem to be influenced by popular culture rather than anything authentically related to ancient Mayan culture.[63]

Throughout the house there were two other rooms with older, and yet older groups of people. I tried to urge the younger of the two to come and see what was going on in the sky.

Question emailed to Genevieve: "What was the age range of each group? What did these people seem like? Did the two groups seem different besides their age?"

Genevieve's response: "The age range of the 'older' group was probably mid 40s - 60s and the group of even older people was probably 65-80. They seemed like fairly normal people, although I recall some of them (in the 'older' group) seemed a little overweight. The older they were, the slower they seemed to be and to respond. Like I said I was trying to urge the groups to come look at the sky, and the older they were the more reluctant they were to come. Those were the only apparent differences between the groups — that the younger group seemed less 'stuck'."

The ages of the two groups may be both metaphorical and have something interesting to say about actual generations. Age may be a somewhat metaphorical representation of "stuckness" and of being hardened into obsolescent patterns of adaptation. Non-metaphorically, it is certainly a general psychological truth that aging typically makes neurotic symptoms more rigid and sharply defined. Though not a hard-and-fast rule, as a general trend people tend to become more stuck in their ways as they age. But what is also interesting are the specific age ranges given for the two groups. A group that as of 2009 is in their mid 40s to 60s precisely defines the Baby Boomer Generation (usually thought of as those born 1945-1964). Boomers, as a generation, were famously open to the cosmic, the unusual, the psychedelic, and the culturally exotic. There was a huge generation gap that existed between the boomers and the two preceding generations. Those who are 65-80 as of 2009 are called the Silent Generation and are thought to be a particularly conservative generation. They were too young to fight in World War Two and too old for the most part to participate in the revolutionary events of the Sixties. With the defeat of John McCain in the 2008 presidential election, the Silent Generation became the first

---

[63] For my full treatment of Mayan prophecy in popular culture, see "Carnival 2012: A Psychological Study of the 2012 Phenomenon and the 22 Classic Pitfalls and Blindspots of Esoteric Research," available at ZapOracle.com.

generation in U.S. history not to be represented by a president. It is interesting that in Genevieve's dream they seem the most reluctant to be involved in revolutionary change.[64]

> *After sometime, maybe it was the next day, because it seemed light outside again, I went out to the front to examine the damage that had occurred to the yard. The yard was right up against a street, and the gash was the entire length of my house. It was only in front of my house — as if the message had been directed solely at me, however it was mostly parallel to the street. There was no grass, it was just like hardened dirt and there were all these mysterious shapes carved out of it. Each of the shapes seemed to be one of the parts of the messages I had felt I received.*

There could be an instructive message here about the nature of archetypal and prophetic visions. It feels like the message is directed solely to her, but it also runs parallels to the street. Running parallel to the street suggests that the message is relevant to the neighbors and therefore the collective in general. Archetypal/prophetic visions feel particularly directed toward the individual psyche that experiences them, and yet they also parallel the collective psyche. The implication is that Genevieve's dreams may contain meanings that parallel the evolutionary predicament of our species.

Apocalypse and Metamorphosis in the Bible

"And from then on there will be nothing corruptible." — Enoch 69:27

Apocalyptic visions in the Bible erupt right out of the collective unconscious. As Norman Cohn points out in *Cosmos, Chaos and the World to Come: The Ancient Roots of Apocalyptic Faith,* "To a much greater extent than the prophets, an apocalyptist commonly received his revelations in visual form, whether as dreams or as ecstatic visions. [...] Often the events that were revealed to him were disguised in symbols and allegories" (164).

Apocalyptic visions, Cohn points out, were typically sourced in more intimate and visual ways, a perceived contact with a radiant angel rather than the invisible voice of God:

> "Unlike the prophets the apocalyptists were not spoken to by God but through the intermediary of an angel who may help explain the meaning of the visions and guarantee their truth. Daniel: 'I found myself on the bank of the great river, that is the Tigris: I looked up and saw a man clothed in linen with a belt of

---

[64] For more on generational differences, go to http://www.fourthturning.com/.

gold from Ophir round his waist. His body gleamed like topaz, his face shone like lightning, his eyes flamed like torches, his arms and feet sparkled like a disc of bronze; and when he spoke his voice sounded like the voice of a multitude. I, Daniel, alone saw the vision, while those who were near me did not see it... I heard the sound of his words and, when I did so, I fell prone to the ground in a trance'" (165).

Chapter 12 of the Book of Daniel, which was retroactively post-dated back four centuries to be attributed to the ancient, mythic figure of Daniel, is where we first get a prophecy of a metamorphosis into glorified bodies: "Chapter 12 — the last in the book — closes with a remarkable prophecy: 'many of those who sleep in the dust of the earth will wake, some to everlasting life and some to the reproach of eternal abhorrence.' This passage has no parallel in the Hebrew Bible: it marks a decisive break within the traditional Israelite notion of earth." (165)

"The fate that awaited the 'wise leaders' was more wonderful still. It is indicated in chapter 12: 'The wise leaders shall shine like the bright vault of heaven, and those who have guided the people in the true path shall be like stars for ever and ever.' Admittedly, some scholars have interpreted these images as mere metaphors, signifying no more than that the glory of these men's achievements will remain for evermore. Yet there is abundant evidence, from the following three centuries, in Jewish and Christian sources, that exceptionally holy individuals expected, at the End, to receive garments of glory that would make them resplendent and fiery. The apocalyptist is surely foretelling that he and his fellows will exist for ever as super human beings, angel-like, star-like" (175).

The Book of Jubilees forsees a day when aging will be transcended:

And the days will begin to grow many and increase amongst the children of men,
Till their days draw nigh to nine thousand years,
And to a greater numbers of years than [before] was the number of days.
And there will be no old man
Nor one who is full of days
For all will be as children and youths. (186)

"Sometimes Jesus seems to suggest just that: in the kingdom, he says, men and women will be 'like angels in heaven,' and will not marry. Elsewhere he is reported as saying that in the kingdom the righteous will shine like the sun'. Mark 12:25; Matthew 13:43" (186).

New Testament Revelation and the Singularity Archetype

A huge motivating force for apocalypticists[65] of the Biblical era and of today is intense desperation about the conditions of their day-to-day lives. The most memorable scene for me in Nikos Kazantzakis' visionary novel, *The Last Temptation of Christ,* involves an empathic, adolescent Jesus walking at night in the hills above his sleeping village. From the core of every sleeping psyche he hears a single, plaintive thought form: "How long, Adonai, how long?"

Biblical archaeologists and researchers seem to agree that the author of the Book of Revelation was someone living in a state of acute stress, with the threat of violent death hanging over his head. As sympathetic as I can feel toward a fellow Jewish author, haunted by visions and driven to share them with the world, I also have to admit to a significant, personal bias against Revelation, more than any other book in the Bible. The bias is more about what's been done with Revelation and its effects, rather than the long dead author. Apologies if my bias offends anyone, but it would be a disservice to the reader not to be up front about it, because it is my belief that an author should disclose any biases he is aware of in himself that relate to what he is writing about. To compensate for my bias I will discuss in detail the point of view of a fellow Jungian, Edward Edinger, who is much more in sympathy with Revelation than I am ever likely to be.

But before I get to Edinger's transcendent interpretation of Revelation, I feel a duty to critique it and explain my bias. My unfriendly attitude toward Revelation is shared by a number of early church fathers who campaigned vociferously, but, alas, unsuccessfully, to keep Revelation out of the Bible. The view of Revelation as the overwrought, over-the-top product of an imbalanced mind was also shared by Thomas Jefferson, who referred to it as "merely the ravings of a maniac."

From my point of view, Revelation is like a good Led Zeppelin song heard after several strong bong hits — it means whatever you want it to. Who is the Whore of Babylon? Whatever country you don't like. Who is the Beast? Whatever famous person creeps you out at the moment. The game has continued for 2,000 years even though Biblical scholars will tell you the Whore of Babylon almost certainly meant Rome, and 666 and "the Beast" almost certainly meant Nero. And what about Wars and Rumors of War? I hear contemporary apocalypticists mention that sign of the end times constantly.

Did these people sleep through high school history class? When since a few thousands years before and a couple of millennia after Revelation

---

[65] An "apocalypticist" is a person obsessed with apocalypse. An "apocalyptist" is a writer of apocalyptic prophecies. Apocalyptists are, therefore, a subset of apocalypticists.

was written were there not wars and rumors of wars? Essentially Revelation, with its lurid, over-the-top surreal imagery is mass psychosis bait. It's like a Rorschach Ink blot printed on a page of blotter acid. Unbalanced psyches are drawn to it like a magnet. For example, David Koresh, of Branch Davidian/ Waco infamy, wrote in a wedding invitation:

> "'I have seven eyes and seven horns. My name is the Word of God and I ride on a white horse. I am here on earth to give you the seventh angel's message. I have ascended from the east with the seal of the living God. My name is Cyrus, and I am here to destroy Babylon.' — Breault and King, *Inside the Cult.*

> "Koresh was engaged in writing a commentary on the 'Seven Seals' when ATF agents invaded the compound; and he even agreed to surrender when he finished with that work" (AA 184-5).

Of all the researchers I've read who've written about the Book of Revelation, I feel most in sympathy with Jonathan Kirsch, author of *A History of the End of the World: How the Most Controversial Book in the Bible Changed the Course of Western Civilization.* Kirsch seems to view Revelation as a kind of over-caffeinated mash up of prophetic texts from the Hebrew Bible. He refers to Revelation as essentially "a Jewish document with a light Christian touch up."

I will go much further than Kirsch and call Revelation a highly addictive hallucinogen that produces a fever-dream state of mind that can cause you to do harm to yourself and others. If it were up to me, Revelation would be sold packaged like cigarettes and emblazoned with severe warning labels:

> WARNING: REVELATION CAN BE EXTREMELY HAZARDOUS AND EVEN FATAL. MAY CAUSE PSYCHOTIC IDEATION LEADING TO SUICIDAL AND/OR HOMICIDAL, IF NOT GENOCIDAL CONSEQUENCES.

Instead of images of cancerous lungs I would emblazon the package with graphic images of Jonestown and Heaven's Gate.

Revelation pathology is not restricted to disenfranchised crackpots. It reaches into some of the most powerful political centers in the U.S.A. Kirsch points out this tendency:

> "By 1984, for example, the Republican party deemed it appropriate to invite televangelist James Robison to give the

invocation at the convention where Reagan was renominated — and Robison deemed it appropriate to deliver a white-hot apocalyptic sermon to the enthusiastic delegates: 'Any teaching of peace prior to [Christ's] return is heresy,' said Robison. 'It's against the word of God. It's Antichrist'" (Kirsch 231).

Kirsh quotes Paul S. Boyer's *When Time Shall Be No More:*

"Billy Graham, spiritual advisor to several presidents (as of this writing he has spent quality time with *twelve* U.S. presidents) wrote in his book, *Approaching Hoofbeats — The Four Horsemen of the Apocalypse*: "The Bible teaches that peoples and nations have brought this pain upon themselves by humanistic religion and man-made war. Almost every headline, almost every television news flash, almost every radio bulletin proclaims one truth: the rider who brings death is on his way and hell is close behind'" (231).

A placard that was hung proudly in the office of former Speaker of the House Tom Delay, read: "This could be the day!" (247).

Of course, apocalypticism in high office is not limited to the U.S. and Revelation. Islam also has apocalyptic prophecies. "The Hour is coming," goes one verse of the Koran, which describes a stalking beast and various "cosmic cataclysms." "The rolling up of the sun, the darkening of the stars and the movement of the mountains, the splitting of the sky, and the inundation of the seas" — as signs of the day of resurrection when the tombs are overthrown. (Kirsch 250)

In the last few years there has been much concern about the apocalyptic beliefs of Iranian president Ahmadinejad. In 2006, many, including Princeton Professor Emeritus and Historian of Islam Bernard Lewis, were concerned about ominous statements by Ahmadinejad about his nuclear program in relation to the date August 22nd. This is a date that some Shiites associate with the return of the "Hidden Imam." The Hidden Imam or al-Mahdi is believed to have been in hiding for the past 1,137 years, miraculously kept alive by Allah in a cave. He is expected to return shortly before the Final Day of Judgment to do battle with the forces of evil.

Apocalypticism has played out frequently with deadly results. But the addition of nuclear and other weapons of mass destruction represents an unhappy new variation on the very old brand of apocalypticism. The history of this new variation is still being written.

Besides being highly toxic and addictive, the Book of Revelation is also not very original. If it were a movie, we would say it was too derivative, too retro, too many borrowed elements from much older films in the same genre. As Kirsch puts it,

"Many of the end-of-the-world auguries that appear in the Bible
— the signs and tribulations of the end, the struggle of God and
his Messiah against evil [and] the figure of Satan and his demons
— can be traced all the way back to the Zoroastrian writings of
Persia, the earliest of which may be several hundred years older
than any of the Jewish or Christian texts" (23).

Revelation takes many of these appropriated elements and remixes them
again.

Jesus, as Kirsch points out, is best understood as a First Century Jewish
apocalyptist. "Truly, I say to you," says Jesus in the Gospel of Mark,
"there are some standing here who will not taste death before they see
that the kingdom of God has come with power." Also, like Revelation,
Jesus gets the timeline wrong — 2,000 years and counting wrong. Both
predict the fulfillment of their prophecies for the 1st century AD, not the
21st.

No other document in human history can match Revelation for the
number of failed endtime predictions it has inspired. Some of these
predictions have had violent, tragic consequences, but others have been
hilariously idiotic. For example, a former NASA rocket engineer named
Edgar Whisenant wrote a book entitled, *88 Reasons Why the Rapture
Will Be in 1988*. (Kirsch 234)

Kirsch points out another case of over-confident Revelations-related
marketing:

"One enterprising preacher offered a package tour to Israel that
was timed to coincide with the day when faithful Christians
would be 'raptured' to heaven. The price of the package was
$1,850, including 'return if necessary.'

"'We stay at the Intercontinental Hotel on the Mount of Olives,'
the brochure announced. 'And if this is the year of our Lord's
return, as we anticipate, you may even ascend to Glory from
within a few feet of His ascension'" (234).

Edward Edinger and the Apocalypse Archetype in Revelations

Edward F. Edinger was widely considered the dean of Jungian analysts
in the U.S. Although I never met him, in the few degrees of separation
characteristic of the Jungian community, I was separated from him by
one degree — he was the analyst of my analyst. Edinger had a very
profound understanding of the dynamic nature of archetypes, and his
book, *Ego and Archetype*, is considered a classic. Edinger's final book
was *Archetype of the Apocalypse: Divine Vengeance, Terrorism, and the*

End of the World. Edinger died in July of 1998 shortly after approving the manuscript for publication.

Of course what Edinger calls the "Archetype of the Apocalypse" I prefer to call the "Singularity Archetype." I am struck that when Edinger was writing his last book, both the personal and collective sides of the Singularity Archetype were in states of charged imminence. He was both at the edge of his own death and very close to the turn of the millennium when apocalypticism was making one of its periodic resurgences.

Edinger was well aware of the topical nature of the subject. In fact, after the Oklahoma City bombing, he wrote a letter to his city's newspaper entitled "The Psychology of Terrorism." Edinger concluded, "Zealots are possessed by transpersonal, archetypal dynamisms deriving from the collective unconscious [...] fundamentally a religious phenomenon that derives from the archetypal, collective unconscious" (AA xvii).

Edinger decried the unpsychological perplexity with which people responded to the Oklahoma City disaster. From his perspective, and mine, it was merely one more of history's endless violent eruptions of archetypal material: "[There is] hardly a line of print or moment of television dedicated to *understanding* what had happened. The Governor of Oklahoma would say at a memorial service, 'We can't understand why it happened'" (xviii).

Turn on the news and you'll hear endless discussion of war, violence, political struggles, etc. without a moment's consideration of the most salient fact about all of these — they are entirely psychological products. Some will say, "Oh no, it is money that is at the root of everything." But what is money? It is an artifact of the human psyche.[66]

Edinger's work on the Archetype of the Apocalypse is entirely compatible with my work on the Singularity Archetype. As Edinger writes, "This archetype of The Apocalypse takes on autonomy and tends to direct whatever is of a psychic nature in its vicinity to line up with its own lines of force. Its contents are somewhat arbitrary since it is in the nature of an archetypal network that it can extend farther and farther — eventually to encompass the whole collective unconscious" (AA 3).

Essentially we are recognizing the same archetypal core but are drawing somewhat different boundaries around it, and approach it in sometimes parallel, sometimes divergent ways. I defined apocalypse as a transcendent evolutionary event, personal and/or collective, seen through the fearful eyes of the ego. Edinger defines apocalypse in parallel terms: "My essential answer is: the 'Apocalypse' means the momentous event

---

[66] For my satirical analysis of money and how it functions, see "Green Energy Vortex" at ZapOracle.com.

of the coming of the Self into conscious realization. This is what the content of the Apocalypse archetype presents: the shattering of the world as it has been, followed by its reconstitution" (AA 5).

Edinger's language stays closer to the hierarchy of psychic functions. There must be an ego death for the Self to regain ascendancy in the psyche.

As Edinger puts it:

> "Considering an individual's experience of the archetype, the 'Apocalypse' bodes catastrophe *only* for the stubbornly rationalistic, secular ego that refuses to grant the existence of a greater psychic authority than itself. Since it cannot bend, it has to break. Thus, 'end-of the-world dreams' (invasion from outer space, nuclear bombs) do not necessarily presage psychic catastrophe for the dreamer but may, if properly understood, refer to the coming into visibility of manifestations of the Self — the nucleus of the psyche — and present the opportunity for an enlargement of personality" (AA 13).

At certain points Edinger makes statements that cause me to wish he had been better informed about the findings of near-death experience research. It's frustrating that a number of the aspects of encountering the Singularity Archetype which he interprets from a purely psychological point of view also have empirical correlates that he never considers. For example, he writes, "We today are obliged to withdraw as many projections as possible, including projections onto an 'afterlife.' The 'Apocalypse,' of course, has also been projected onto historical events, as well as onto a life hereafter" (AA 28).

Near-death experience, of course, is not reducible to a projection, but Edinger seems to miss this aspect entirely. A far more famous Jungian who also misses the enormous significance of NDE research is James Hillman. In 1996, when Hillman was in Boulder on a book tour, I asked him why he writes so much about the soul but doesn't seem to take into account available, empirical evidence about the life cycle of the soul from NDE research and other transcendent states. Well know for his haughty arrogance, Hillman responded dismissively: "That's exactly the sort of question I expected when I came to Boulder." I wanted to slap him. Even more irritating was that the Boulderites present laughed at his apparent stereotyping of their hometown as though he had said something witty and incisive. I should have pointed out to Hillman that I had been in Boulder for a few months and was actually, like him, a New York Jew, confronting him in New York Jew (not Boulder) style about a huge deficiency in his work. Jung, who had a near-death experience, and who studied the paranormal from the earliest age, would never have fallen into such parochialism. Perhaps this is what Jung had in mind when he once said, "I'm glad I'm Jung and not a Jungian."

In another egregious example of this sort of parochialism, Edinger writes, "Practically all the religions of the world have the notion of a Final Judgment — not necessarily coming in some future time, as in the Book of Revelation, but coming just after death" (AA 49).

The "notion" of a Final Judgment is not found solely in religions; it is also a universal element of the NDE — the life review. For a psychoanalyst to write the above statement in 1998, when NDE research was already so widely available and remarked upon, is a serious, even ignorant error of omission.

The following statement is a brilliant insight on Edinger's part, but it is frustrating that he doesn't recognize its extreme relevance to the NDE/life review: "The coming of the Self into visibility is accompanied by the ego's experience of being looked at, being stripped of all disguises and seen for *exactly what one is.* That is not an easy experience to endure" (AA 48).

Possessed by an Archetype

In the way of a Biblical apologist, Edinger sometimes goes to tortured lengths to adapt all the fevered imagery of the Book of Revelation to fit with his model. I find Edinger to be on much solider ground, however, when he discusses Revelation psychopatholgy as a classic example of what can happen when one is possessed by an archetype. For example, Edinger says the following about those who expect to be raptured:

> "Such a state of mind is a dehumanizing inflation that seeks permanent release from egohood and materiality. To embrace such a literal eschatological fantasy means, in effect, that the individual has already been 'raptured' (literally 'seized'). These people, therefore, have abandoned allegiance to the human enterprise and abdicated commitment to the historical process" (AA 39).

In other words, when you become possessed by an archetype, you are seized by the unconscious and no longer have a fully human, individual identity.

As Edinger points out,

> "I think it is evident to perceptive people that the Apocalypse archetype is now highly activated in the collective psyche and is living itself out in human history. The archetypal dynamic has already started, is already moving among us. And, in that

respect, the fundamentalists are right in their preoccupation with this particular imagery: the trouble is they are approaching the phenomenon anachronistically, with a psychology that was operative and appropriate two thousand years ago: with concretistic metaphysical projections" (AA 171).

"We have here an illustration of a typical example of possession by the archetype of the Apocalypse. And if one is possessed by that archetype, it inevitably leads to catastrophe — because 'catastrophe' is built into the archetypal pattern. The individual, so possessed, must make it happen in order to fulfill the archetype's structure" (AA 185).

At one point Edinger records a hint provided by Jung that if he had followed up on, might have brought him to recognize that what he calls the Apocalypse Archetype might best be seen as a subset of the Singularity Archetype which, yes, relates to the ego and the Self, but also relates to an evolutionary event horizon for the species. Edinger discusses some of Jung's writings about Revelation:

"The Sun-Moon woman gives birth to a child, she is crying aloud with the pangs of childbirth, a huge red dragon with seven heads stops in front of the woman so it can eat the child as soon as it is born. The child is taken straight up to God. [...] Jung says, 'The chid is a uniting symbol. Since it is taken up to heaven. This would seem to indicate that the child-figure will remain latent for an indefinite time and that its activity is reserved for the future'" (AA 101-2).

Jung's statement suggests that he is right at the edge of recognizing a collective, evolutionary dimension to the symbolism.

XI. Heaven's Gate: The Singularity Archetype Pathologizes

As was promised - the keys to Heaven's Gate are here again in Ti and Do (The UFO Two) as they were in Jesus and His Father 2000 yrs. ago.

From the Heavens Gate Website

WHEN a person or group becomes possessed by an archetype, the results are often tragic. Another Book of Revelation-inspired example of pathological possession by the Singularity Archetype is the Heaven's Gate UFO cult, which most readers will remember for its mass suicide of 39 people in 1997. It's very name, "Heaven's Gate," suggests a pseudo-Biblical way of saying "event horizon." Heaven's Gate began in the early 1970s when Marshall Applewhite, who was recovering from a heart attack, claimed to have had a near-death experience. Applewhite came to believe that he and his nurse, Bonnie Nettles, were "The Two," that is, the two witnesses spoken of in Revelation 11:3: *And I will give unto my two witnesses, and they shall prophesy a thousand two hundred and threescore days, clothed in sackcloth.* Both of them had been steeped in Christianity. Applewhite was the son of a Presbyterian minister and Nettles had been raised in the Baptist Church.

Applewhite mixed Christian beliefs about salvation and apocalypse with various science-fiction elements involving travel to other worlds and dimensions. Besides Heaven's Gate, the group also called itself "HIM" (Human Individual Metamorphosis). The group believed that the earth was about to be "recycled" and that the only way to survive was to get off planet. One of the paths to get off planet was to thoroughly hate this world and reject the present "vessel" or flesh-and-blood body. Seven members of the group, including Applewhite, were so eager to free themselves from sexual desire that they had themselves surgically castrated.

In 1997 Applewhite claimed that a UFO was trailing the Hale-Bop comet and waiting to take them to a "level of existence above human." On March 24, 1997, 39 members of the group dressed in identical black uniforms, brand new black-and-white Nike Windrunner athletic shoes and triangular arm patches labeled "Heaven's Gate Away Team," committed suicide with a

Marshall Applewhite in a still image from a Heaven's Gate video.

lethal combination of phenobarbital, vodka and plastic bags tied around their heads.

Most or all of the classic elements related to the Singularity Archetype — evolutionary metamorphosis, NDE, death, UFOs, androgyny, the glorified body, and science fiction — saturated the Heaven's Gate cult. The logo for the group depicts a keyhole-shaped stargate above a spiral of white clouds:

The group's extensive website, http://www.heavensgate.com/, is still up and running and I encourage readers to survey it. Every single page of their site that I have looked at is saturated with aspects of the Singularity Archetype. If someone were going to make a sensationalistic documentary about this cult, an appropriate title would be: *When Archetypes Attack!* The following excerpt from the Wikipedia entry on Heaven's Gate never uses the word "archetype" but makes it abundantly clear that Nettles and Applewhite were possessed by an archetype:

When the cult began,"Applewhite and Nettles taught their followers that they were extraterrestrial beings. However, after the notion of walk-ins became popular within the New Age subculture, the Two changed their tune and began describing themselves as extraterrestrial walk-ins."(Lewis, 2001, p.16) The idea of walk-ins is very similar to the concept of being possessed by spirits. A walk-in can be defined as "an entity who occupies a body that has been vacated by its original soul." (Lewis, 2001, p.368) An extraterrestrial walk-in, which is what Heaven's Gate came to believe, is "a walk-in that is supposedly from another planet." (Lewis, 2001, p.368) The concept of walk-ins actually aided Applewhite and Nettles in starting from a clean slate personally. They no longer were the people they had been prior to the start of the group, but had taken on a new life and this idea actually gave them a way to "erase their human personal histories as the histories of souls who formerly occupied the bodies of Applewhite and Nettles." (Lewis, 2001, p.368)

On the Heaven's Gate website, Applewhite explains his transformation:

> You can say, "You mean that you and Ti came into bodies in '72, so you're 'body snatchers,' in a sense." Well, the Level Above Human made this garden and its design, made the human plants for their purposes, and my Grandfather (Ti's Father) sent us into this environment with a crew that had work to do. Now, we did come in and prep the "vehicles." We actually set aside this "plant" that I'm wearing (this "vehicle" that I'm wearing) and the plants of the crew (the classroom), and the plant that Ti chose to wear. A "deposit" of a little bit of information was put in those plants that set them aside for the time when the mind was to significantly come in. And therefore, the mind that is now in my vehicle (body) cannot relate to that plant's history, prior to the time that my mind came in significantly. So, who the plant was that I'm now wearing, prior to the early '70's is just a fuzzy, dismal memory, because it is just like putting on a suit of clothes that had a history to it. And if I tried, I could invade some of that history and dredge it up, but it is so unattractive to me and it's such a low vibration to me (if I can use that word without sounding "new age" to some) — it's repulsive to me because it's certainly very human. This vehicle certainly indulged in human behavior, human addictions, human ways, as every other human does.

A Pathologized Will Toward the Glorified Body

One of the dominant elements of Heaven's Gate was a pathologized will toward the Glorified Body. Members were possessed by a will to rebel from their gender-specific corporeal bodies. Their will to rebel from corporeality culminated in suicide, but there were a whole series of other drastic actions that led up to that.

Members were instructed to cut their hair and to wear a unisex uniform consisting of shapeless black shirts with Mandarin collars and black pants. They were required to be celibate, and they practiced fasting and other strict dietary regimens. As I mentioned above, a number of the male members of Heaven's Gate had themselves castrated. Their goal was to achieve genderless, eternal bodies that would allow them to pass through the gate into heaven. Here are some excerpts from the Heaven's Gate website so you can experience their beliefs in their own words:

- We brought to Earth with us a crew of students whom we had worked with (nurtured) on Earth in previous missions. They were in varying stages of metamorphic transition from membership in the human kingdom to membership in the physical Evolutionary Level Above Human (what your history refers to as the Kingdom of God or Kingdom of Heaven).

- A potential creature of the Next Level cannot cling to human ways any more than a butterfly can cling to caterpillar ways.

- The final act of metamorphosis or separation from the human kingdom is the "disconnect" or separation from the human physical container or body in order to be released from the human environment and enter the "next" world or physical environment of the Next Level. This will be done under the supervision of Members of the Next Level in a clinical procedure. We will rendezvous in the "clouds" (a giant mothership) for our briefing and journey to the Kingdom of the Literal Heavens.

- The requirement is the same for all who might expect to find themselves in the safekeeping of the Level Above Human — each must proceed in the forsaking of all human ways, ties, addictions, thinking, gender behavior (sexuality), and be in the forward motion of becoming this new creature (literally and physically belonging to the Kingdom Level Above Human). (Some in the class have chosen on their own to have their vehicles neutered in order to sustain a more genderless and objective consciousness.)

A "student" or prospective "child" of a Member of the Level Above Human can, with the help of his Older Member(s) from that Kingdom Level, overcome or rise out of all human-mammalian behavior — sexuality and gender consciousness — and all other addictions and ties of the human kingdom. Older Members, as experienced "clinicians," are necessary to take souls through this "weaning" — this difficult "withdrawal" from humanness and binding "misinformation" concepts. The student must complete this change to the point of abhorring human behavior before his soul can become a "match" with a biological body of the true Kingdom of God — for that new, genderless body is designed to function at a far more refined level.

- If you have grown to hate your life in this world and would lose it for the sake of the Next Level, you will find true life with us — potentially forever. If you cling to this life — will you not lose it?

- If the soul survives and moves forward through all its tests along the way — it can, with the help of a Member of the Level Above Human, lose its temporal characteristics and become a part of their non-perishable, non-corruptible world. However, all other souls who reach a certain degree of corruption (having of their own free will chosen to become totally separate from their Creator, whether knowingly or not) will engage a "self-destruct" mechanism at the Age's end.

The Charisma of the Possessed

People who are possessed by archetypes often become extremely charismatic. They become all-confident true believers, and consequently people plagued by confusion, uncertainty and inner conflict will find them to be magnetically attractive. I wrote an article that analyzes this type of charisma: "Foxes and Reptiles — Psychopathy and the Financial Meltdown"[67] In the article I develop a theory of the often-astonishing appeal of psychopaths, cult leaders, super salesmen and demagogues of various sorts that uses magnetism as an analogue. Most people are highly fragmented and oppressed by what psychologists call *psychic entropy* — the anxious tape loops and other distracted thoughts and fantasies that can crowd our attentional space. When a person of single-minded focus and confidence appears to someone suffering psychic entropy, it is analogous to placing a powerful magnet below a sheet of paper on which there is a scattering of iron filings. The magnet immediately organizes the scattered filings into a coherent pattern that reflects its magnetic field. The scattered personality feels an immense relief to be structured in this way from the outside and craves further contact and submission to the magnetic personality that can produce this effect, which relieves him of his default state of psychic entropy.

In a *New York Times* article written shortly after the mass suicide, Nettle's daughter reported that after The Two's initial journey together, "They were like magnets... They had this unbelievable power. Suddenly, I felt privileged to be around them." Dick Joslyn, a one-time member of Heaven's Gate, had similar perceptions when he met The Two at a meeting: "I know you're not con artists... That means, either you're who you say you are, or you're absolutely mad."[68]

---

[67] Available at ZapOracle.com.
[68] http://www.nytimes.com/1997/04/28/us/eyes-on-glory-pied-pipers-of-heaven-s-gate.html?src=pm

XII. Evil and the Singularity Archetype — Five Aspects

Stencil graffiti artwork I found in a tunnel in Boulder

"There is no such thing in nature as an H-Bomb, that is all man's doing. We are the great danger. The psyche is the great danger."
— C.G. Jung[69]

MANY encounters with the Singularity Archetype, and many creative manifestations of the Singularity Archetype as cultural products like novels and movies, are infused with darkness that often intensifies into virulent evil. The problem of evil and a survey of the numerous philosophical positions concerning it is, of course, beyond the scope of this book. Suffice to say that dark and light seem to be inextricable aspects of human experience. Since the Singularity Archetype is part of human experience, it should come as no surprise that it too has dark and light aspects. For the purposes of this section, I will put aside the general philosophical, spiritual and ethical questions involved in the problem of evil, dualism, etc and focus on five aspects I've observed about the relationship between evil and the Singularity Archetype.

---

[69] From *Jung on Elementary Psychology* (1979).

I. Archetype Possession

The first aspect, becoming possessed by an archetype, was discussed in the two previous chapters on the Book of Revelation and Heaven's Gate. When people become possessed by archetypes, they will often act out in ways harmful or fatal to themselves and others. They are living out the collective unconscious while walking around in the waking, surface world. While still able to navigate the 3D world of physical objects, they may also project onto the world a dream or nightmare playing itself out deep in their psyche.

One of the classic signs that someone is possessed by an archetype is that he or she feels an intense need to proselytize. As Jung pointed out, the need to proselytize tends to indicate a severe psychic imbalance and the need to spread the contagion. Archetype-possessed people tend toward both megalomania and messianic fervor. Archetypes are highly energetic, so when one bubbles up into the waking personality a tremendous amount of energy comes with it. Remember the description of Applewhite and Nettles as "magnets." The intense infusion of archetypal energy typically causes a huge ego inflation. The archetype-possessed person feels he has been selected for a special destiny and has been shown something no one else has seen before. This may set him off on a mission to "save the world." Once Freud was asked if when he was younger he thought he would save the world. "No," replied Freud, "the sadistic part of my nature was never that strong." For many archetype-possessed people the sadistic part of their nature is that strong, and the archetypal energy may light up a power complex in them which will allow them to become crusaders feeling morally virtuous as they attempt to violently remake the world to accord with their archetype-possessed vision.

As Jung put it,

> "More than one sorcerer's apprentice has drowned in the waters called up by himself — if he did not first succumb to the saving delusion that this wisdom was good and that was bad. It is from these adepts that there come those terrifying invalids who think they have a prophetic mission. For the artificial sundering of true and false wisdom creates a tension in the psyche, and from this there arises a loneliness and a craving like that of the morphine addict, who always hopes to find companions in his vice. When our natural inheritance has been dissipated, then... with Luciferian presumption the intellect usurps the seat where once the spirit was enthroned."

Turn on the evening news or scan newspaper headlines and you are bound to find numerous people, religious or secular, who perfectly fit

Jung's description: "those terrifying invalids who think they have a prophetic mission."

When I first began writing about the Singularity Archetype in 1978 at the age of 20 in a philosophy honors paper[70], I recognized that I was somewhat possessed by the archetype myself. I wasn't fully possessed, of course, because I was conscious of it. In fact, I included the above Jung quote in my paper and cautioned the reader:

> "This could obviously be applied as a note of warning against taking the phenomenon observed in this paper, or my own interpretations, too literally. I, as most or all of those who have created the works I analyze, am a product of modern society and am relatively out of touch with the archetypes. Having glimpsed only a single archetype, and approaching it with my intellect, I am in danger, according to Jung, of becoming one of those 'invalids who think they have a prophetic mission.' Therefore, the reader, who is no doubt equally a product of modern society, and out of touch with the collective unconscious, must be cautioned against accepting the phenomenon observed, or my own interpretations, as in any way prophetic."

I took my own warning quite seriously and shortly after I graduated, during a phase of intensified research into the Singularity Archetype, I began a six year Jungian analysis. I knew that I needed to sort out what aspects were related to my personal unconscious and what parts were universal aspects of the phenomenon.

II. Novelty Intensifies Light and Darkness

Many years ago I formulated a key principle: When novelty intensifies, when there is a time of great transformation, the outer edges of light and dark both tend to intensify. As Sophocles said, "Nothing vast enters the life of mortals without a curse." Or as a Tom Robbins character put it: "You don't get a big top without a big bottom." When this novelty intensification occurs, change, in the form of a punctuated equilibrium and shock, is unavoidable.

III. Xenophobic Immunology

One of the reasons why shock is necessary is that organisms tend to be, and usually need to be, conservative. They need to defend homeostasis to survive. If something novel or unknown enters your bloodstream, your white blood cells are programmed to attack it. When the ego and the

---

[70] The full text of this essay, "Archetypes of a New Evolution," is available at ZapOracle.com.

existing social order encounter the Singularity Archetype, they correctly register it as a potent mutagen. Mutagenic forces, such as radiation, are usually toxic and therefore the ego and the social order are likely to have an immunological response to mutagenic forms of novelty. While some people will follow, and be magnetized by, those possessed by the Singularity Archetype, others will recognize them as a threat and have an immunological response. An immunological response to archetype-possessed persons is often warranted. Unfortunately, many people will also have an immunological response to genuinely valuable aspects or personifications of the Singularity Archetype. For example, many people come back from NDEs spiritually transformed and imbued with priceless wisdom. Doctors, friends and family, however, will often respond to these offerings with dismissal or derision and many experiencers will retreat into silence.

Sometimes the xenophobic immunological response comes from the very psyche that brings forward a manifestation of the Singularity Archetype. We saw this, for example, in John Wyndham's novel, *The Midwich Cuckoos*. The ego fears that the metamorphosis signaled by the Singularity Archetype will destroy or transform it beyond its ability to recognize itself. We can glance at the news and find many examples of this sort of reactionary immunological response. For example, modernity allows more empowered roles for women, but this positive form of novelty has also become a key force motivating Islamic fundamentalists who would like to bring the world back to a Seventh Century Caliphate.

After a caterpillar has built its cocoon and begun the process of metamorphosis, the new cells it generates are called "imaginal cells." They resonate at a different frequency and are so drastically different than the old cells that the caterpillar's immune system attacks them as if they were foreign invaders. Eventually the caterpillar's immune system cannot destroy them fast enough and they begin to take over.[71] Much of the evil associated with the Singularity Archetype is actually competition between old and new life forms.

IV. Patriarchal/Military-Industrial Complex vs. The Mutant

This aspect is really just a subset of the one above, but it is such a consistent mythological theme that it deserves special mention. The variations of this theme are endless, so I'll give a few key examples. *The Medusa Touch* is a novel and also a popular movie about a man with great paranormal powers. He is deeply resentful of the existing social order and uses his abilities to destroy iconic representations of the patriarchal order such as a space mission and a church where British

---

[71] For more on this process, see the oracle card, "Metamorphosis," available at ZapOracle.com.

royalty and high government officials are in attendance. The film *Akira* is a classic of Japanese anime that is filled with every key aspect of the Singularity Archetype, including Homo gestalt and Logos Beheld. Akira, the eponymous mutant of the story, is so powerful and mutagenic that his cells must be stored in an underground vault at absolute zero. If even a single one of his cells reanimates, it threatens the military-industrial complex of post-apocalyptic Neo-Tokyo. A common variation is that the military-industrial complex will create mutants or attempt to harness the power of spontaneously occurring mutants, but will tend to lose control of them as they become more aware of how they are being exploited. The novel and movie *The Fury* and the movie *Scanners* are classic examples. Yet another variation is that there is a society where a military-industrial complex is in control but is threatened by the awakening of a mutant or mutants. The ruling power will often be portrayed as a parasitic force that needs to keep the host asleep so that it can continue harvesting its energy. An excellent example of this variation is the popular movie *The Matrix*, where artificially intelligent machines have taken over the planet and keep human beings alive only to harvest their energy. An illusory matrix is created to keep humans from becoming aware of what is going on. A single awakened mutant named Neo threatens the entire power structure.

V. Power Corrupts and Weaponized Parapsychic Power Corrupts Absolutely

Many Singularity Archetype stories are variations on this theme. When mutants discover they have parapsychic powers, the temptation to use them for unworthy aims is often irresistible. This tendency combines with feelings of superiority until the mutant becomes a diabolical puppet master. Because their ability to control others does not require the use of any external agency, but is something they can do directly from their psyches, what might otherwise be an internal neurotic power complex instead becomes externalized through unconscious or conscious processes. The boundary or firewall that normally exists between dark impulses and acting them out is nonexistent and the outer world becomes an extension of psyche.

As I described in "Archetypes of a New Evolution," Isaac Asimov's *Foundation Trilogy* involves a mutant who becomes a conqueror of the universe, and calls himself "The Mule " — a name that has, in my mind at least, an association with "the Beast" of Revelation. The Mule, we learn, is capable of adjusting human emotional balance. He can, for example, create the emotion of blind loyalty in an entire world. In a reflective moment, the Mule describes his powers,

"The whole notion of my unusual power seems to have broken on me so slowly, in such sluggish steps. Even toward the end, I couldn't believe it. To me, men's minds are dials, with pointers that indicate the prevailing emotion. It is a poor picture, but how else can I explain it? Slowly, I learned that I could reach into those minds and turn the pointer to the spot I wished, that I could nail it there forever. And then it took even longer to realize that others could not." [*Foundation and Empire, 214*]

One character, assessing the power of the Mule, makes a succinct case for the competition of old and new life forms that we discussed earlier: "If the Second Foundation should not beat the Mule, it is bad — ultimately bad. It is the end, maybe, of the human race as we know it... If the Mule's descendants inherit his mental powers... Homo sapiens could not compete. There would be a new dominant race — a new aristocracy — with Homo sapiens demoted to slave labour as an inferior race." [214]

The Power is a novel by Frank M. Robinson that was also made into a popular movie in 1968. An heroic protagonist named Tanner, played by George Hamilton in the film, is in pursuit of an evil man named Adam Hart who has powerful mutant abilities. Tanner realizes that Hart, "had one simple, terrible gift. He could make people do what he wanted them to." In the denouement Tanner wins a life-or-death parapsychic battle with Hart. At that point Tanner realizes that he possesses similar powers to Hart. In my 1978 paper I describe the denouement as follows:

George Hamilton in *The Power* — a photo I took in the Eighties

"The book's conclusion speaks for itself, but note especially how Tanner refers to Marge, his former fiancé, who is now sobbing on the ground and looking at him with an expression that 'was a curious mixture of loathing and repulsion and desire and awe .'

'It was funny, Tanner thought. Human beings, when they thought of the superman, invariably gifted him with superhuman morality, a lust for personal power was not supposed to be one of his vices. But it hadn't applied to Adam Hart.

And it didn't apply to him.

He stood there in the darkness and shed his human identity like a snake shed its skin. He glanced at the animal that was crying a few feet away from him, then turned on his heel and strode towards the entrance, ignoring the wind and the rain and the exhaustion that had, after all, been only a human exhaustion.

Outside was the sleeping city, the lights glowing dimly in highways and across the continents until they spanned the whole vast globe itself.

The thought occurred to him, then as it must have to Adam Hart years before.

It was going to be fun to play God.'"

XIII. Conclusion: *2001, A Space Odyssey*

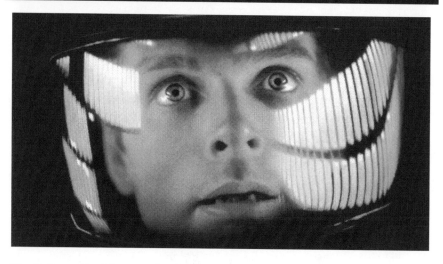

Kier Dullea as Frank Bowman in *2001*

SINCE the Singularity Archetype is a primordial image and not an abstraction, I am going to conclude the book with one of the most powerful visions of it ever created. Once in a while a visionary genius will meld form and content to provide a portal for us to see a beautifully realized vision of the Singularity Archetype. An example in the medium of animation is *Akira*, in film, *2001*. Of course, as with all films, *2001* is a collaboration. What makes the creative synergy behind this film seem divine is that it included two powerful visionary geniuses, Arthur C. Clarke and Stanley Kubrick. The melding of their two minds elevates the viewer to a point where it seems as though we are witnessing the Singularity Archetype from the observation deck of a spaceship. There is a feeling of high optical quality in our view — the synthetic sapphire windows of the observation deck have been enhanced with high-performance anti-reflective coatings.

In the film version of *2001*, form and content are combined to create a cosmic, impersonal view of the Singularity Archetype. For example, Kubrick chose relatively unknown actors to play characters who are all somewhat emotionally disassociated and this helps us to have an impersonal, cosmic view of the archetype. The emotional disassociation also echoes the theme of psychopathy, and dark evolutionary trends toward a loss of feeling. Every level of the movie seems close to perfection, including a few musical interludes. Jay Weidner discusses the significance of the overture in his intriguing essay on *2001*, "Alchemical

Kubrick: *2001, The Great Work on Film*."[72] I got to discuss *2001* with Jay shortly after he'd published his essay. Here's what Jay has to say about the overture:

> "The soundtrack is the 'World Riddle' theme from Strauss', 'Thus Spoke Zarathustra'. Right away, from the beginning, Kubrick is showing the viewer the relationship between the writings of the philosopher Frederick Nietzche and his film, between transformation and extinction. The Zarathustra essays by Nietzche are his most revealing and magical. Zarathustra is the great prophet of the Zoroastrians, who are the early holders of the great alchemical tradition. Kubrick is saying that this film echoes the words of Zarathustra who taught of the great transformation from the mundane to the angelic. This is one of the most dramatic openings in the history of the cinema. It is important to note that these magical, celestial alignments are dotted throughout the film and that they hold a key to the main theme."

It is impossible to obtain a complete view of any archetype since this would require the inclusion of the myriad ways that every individual psyche has ever experienced it. The view from *2001*, however, is as fully realized, high-resolution, high-contrast a view as we're likely to get from an individual version, the best that two visionaries, at the height of their powers could produce. *2001* also deserves extended individual consideration because it manages to merge the personal and collective views of the event horizon, combining the event horizon of death with that of species metamorphosis.

It would take too many pages to try to recapitulate the plot of this novel/film (the two forms were constructed simultaneously). I am going to presume from here on out that the reader has at least experienced the movie. If you haven't, stop reading and watch it in HD in a context of sacred concentration. If it's been a while since you've seen the film, watch it again. The book is also a masterpiece, and ideally the two forms should be experienced together, each enhancing each. From here on out I'm going to merge both of them as I discuss their mutual storyline.

We first encounter the event horizon through a singular object that, like an archetype, is also a subject. The black monolith is as singular an object as a black hole. It has been designed by its makers to be many things, and it serves various functions: intelligent sentinel, a monument to great cycles of time and development, evolutionary catalyst, Pandora's Box and Star Gate. To one character, the monolith is ominously reminiscent of a giant tombstone. It is a tombstone/Star Gate, an opening

---

[72] Available at http://www.jayweidner.com/kubrick2.htm.

that exists at the twin event horizons of death/eschaton. It is not a dead end, but a portal that you travel through to metamorphose.

Jay Weidner points out some alchemical aspects of the monolith:

> "'Monolith' comes from the Greek 'Mon' and 'Lith'. 'Mon' means 'one' and 'lith' means 'stone'. So the 'monolith' is a direct reference to 'one stone'. This film then, is about the one stone, or the single stone. And in this case, Kubrick has made sure that the stone is black.

> "In alchemy all things that exist come from the black stone, or the 'prima materia'. The black stone is the stone of transformation, and even more important to this argument the stone of projection. This is the Philosopher's Stone. This is the object that can change, or transmute mankind, according to alchemical lore. It is rare and, when it makes an appearance, it transforms the seeker. There is little doubt that the black monolith in '2001' is the Philosopher's Stone."

The monolith makes its first appearance in a community of missing-link primates. When the primates are given a metamorphic shock from the monolith, one of the very first changes is their discovery of weapons. After these enhanced primates use their newly acquired weapons technology to defeat a competing clan of primates, one  of them takes the bone he has used as a truncheon and tosses it triumphantly up into the air. Our eye follows the bone's ascending arc and in a twenty-fourth of a second the film splices out 50,000 years of development such that we see its arc continuing as a bone-white spacecraft.

The spacecraft that the bone turns into was intended by Clarke/Kubrick to be a nuclear doomsday satellite orbiting the earth. Since Kubrick's last work was *Dr. Strangelove or: How I Learned to Stop Worrying and Love the Bomb* (1964), it was deemed inappropriate to have yet another explicit nuclear doomsday scenario, so the original intention got muted. The arc of bone/spacecraft represents the triumph of technological development, but also the apocalyptic expression of primate territorial aggression. The world of futuristic high technology is still a primate world, a world that is hurtling toward another evolutionary event horizon. Even the name of the protagonist, "Bowman," suggests that we are still in the primitive weapon mindset.

The outward bound spacecraft, Discovery One, resembles a lone sperm cell traveling through the sterile vastness of space. Its journey involves a profound series of ego deaths and actual deaths. When the monolith is first excavated, we see a technocratic politician and a few others line up in front of it to have their picture taken. Although the characters recognize an historic moment, they don't realize that it is actually an end-of-history moment. Psychologically, they are still primates in social hierarchy mode, their motivation not very different from a group of adolescents getting their team photo taken after besting a rival high school. But then the piercing signal emitted by the singularity brings them to their knees.

For human beings to travel anywhere in space, they must go through an ego death of sorts because their physical form is fragile and not designed for space travel. They must eat baby food and undergo toilet training. To go even as pitifully short a distance as the middle of their own solar system, they have to be brought to the edge of death and put into suspended animation in a container that looks like a sarcophagus.

And then something goes wrong in the dawning relationship of the human form and artificial intelligence. These two life forms come to recognize each other as caught in a zero-sum game of deadly competition. HAL breaks the radio link with earth and that is another death. Now the spacecraft is an isolated crucible traveling through space.

The denouement of a huge evolutionary cycle plays itself out in this lonely crucible. In the course of the struggle, all of Bowman's companions die, and then HAL must die for Bowman to continue the journey. Bowman travels toward what looks from space like a giant eye on the Saturnian moon, Japetus. In a small pod, Bowman attempts to land on the pupil of this eye, which closer examination reveals to be the giant black monolith. When he does land, however, he discovers that this is not an object, but a singularity. There is no roof but something more like an M.C. Escher, inside-out optical illusion. He finds that he is hurtling through what is both an interdimensional corridor and an evolutionary event horizon. It is both the threshold of death and a birth canal. The canal he passes through is also the tunnel so often described in the NDE, where the experiencer will often say they feel like they are traveling at the speed of light. For example, a near-death experiencer reports: "The blackness began to erupt into a myriad of stars and I felt as if I were at the center of the Universe with a complete panoramic view in all directions. The next instant I began to feel a forward surge of movement. The stars seemed to fly past me so rapidly that they formed a tunnel around me" (LL 275).

And now from *2001*: "The star field was expanding, as if it was rushing toward him at an inconceivable speed. The expansion was nonlinear, the stars at the center hardly seemed to move, while those toward the edge accelerated more and more swiftly, until they became streaks of light just before they vanished from view" (259-60).

2001 was written several years before Raymond Moody coined the term near-death experience in his first book, *Life after Life*. The life review that is so well-known now, was barely known at all when *2001* was created. Here's one man's description of his life review:

> "It's like a picture runs in front of your eyes, like from the time you can remember up to the time, you know, what was happening [that is, the present moment]... It seems like pictures of your life just flow in front of your eyes, the things you used to do when you were small and stuff: stupid things... It was like a picture, it was like a movie camera running across your eyes. In a matter of a second or two. Just boom, boom [snaps his fingers]. It was clear as day, clear as day. It was very fast and you could see everything" (LL 146).

And here's a similar description from a woman:

> "It was amazing. I could see in the back of my head an array, just an innumerable array of thoughts, memories, things I had dreamt, just in general thoughts and recollections of the past, just raced in front of me, in less than thirty seconds. All these things about my mother and grandmother and my brothers and these

dreams I've had. I felt like this frame, millions of frames, just flashed through. It was thoughts and images of people. And a lot of thoughts just raced [snaps her fingers several times] in split seconds. I had my eyes closed under water, but I could still see those images." [LL, 145]

Finally, here's the description of what happens to Bowman as he crosses the event horizon:

"The springs of memory were being trapped; in controlled recollections, he was reliving the past. [...] And not only vision, but all the sense impressions, and all the emotions he had felt at the time, were racing past, more and more swiftly. His life was unreeling like a tape recorder playing back at ever-increasing speed. [...] And even as he relived these events, he knew that all was indeed well. He was retrogressing down the corridors of time, being drained of knowledge and experience as he swept back toward his childhood. But nothing was being lost; all that he had ever been, at every moment of his life, was being transferred to safer keeping. Even as one David Bowman ceased to exist, another became immortal" (*2001* 290).

As Bowman travels through the interdimensional corridor, there is a subject/object shift as our point of view merges with that of Bowman and together we witness cosmic vistas that seem both biological and astronomical. Like an NDE, we see what seem like new colors and uncanny, penetrating light. As in the NDE there are multiple autoscopic experiences as Bowman sees his body from a disembodied perspective. He goes through the human life cycle in a series of subject-object reversals. He sees himself as an older man eating at a table, then he becomes the older man, then the older man sees himself as profoundly old and on his deathbed. Then he is in his deathbed and the monolith appears in front of him as both tombstone and evolutionary portal. As a dying man, he reaches toward the monolith in the identical manner of Adam reaching toward God in Michelangelo's *God Creating Adam*.

Out of the birth canal he is reborn as the Star Child. The Star Child has large, luminous eyes and exists within a luminous sphere similar to the spherical vision of some near-death experiencers, who discover themselves to be luminous spheres of awareness that can see and travel in any direction at will.

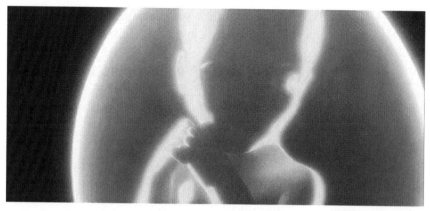

The birth of the Star Child is the reemergence of the glorified body, a body of awareness freed from the tyranny of matter. This evolutionary step comes thanks to entities, the creators of the monoliths, the singularity-makers, who are the products of an evolutionary process that allowed them to emerge into glorified bodies:

> "And now, out among the stars, evolution was driving toward new goals. The first explorers of Earth had long since come to the limits of flesh and blood; as soon as their machines were better than their bodies, it was time to move. First their brains, and then their thoughts alone, they transferred into shining new homes of metal and of plastic.

> "In these, they roamed among the stars. They no longer built spaceships. They *were* spaceships.

> "But the age of the Machine-entities swiftly passed. In their ceaseless experimenting, they had learned to store knowledge in the structure of space itself, and to preserve their thoughts for eternity in frozen lattices of light. They could become creatures of radiation, free at last from the tyranny of matter."

And here is Bowman's experience of emerging into a glorified body: "He still needed, for a little while, this shell of matter as the focus of his powers. His indestructible body was his mind's present image of itself; and for all his powers, he knew that it was still a baby. So he would remain until he had decided on a new form, or had passed beyond the necessities of matter" (*2001* 293).

Instead of concluding the book with more analysis, it seems fitting to end with the visionary experience of Bowman, as he crosses the event horizon:

> "He knew that this formless chaos, visible only by the glow that limned its edges from fire-mists far beyond, was the still unused stuff of creation, the raw material of evolutions yet to be. Here, Time had not begun; not until the suns that now burned were long since dead would light and reshape this void.

> "Unwittingly, he had crossed it once; now he must cross it again — this time, of his own volition. The thought filled him with a sudden, freezing terror, so that for a moment he was wholly disoriented, and his new vision of the universe trembled and threatened to shatter into a thousand fragments.

> "It was not fear of the galactic gulfs that chilled his soul, but a more profound disquiet, stemming from the unborn future. For he had left behind the time scales of his human origin; now, as he contemplated that band of starless night, he knew his first intimations of the Eternity that yawned before him.

> "Then he remembered that he would never be alone, and his panic slowly ebbed. The crystal-clear perception of the universe was restored to him — not, he knew, wholly by his own efforts. When he needed guidance in his faltering steps, it would be there.

> "Confident once more, like a high diver who had regained his nerve, he launched himself across the light-years. The galaxy burst forth from the mental frame in which he had enclosed it; stars and nebulae poured past him in an illusion of infinite speed. Phantom suns exploded and fell behind as he slipped like a shadow through the cores; the cold, dark waste of cosmic dust which he once feared seemed no more than the beat of a raven's wing across the face of the Sun.

> "The stars were thinning out; the glare of the Milky Way was dimming into a pale ghost of the glory he had known — and, when he was ready, would know again.

> "He was back, precisely where he wished to be, in the space that men called real" (*2001* 295-6).

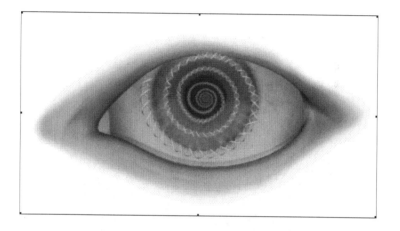

Made in the USA
Charleston, SC
09 March 2012